Rethinking Liberalism

Richard Bellamy

D1477318

PINTER

London and New York

Pinter
A Continuum Imprint
Wellington House, 125 Strand, London WC2R 0BB
370 Lexington Avenue, New York, NY 10017–6550

First published 2000

British Library Cataloguing in Publication Data
A catalogue record for this book is available from the British Library.

ISBN 1–85567–484–X (hardback)
     1–85567–485–8 (paperback)

Library of Congress Cataloging-in-Publication Data
Rethinking liberalism/[selected by] Richard Bellamy.
     p.   cm.
   ISBN 1–85567–484–X (hb).–ISBN 1–85567–485–8 (pb)
   1. Liberalism.   2. Liberalism–History.   I. Bellamy, Richard
(Richard Paul)
JC574.R47   2000
320.51–dc21

Typeset by York House Typographic Ltd, London
Printed and bound in Great Britain by Creative Print and Design (Wales), Ebbw Vale

Contents

CONTENTS

Acknowledgements

Most of these essays have been revised only slightly to avoid the odd overlap and occasionally to add some passage that for various reasons was omitted from the original version. Otherwise, they are much as first published. Consequently, some express views that I have rightly or wrongly come to modify – sometimes in later essays in this collection.

Specific debts are recorded for each chapter, but I am grateful more generally to the various institutions and colleagues who have supported me over the years, most especially: Quentin Skinner, Jonathan Steinberg and Richard Tuck at Cambridge; David Miller and Raymond Plant at Oxford; Malcolm Anderson, Richard Gunn, John Holmwood, Zenon Bankowski and Neil MacCormick at Edinburgh; the late Martin Hollis, Timothy O'Hagan, John Street, John Greenaway, John Zvesper and Alan Scott at UEA; and Barry Holden, Barry Jones, Andrew Mason, Jonathan Dancy and Tony Downes at Reading.

For the past six years I have also collaborated with Dario Castiglione of the University of Exeter on a string of Economic and Social Research Council (ESRC) projects, and as Chapter 12 – the only one of our numerous joint publications I have included – indicates, the results of that collaboration have fed into many of the pieces collected here.

Finally, I am indebted to my publishers, editors and co-authors for allowing me to reproduce these essays. They first appeared as follows:

1. 'Hegel and Liberalism', *History of European Ideas*, 8 (1987), pp. 693–708; reprinted in R. Stern (ed.), *Hegel: Critical Assessments*, 4 vols (Routledge, 1993), IV, pp. 325–44. Published here by kind permission of Elsevier Science.
2. 'Isaiah Berlin, T. H. Green and J. S. Mill on the Nature of Liberty and Liberalism', in R. Harrison and H. Gross (eds), *Jurisprudence: Cambridge*

Essays (Clarendon Press, 1992), pp. 257–85. Published here by kind permission of Oxford University Press.

3. 'Idealism and Liberalism in an Italian "New Liberal" Theorist – Guido de Ruggiero's *History of European Liberalism*', *Historical Journal*, 30 (1987), pp. 191–200. Published here by kind permission of Cambridge University Press.

4. (with Peter Baehr) 'Carl Schmitt and the Contradictions of Liberal Democracy', in R. Bellamy (ed.), *Capitalism, Socialism and Democracy Fifty Years On*, a special issue of the *European Journal of Political Research*, 23 (1993), pp. 163–85. Published here by kind permission of Kluwer Academic Publishers.

5. 'Schumpeter, and the Transformation of Capitalism, Liberalism and Democracy', *Government and Opposition*, 26 (1991), pp. 500–19.

6. (with Martin Hollis) 'Liberal Justice: Political and Metaphysical', *Philosophical Quarterly*, 45 (1995), pp. 1–19. Published here by kind permission of Blackwell Publishers.

7. 'Moralising Markets', *Critical Review*, Summer (1994), pp. 341–57.

8. 'Liberal Rights and Socialist Goals', W. Maihofer and G. Sprenger (eds), *Revolution and Human Rights*, *Archiv für Rechts- und Sozialphilosophie*, Beiheft Nr. 41 (1990), pp. 249–64; reprinted in a revised form as 'Liberal Rights, Socialist Goals and the Duties of Citizenship', in David Milligan and W. Watts Miller (eds), *Liberalism, Citizenship and Autonomy* (Gower Press, 1992), pp. 88–107; and partially translated into Italian in V. Mura *et al.* (eds), *I dilemmi del liberalsocialismo* (La Nuova Italia Scientifica, 1994), pp. 359–73. Published here by kind permission of Gower Press.

9. 'Citizenship and Rights', in R. Bellamy (ed.), *Theories and Concepts of Politics* (Manchester University Press, 1993), pp. 43–76; reprinted in a slightly revised Italian translation as 'Tre modelli di cittadinanza', in D. Zolo (ed.), *Cittadinanza: Appartenenza, Identita, Diritti* (Laterza, 1994), pp. 223–62. Published here by kind permission of Manchester University Press.

10. 'Liberalismo e la sfida del pluralismo', *Iride*, 10 (1997), pp. 494–511; also published as 'Liberalism and the Challenge of Pluralism', in I. MacKenzie and S. O'Neill (eds), *Reconstituting Social Criticism: Political Morality in an Age of Scepticism* (Macmillan, 1999), pp. 153–70. Published here by kind permission of Macmillan Press Ltd.

11. 'The Anti-Poll Tax Non-Payment Campaign and Liberal Concepts of Political Obligation', *Government and Opposition*, 29 (1994), pp. 22–41.

12. (with Dario Castiglione) 'Building the Union: The Nature of Sovereignty in the Political Architecture of Europe', *Law and Philosophy*, 16 (1997), 421–45. Published here by kind permission of Kluwer Academic Publishers.

Introduction

This volume collects various essays written over the past decade on the changing character of liberalism. I have selected those pieces that complement rather than overlap with my two monographs on this topic. Part I consists of articles that either prepared the way or developed the historical analysis of liberalism in my *Liberalism and Modern Society: An Historical Argument* (Polity Press, 1992). Parts II and III contain studies on the contemporary thinkers and themes addressed in *Liberalism and Pluralism: Towards a Politics of Compromise* (Routledge, 1999). The two other main topics on which I have published in this period – Italian political thought post-1700 and the relationship between constitutionalism and democracy (especially with regard to the European Union) – are represented respectively by Chapters 3 and 12 alone. Book-length treatments of these subjects are currently in preparation.

To their author at least, these chapters evidence a fairly consistent evolution of my views. When I began work on liberalism in the early 1980s, the liberal–communitarian debate had just begun. The publication of important books by 'communitarian' thinkers such as Alasdair MacIntyre, Charles Taylor, Michael Sandel and Michael Walzer had challenged the post-Rawlsian consensus concerning the methods of political philosophy and the nature of liberal societies and institutions. Though their criticisms were often directed more at New Right libertarians than social liberals such as Rawls, they believed the latter had made way for the former by conceiving the state as neutral with regard to different conceptions of the good and concerned only to defend the equal rights of individuals. I intended initially to transcend this dispute by showing how liberal and communitarian arguments had been intertwined in the past. Throughout the nineteenth century – the era of liberalism – liberal thought had fused enlightenment and romantic elements. A synthesis achieved most self-consciously in the work of Hegel, it characterized the British liberal tradition from Mill to Hobhouse. Historically liberalism had a strong ethical commitment to a particular conception of the good rather than being neutralist and rights-based, as most contemporary liberals now argued. This older conception of liberalism valued characteristically liberal social practices, such as the market and democracy, because they fostered a certain type of individual flourishing. It linked a perfectionist account of human development to a belief in social progress. Traditionally, therefore, liberalism might best be designated as communitarian liberal – a position I sought to defend on substantive as well as historical grounds.

This thesis is developed in Chapters 1 and 2 (the second, though published in 1992, was written in 1984). However, further historical investigation, especially the comparison of the British with other European liberal traditions, led me to modify my position. Most continental liberals were Anglophiles. But the establishment of liberal regimes, notwithstanding a modernizing economy and society, proved harder on the continent than in Britain, forcing these theorists to investigate more fully than their English (if not their Scottish) counterparts the social and cultural preconditions of liberal institutions. They came to question whether modern societies necessarily developed so as to support the values and forms of individual development liberals favoured. Social differentiation, increased complexity and the associated pluralism of ideals and interests, on the one hand, and the development of bureaucratic forms of organization within both economy and the state, on the other, rendered individual lives more conflictual and less autonomous than earlier liberals had thought. Markets and democracy became less entrepreneurial and deliberative respectively, thereby ceasing to promote the attributes traditionally associated with a liberal character. As a result, continental theorists were obliged to rethink liberalism in more realist terms and explore how liberal political systems might operate within complex, pluralist and bureaucratic societies. In *Liberalism and Modern Society*, Italy and Germany provided my main examples of the transformation and disenchantment of continental liberalism between 1870–1930, with Max Weber singled out as the most profound analyst of the fate of liberal ideas and practices in modern conditions. Writing Chapter 3 on Guido de Ruggiero, whose classic if much misunderstood *History of European Liberalism* inspired my own project, first set me on this line of enquiry. Chapters 4 and 5 on Joseph Schumpeter and Carl Schmitt, whose work paralleled and was influenced by that of Weber, were written after the book was completed and seek to deepen and carry forward its arguments.

Parts II and III chart my no doubt foolhardy attempt to extend the historical argument of *Liberalism and Modern Society* into the contemporary era, and to examine how liberalism might be rethought in the context of today's complex, pluralist and globalizing societies. The brief discussion of recent liberal philosophers and even briefer gestures towards an alternative democratic liberalism had been the most criticized sections of the book. I now tried to meet these criticisms. In fact, many liberal theorists had begun to move in directions I found congenial. For a start, there had been something of a rapprochement between liberal and communitarian thought. Certain theorists, notably William Galston and Joseph Raz, had given an avowedly perfectionist and to some degree communitarian defence of liberalism. Others, such as Will Kymlicka, contented themselves with arguing that liberalism incorporated most of the insights of communitarians, so that they had been shooting at a straw target. Even the New Right protested they were not anti-communitarian but merely believed communities were a private affair more damaged than helped by state action. Meanwhile, communitarians such as Taylor and Walzer argued they too were closet liberals. Their differences with other liberal thinkers lay largely at the level of ontology rather than advocacy.

Some liberals also accepted the need to rethink liberalism in a more explicitly political and less metaphysical or ethical direction than hitherto. Thus, Rawls recast his theory as an avowedly political conception of liberalism designed to confront 'the fact of pluralism', whilst Will Kymlicka tried to extend liberal arguments concerning rights and equality to the protection of distinct cultures to meet the challenge posed by multiculturalism. However, more robust liberals regarded such moves as selling the pass. Raz, for example, contended that Rawls's 'epistemic abstinence' deprived his theory of the very arguments needed to generate its liberal conclusions. Fortunately, such self-abnegation was also unnecessary, since the deep ethical commitments of liberalism were far less contentious than Rawls supposed. Reviving the perfectionist and progressive arguments of traditional liberalism, Raz contended that liberal autonomy and the pluralism of modern societies were mutually supporting. *Pace* Kymlicka, non-pluralist and illiberal cultures were destined to wither away, although liberals had prudential and justice-based reasons to make this process as painless as possible. Libertarians were somewhat more hard-nosed but made a parallel point. They argued the market gave individuals the possibility to choose any way of life or culture, so long as they were willing to bear the costs. As such, it offered the fairest and most efficient means for determining which should survive, with the least popular and viable rightly going to the wall.

The essays in Part II engage with these debates. Chapter 6 questions whether even a political liberalism can forgo all metaphysical claims, whilst contending the strong conception of ethical community advocated by Raz and others is no longer plausible in pluralist societies. Chapter 7 argues markets cannot fill this space, for they too rely on moral and social resources they do not create and may even subvert. Chapters 8 and 9 criticize the attempts of 'political' and 'economic' liberals alike to evade these dilemmas by grounding their arguments in a set of abstract, universal rights that might frame the democratic and market activities through which individuals pursue their various conceptions of the good. These rights supposedly reflect a minimal consensus on the necessary preconditions for any such practices. However, rights do not establish these practices – they derive from them and the goods they promote. In consequence, they have a collective as well as an individual dimension, and are themselves subject to incommensurable and often incompatible judgements. Freedom of speech, for example, is valued less as an individual right, which few, after all, choose to exercise, than for its contribution to sustaining a certain kind of society which provides its members with a desirable quality of life. As debates over issues such as pornography reveal, one cannot specify the scope and limits of this right without invoking considerations about the good, both of individuals and of the broader community. Since people will disagree about these issues, it proves impossible to exclude conflicting ideals and interests from the public sphere, as contemporary liberals propose. No compossible set of rights exists, no matter how minimal. Thus, we need mechanisms to resolve these disputes in a fair and mutually acceptable manner. Chapter 10 reveals neither markets nor judicial review are suited to this task, and advocates (as do the concluding sections of Chapters 6, 8 and 9) employing democratic politics to build community by negotiating reciprocal compromises between conflicting views.

This argument draws on the civic republican tradition as described by Quentin Skinner and more recently by Philip Pettit. Whereas the republicanism favoured by certain communitarians, such as Taylor and Sandel, looks to Aristotle and assumes an intrinsic connection between political participation, individual development and the unfolding ethical life of the polity, this view derives from Machiavelli and the Roman tradition of Cicero and Livy. As Isaiah Berlin noted in a famous essay, part of Machiavelli's 'originality' lay in his appreciation of the clash between mutually exclusive yet ultimate moral visions and types of moral claim, and his perception of the distinctive role of politics in deciding between them. Unlike contemporary communitarians, he did not believe societies can be united around a common conception of the good. A society of any complexity was inevitably riven by class conflict and competing interests and ideals. Rather than trading on a moralistic conception of positive liberty, therefore, Machiavelli urged civic involvement to avoid the domination of tyrants or elites. A negative view of liberty, freedom from domination nonetheless involves an appreciation of how individual liberty is tied to the collective actions of citizens in the maintenance of a free society.

As Machiavelli's modern heir, Max Weber, saw, his understanding of the irreducible character of moral conflict and his realist approach to politics are well suited to the pluralist dilemmas thrown up in contemporary societies. However, Weber, like (if more profoundly than) his contemporary Italian Machiavellians, gave a Nietzschean twist to the Florentine's position, that led him to see latter-day Princes as the only possible political actors. This aristocratic and neo-existentialist argument takes the liberal notion of autonomy to extremes. Only the radical and life-defining choices of exceptional individuals, possessing what Iris Murdoch memorably termed 'a brave and naked will', can decide between conflicting values. Although compatible with an elitist view of democracy, as the analysis of Schumpeter – who followed Weber in this respect – reveals, it can yield the distinctly more sinister notion of the Führer principle, a path tragically followed by Carl Schmitt and in Italy by Vilfredo Pareto and Giovanni Gentile. By contrast, I argue (in the final sections of Chapters 4 and 5) we need not be so pessimistic. The democratic settlement of pluralist disputes and the political regulation of complex societies remain both possible and highly desirable. Delivering on this promise involves showing one can mediate in a manner at once realistic and reasoned between incommensurable and incompatible ideals and interests. Drawing on the democratic potential of Machiavellian republicanism, I try to meet both these conditions.

The key to republicanism, on my interpretation, lies in devising a political system that mixes the social interests and moral ideals in play, constraining the ability of anyone to dominate another and leading each to seek mutually acceptable solutions that track the common, shareable concerns of those affected by the decision. A position I develop in detail in Chapters 4 and 5 of *Liberalism and Pluralism*, and more sketchily in this volume in the final sections of Chapters 4, 5, 6, 8, 9 and 10, its origins lie in the classic republican conception of a mixed and balanced constitution. Social complexity and the undercutting of state sovereignty occasioned by globalization aid this dispersal of power. The resulting mixed polity forces a process of justification similar to that described by recent post-Rawlsian contractarian theorists, such as Thomas Scanlon and Brian Barry, but adds three ingredients missing from their writings yet vital to real-world politics. First, it provides a mechanism that allows individuals to push their interests and ideals for themselves and complain if these are overlooked or unjustifiably overridden. Second, that same mechanism allows the negotiation of compromises that help construct common interests and consensual values, at least with regard to particular policies. Third, the involvement of citizens helps legitimize the result in their eyes and fosters compliance with it. I dub this strategy democratic liberalism because it treats liberal virtues and values as intrinsic to democratic processes rather than preconditions for them, as liberal democrats suppose.

The democratic liberal approach takes the opposite tack to the neutralist liberal constitutional one. Advocates of the latter position try to arrive at a consensus on a constitutional framework by excluding contentious opinions from the political arena and placing hard cases in the hands of a constitutional court. However, such a primordial consensus proves a chimera. At best it ends up being so abstract that its implications for particular circumstances are hard to fathom; at worst it fails to gain acceptance amongst those to whom it applies and has to be imposed. A democratic liberalism aims at compromises through the expression and discussion of controversial views. It is the specificity of plural conflicts, the fact that they occur between particular bearers of value in given contexts, that provide the commonalities and the possibilities for bartering and alternative rankings that make compromises possible. A democratic liberalism exploits these circumstances, in the process generating policies that are both well adapted to complex situations and acceptable to a plurality of agents. The trick is to so design institutions that the negotiation of compromises occurs in a fair manner that obliges each party to hear and engage with the other side.

Part III applies these criticisms of liberal theory and its proposed democratic reworking to the analysis of liberal practice. Chapter 11 sees in the Poll Tax the unravelling of neutralist, rights-based liberalism and its privatization of community obligations. Chapter 12 argues that the erosion of national political communities by global markets has not led to agreement on a cosmopolitan moral and political framework, as certain liberals hoped. Instead it has produced a fragmentation of communitarian allegiances – a situation that requires a complex political system to mediate between them. The mixed and balanced constitutional regime characteristic of republicanism proves highly suited to this task. The reconfiguration of sovereignty and national identity within the EU offers an example of how such a transnational republic might be constructed.

Taken together, these essays present a rethinking of liberalism's past, present and future. They map a passage from the liberal democratic norms and forms characteristic of nineteenth-century nation-states to an agonistic, democratic liberal politics suitable for the transnational, complex and plural societies of the next millennium. This transition involves a shift of focus from consensus to compromise. The result is a democratic system that incorporates liberalism by combining the concern for fairness and justification traditional to liberals with the flexibility and popular legitimacy rightly valued by democrats.

PART I

The Transformation of Liberalism

CHAPTER 1

Hegel and Liberalism

Contemporary liberals generally regard Hegel's political theory as totally antithetical to liberalism. They take issue with his claim that a political community is defined by a number of common moral goals that are logically prior to those of its members; and that the legitimacy of the state flows from upholding these, rather than the particular interests of individuals in society. They argue that the state is simply a means to the fulfilment of our private projects. It is therefore subordinate to society, merely providing a legal and institutional framework for the adjustment and reconciliation of the divergent pursuits of its different members. Hegel is charged with substituting the plurality and freedom of society for the imposed uniformity of a preconceived metaphysical entity, the 'supra-individual' state.[1]

Recent critics of modern liberalism have come to Hegel's defence. They maintain that the individualist framework adopted by contemporary liberals is incapable of explaining the myriad relationships which make up society and define the preferences and ideals of its members. However, they are equally uneasy about his metaphysical explanation of politics. They regard the community as a product of its history and tradition and refrain from following Hegel and interpreting these processes as stages in the development of Spirit or the Idea, which gives to human affairs an inner meaning and rationality.[2]

However, by so arguing, Hegel's defenders would appear to concede the modern liberal's accusations that his philosophy is implicitly conservative; the endorsement of existing social relations as the product of a benign, if unknowable, demiurge, the 'cunning of reason'. In the first section of this chapter I shall contest these interpretations, and show how Hegel's concepts of *Geist* and *Sittlichkeit* function in support of his ontological analysis of human existence. This theory completes, rather than undermines, many central liberal claims regarding the primacy of the individual in the social process. As the second section illustrates, Hegel built upon his conception of the individual to explain the workings of the characteristic liberal institutions of private property, the economic market and representative democracy. Again, his achievement was to dissolve a number of inconsistencies within liberalism, particularly as regards the relations between the two last elements. Contrary to traditional interpretations, he did not dispute their validity as a means of distributing goods and making decisions which respect and reflect the various preferences and rights of different members of society. However, he did deny that they could be interpreted as neutral procedural mechanisms which adjudicated between essentially self-regarding individuals. In the final section, the virtues of the Hegelian approach will be highlighted by comparing his ethical view of liberalism, as a complex of customs and self-understandings orientated around the pursuit of the common good, with the neutralist stance of contemporary liberals.

Individuality and Community

Many liberals accept Marx's contention that Hegel makes the men and women, who are the real subjects of history, predicates of a metaphysical fiction, the Idea or Spirit. This interpretation of Hegelian metaphysics underpins their claim that Hegel conceives of the state as the bearer of the collective identity of its members.[3] Hegel's position, though, is much more complex.

His entire project is an attempt to come to grips with human freedom and individuality. He recognized that the close-knit solidarity of traditional societies had broken down under the twin impact of Christianity (para. 124 R)[4] and the growth of commerce (para. 182 A). The first, in its Protestant interpretation, asserted the primacy of the individual conscience as the fount and locus of all value. The second fostered, in a variety of ways, the possessive individualism characteristic of capitalism. Both are important features of the liberal defence of individuality, and Hegel did not seek to deny either aspect. Whilst he shared his contemporaries' fascination with the Hellenic ideal of political community, he believed that the conditions of modern society entailed a fundamental rethinking of its main tenets. 'The right of the subject's particularity', he remarked,

> his right to be satisfied, or in other words the right of subjective freedom, is the pivot and centre of the difference between antiquity and modern times. This right in its infinity is given expression in Christianity and it has become the universal effective principle of a new form of civilization. (para. 124 A)

The Platonic republic, which he is often seen as emulating, is vitiated by its repression of both aspects of individuality (para. 185 R). However, Hegel disputed the conclusion, drawn by many liberal theorists, of an inherent

4

incompatibility between the individual and community, summed up in Bentham's claim that 'the community is a fictitious *body*, composed of the individual persons who are considered as constituting as it were its *members*'.[5]

Hegel aimed to avoid the extremes of both Benthamite individualism and the Platonic organicism normally attributed to him, and explain how the community provides the medium for social interaction and the fashioning of personal identity.[6] This project involved the criticism of the two alternative accounts of individual agency prominent in the contemporary liberal literature, and briefly outlined above. The empirical model, associated with Hobbes and Bentham, regards the individual as having a number of set desires and powers which he seeks to satisfy by an instrumental calculation of how best to maximize his utility. This model corresponds to the notions of agency appropriate to commercial transactions. The rationalist model, of which Kant is the forebear, conceives the agent as an autonomous chooser of ends, who stands aloof from his natural inclinations. This model derives from the role played by the individual conscience in Christian ethics. Both theories view society as a contract between individuals for the realization of antecedently arrived at goals. Hegel, in contrast, provides a dialectical criticism of the two accounts and attempts to show how the individual's will is realized in particular objects and mediated by certain universal norms of behaviour which are social in origin. Far from denying these two liberal views of the individual, he aims to render them coherent.

He begins by disputing the empiricist thesis, which conceives our will to act 'as an immediate existing content, i.e., as the impulses, desires, inclinations, whereby the will finds itself determined in the course of nature' (para. 11). If our character was defined by a number of accidental wants, then our identity would consist of little more than

> a medley and multiplicity of impulses, each of which is merely 'my desire' but exists alongside other desires which are likewise all 'mine', and each of which is at the same time something universal and indeterminate, aimed at all kinds of objectives and satiable in all kinds of ways. (para. 12)

Hegel questions whether the consistent willing of certain types of objects over others, which define each individual's distinctive personality, could ever emerge from this picture. Outside of a totally regulated environment, our preferences would be perennially subject to change and irreconcilable clashes would arise between incompatible wants.

A utilitarian might counter that I could consistently will to maximize my satisfactions, and hence order them appropriately. Thus I could control my desire for drink on the grounds that the hangover the following morning causes me greater pain than the immediate pleasurable feeling of intoxication. Hegel denies the validity of this approach. First, he argues that such an ordering would still be liable to uncontrollable alterations. The possible combinations of wants by the introduction of new desires, resulting from changing circumstances or new considerations, can increase *ad infinitum* (para. 16). Choosing between them will be entirely arbitrary, for '[a]n impulse is simply a unidirectional urge and this has no measuring rod in itself' (para. 17). Second, he contends that for this reason we could not rank different pleasures according to their empirical properties. Instead, an individual makes qualitative judgements concerning the desirability of different wants on the basis of how he conceives himself, not as a result of certain contingent impulses. I refrain from habitual drunkenness on the grounds that permanent inebriation would be unworthy of me, and a waste of my mental faculties. I help an old lady who has collapsed in the road, even if I have pressing business elsewhere and am tempted to let someone else do it, because I value concern for others and aspire to be a caring person. The possession of such standards of behaviour constitute my identity, providing my actions with meaning and continuity (para. 105). Thus, far from being a slave to the passions, individuals fashion their conduct to their will, just as through their labour they mould the natural world into a design of their own.

However, Hegel does not believe that these norms of conduct are solely products of our rational autonomous will, that we could or should completely transcend our nature. He agrees with Kant that the free will is 'self-determining universality' (para. 21). But the Kantian attempt to ground morality on the formal criterion of universalizability is ultimately vacuous. It is insufficiently determinate in itself to provide us with moral maxims; it can only test some existing precept. Moreover, it fails even in this capacity; for with a little ingenuity I could dress up any precept with sufficient qualifications to enable it to pass the test. The will of the completely autonomous agent, therefore, is as unstable as that of the utilitarian rational calculator. It has no real content beyond the whims of the agent, which in turn derive from his or her natural impulses. Thus the second liberal model of the individual tends to collapse into the first, with all its attendant weaknesses (paras 122–4, 135 and A).

Neither the empiricist nor the Kantian theory of human agency can provide a coherent ordering of preferences suitable as a basis for social co-operation. Hegel sought a resolution to this dilemma by a synthesis of the two. He invokes a universal element to mediate between the particularity of our wants and needs and the individuality of the subjective will. This is supplied by his concept of *Geist* or Spirit. Every community has a characteristic set of cultural norms and values inherent to the collective practices of its members, in Hegel's terminology a *Volksgeist*. The individual shares many of the concepts of his fellows as 'a form of necessity' by virtue of the normal processes of socialization.[7] But this does not entail the complete identification of individual and social context, 'for this consciousness emanates from the individual himself and is not instilled into him by others: the individual *exists* within the substance'.[8]

The community stands in relation to the individual in much the same way as the rules of language relate to speech. Whilst vocabulary and grammar do not absolutely determine what we think and say, they do structure it. When we add or alter common usage, it is necessarily in ways compatible with intersubjective intelligibility if we are not to withdraw into a private world of our own. Even then we would necessarily retain part of this common language to think and act at all, for it is precisely this Spirit which provides the evaluative principles necessary for coherent thought and action, preventing us from falling into the arbitrariness of the subjective will or mere impulse.

The existence of intersubjective modes of understanding are basic to the development of personality. We are social beings and can only acquire the distinctive human capacities to communicate, form relationships and develop goals which render our lives meaningful, through society. Individuals draw upon the concepts and understandings of social life in the framing of their plans of life. However, this does not mean that society imposes a role upon us. Rather, we self-consciously use it to determine our own aims and purposes, just as we use language to write a novel, philosophize, ask a favour, and so on. As a result, we do not uncritically accept all the norms and rules of our community; we can deploy them in ways that enable us to envisage alternative ways of living. The evolution of society is thus an integral part of an individual's self-realization.

If the above account is correct, then Hegel can be absolved from the accusation that he reduces the individual to a cypher of society or a metaphysical entity, *Geist*. He does not impose a real will on the empirical wants and desires of the agent, nor does he reduce his or her autonomy of action. But he does regard these attributes as developing within the context of society, rather than as antecedent to it. Thus the state cannot abolish society, as some critics of Hegel's political theory suggest, since it is integral to our formation as political actors. Instead he proposed an institutional framework which would provide an arena for individuals to voice criticism of their social bonds and hence develop them as human needs change, without returning to a putative asocial state of nature of the war of all against all – the perspective of liberal contractarian theories. In the next section I shall show how Hegel's theory of the state provides the institutional counterpart to this conception of individual agency.

Private Property, the Market and the State

Hegel's description of the development of personality, through the use of particular objects to further projects conceived within the context of certain social rules and norms, can be rendered in Hegelian language as reflecting the relationship between Universal, Particular and Individual. He believes these three terms are interdependent, so that 'Everything rational shows itself to be a threefold union or syllogism [of Universal, Particular and Individual], in that each of the members takes the place both of one of the extremes and the mediating middle.'[9]

Even the most casual acquaintance with the *Philosophy of Right*, a glance at the table of contents for example, reveals this 'threefold mediation or syllogism' to be the organizing principles of the work. Thus the first syllogism – of Individual, Particular and Universal – forms the basis for the section on Abstract Right. Here the individual will finds the universal through seeking the fulfilment of the particular inclinations, needs and passions with which he or she was born via the possession of property. Yet even within this section there is a threefold mediation of the Idea. The second mediation (adopting Hegel's abbreviation) U–I–P, deals with contract – that is, the regulation of individual wills once they come into contact with each other for the purposes of commerce and exchange. The final mediation P–U–I, having the Universal as its mid-point, deals with the morality of commerce and exchange, the notions of fraud and crime. Similarly the third part of the *Philosophy of Right*, ethical life, is both the final mediation of the syllogism, P–U–I, whilst containing within it all three mediations. Thus the family is a unity founded on the immediacy of feeling, civil society is a 'system of needs' based on the satisfaction of particular desires through the forces of production, whilst the state is the unity mediated by the Universal, the common good. Finally, within the state itself there are the three moments of the concept. As Hegel explained in the *Encyclopaedia*:

> the state is a system of three syllogisms: (i) The individual or person, through his particularity or physical or mental needs, ... is coupled with the Universal, i.e. with society, law, right, government. (ii) The will or action of individuals is the intermediating force which procures for these needs satisfaction in society, law, etc ... , and which gives to society, law etc ... , their fulfilment and actualization. (iii) But the Universal, i.e. the state, government, and law, is the permanent underlying mean in which the individuals and their satisfaction have and receive their fulfilled reality, intermediation and persistence. Each of the moments of the concept, as it is brought by intermediation to coalesce with the other extreme is brought into union with itself and produces itself ... It is only by this triad of syllogisms with the same terms that the whole is thoroughly understood in its organization.

This rather formal working out of the logic of the state may seem at first glance to have fully justified the chief qualms of Hegel's detractors. However, it merely summarizes and extends the thesis outlined in the first section. Hegel argues that our individuality, the feelings and desires we have, become particularized, made concrete, by finding satisfaction in the possession and creation of objects. Our rights of personality and property originate in this activity. However, human action does not occur in a social vacuum, and so 'rights collide' (para. 30). We can only prevent the upshot of this contest being the rule of the strongest through a public authority, which represents the complex of rights of all its individual members and facilitates their private projects. Hegel contends that these arrangements develop out of social life and the intersubjective norms which make personal relationships possible: in Hegelian language, the moment of universality.

This logic informs his understanding of the interrelationship of the three main aspects of the liberal political settlement: personal and property rights, the economic market and representative democracy. I shall argue below that Hegel reveals how these institutions assume the theory of individual agency outlined in the previous section, their rationale being to facilitate the development of essential human powers and capacities through social co-operation.

Personal and property rights play a vital part in Hegel's theory. Developing Lockean themes,[10] he asserts that a 'man actualizes himself only in becoming something definite, i.e. something specifically particularized' (para. 207). Possession of property enables us to gain a sense of self-hood, it externalizes our impulses and will, making us aware of our tastes and capacities (paras 34, 41 and 57). Using our property, transforming it through our labour, liberates us from our desires, moulding them to our will (paras 45, 46 and 59). This process of progressive self-determination becomes complete when we alienate our property and enter into exchanges with others (para. 62). Private property provides the basis for personal rights, since it is a precondition both for the development of our personality and for moral action (paras 49, 66 and R). Communal ownership, by contrast, would undermine the independence necessary for the free development of the will (paras 46 and 186 R). An important corollary of this analysis is Hegel's contention that I cannot treat my person or liberties as property, since this would negate the subject of possession and entail a form of suicide (paras 66 and 70).

Private property secures the necessary, but not the sufficient, conditions for individual freedom. To identify with one's possessions involves a continued subservience to desire and externalities. Transcending this state is partially achieved through contract. Goods take on universal attributes for the purposes of exchange; we measure their worth in terms of their human use value (para. 77). However, he disputes the belief that social and contractual relationships can be regarded entirely individualistically, as instrumental calculations for maximizing personal utility (para. 187). This criticism refers back to his theory of human agency, examined earlier. If property merely served to satisfy existing impulses and desires, as an end in itself rather than a means for self-development, then there would be no reason to go beyond mere subsistence. Any increasing pressure of population on resources would yield Malthusian consequences rather than new forms of production and social co-operation. The market does not simply allow the competition of the state of nature to continue at a higher level; it transforms the individual by developing his or her capacity for self-realization (paras 187 and R). An awareness of others, as we saw, is vital for the individual to move beyond mere particularity. Hegel illustrates this by demonstrating how even the mutual security of possession evinces a pre-existing social bond: for 'I hold my property not merely by means of a thing and my subjective will, but by means of another person's will as well and so hold it in virtue of my participation in a common will' (para. 71).

Market relations, which characterize civil society, only appear to have mutual self-interest as their basis when viewed externally, by the Understanding (*Verstand*) (para. 189 A). Their true rationale, as provided by Reason (*Vernuft*), derives from the social character of the capitalist system. Building on the work of classical political economists, particularly Adam Smith and Sir James Steuart,[11] Hegel describes how the economic advances of commercial society had not only increased the scope for personal autonomy, but also generated new forms of communal attachment and solidarity.[12] Our release from a primitive dependence on nature comes with an appreciation of more universal aspects of human existence, which arises through social contacts and the search for stable shared norms to regulate our affairs. He criticizes Rousseau's belief, implicit in the contractarian tradition, that society puts a constraint on the natural freedom of the state of nature:

> Since in social needs, as the conjunction of immediate or natural needs with mental needs arising from ideas, it is needs of the latter type which because of their universality make themselves preponderant, this social moment has in it the aspect of liberation, i.e. the strict natural necessity of need is obscured and man is concerned with his own opinion, indeed with an opinion which is universal, and with a necessity of his own making alone, instead of with an external necessity, an inner contingency, and mere caprice. (para. 194 and R)

The 'system of needs' does not evolve from the satisfaction of the naturally given wants of isolated individuals; it provides the context in which social bonds arise through the network of reciprocal relationships, formed on the basis of a mutual recognition of certain universally valued goods (paras 190–2). Commodities cease to have any value in themselves but derive their worth from human need. This facilitates the development of a money economy, whereby incommensurables can be exchanged using a single medium (para. 63 A).

Outside a subsistence economy we need others to provide certain of our basic needs. This requirement increases as the division of labour extends and our wants get more complex; for example, today not only have our stable foods passed through a network of different producers, refiners and brokers but we have developed needs and tastes for goods, such as cars and home computers, which can only be co-operatively produced. Even if 'each a member is his own end', locked in the pursuit of self-interested particularity, 'except in contact with others he cannot attain the whole compass of his ends' (para. 182 A). A quasi-Smithian 'invisible hand', re-christened the 'cunning of reason', is at work in commercial transactions, so that 'if I further my ends, I further the ends of the universal, and this is turn furthers my end' (para. 184 A). My self-interest causes me to add to the community's wealth by both producing more and increasing my demand for the goods of others:

> That is to say, by a dialectical advance, subjective self-seeking turns into the mediation of the particular through the universal, with the result that each man in earning, producing and enjoying on his own account is *eo ipso* producing and earning for the enjoyment of everyone else. (para. 199)

Despite these advantages, Hegel appreciated that the complexity of modern industrial society put this sense of community under a severe strain, and that on a conscious level 'in civil society universal and particular have fallen apart' (para. 184 A). Hegel identified two threats to community feeling within the industrial system. First, although the division of labour ties individuals together through various forms of economic interdependence, it shuts them off socially from their fellows. People increasingly identify with the particular groups they belong to, their family and workmates, and lose a sense of membership of a wider community. Second, as industrial labour becomes increasingly mechanical and monotonous it has an ennervating effect on the worker, subduing his will to rise above basic natural needs (para. 243).[13] Personal and economic relations in civil society are conducted within a legal framework which applies certain universal criteria of justice. These regulations reflect the interconnectedness of civil society and the interest each individual has in the universal observance of rules securing possession (para. 235). However, the atomism of modern life threatens the system, for the pursuit of personal satisfactions increasingly takes precedence over a knowledge of, and hence a concern for, the common interest (para. 236 R).

Hegel illustrates this dilemma by addressing the problem of poverty.[14] A purely economic theory of justice, such as Hume's, based on a mutual interest in maximizing production, proves self-contradictory. The 'unimpeded activity' of civil society, centred simply on the unrestrained gratification of human desire, leads to periodic crises of over-production (para. 243). When the demand for a particular commodity ceases, the workers, who, due to the increasing specialization of labour, depend for their livelihood on this product, lose their jobs. Whilst a safety net of state benefits and voluntary charity may prevent the indigent from actually starving (paras 242 and R), Hegel appreciates that it is the drop in relative standing which counts. The unemployed lose the sources of self-respect deriving from labour and become 'a rabble of paupers'. At the same time this brings with it 'conditions which greatly facilitate the concentration of disproportionate wealth in a few hands' (para. 244).

Plant, Avineri, Cullen and others have followed Marx and argued that Hegel has no solution to this problem.[15] His philosophy commits him to offering a redescription of society capable of reconciling us to it, but eschews the structural changes necessary to alter the social practices which produce the poor and oppressed in the first place. Paradoxically, whilst Marx and liberals agree that Hegel's philosophy amounts to a 'pantheistic mysticism', Marx maintains that he deploys it to defend the economic system underlying liberalism.[16] However, as we saw in section one, Hegel clearly rejects the possessive individualist mentality Marx imputes to liberal theory. With extraordinary prescience, Hegel foresaw that if economic competition went unchecked then the only solution to over-production would be the creation of new markets by colonization, a path already taken by England (para. 246). But he did not advocate this solution. As long as we remain within the perspective of political economy, of instrumental action to realize self-interested goals, then unrestricted economic expansion seems the only answer to this problem. However, for Hegel the unchecked pursuit of particularity is a pathological state. As we noted in section one, our projects only gain meaning and purpose, become expressions of our individuality and autonomy, within the context of a shared set of norms. These norms make social life possible, since they enable us to relate our own interests with those of others as part of the complex tapestry of universal values which make for a worthwhile life. The restricted mentality of the market is transcended through political institutions capable of fostering a general commitment to providing the social conditions necessary for the realization of human capacities generally, rather than mere individual self-interest.

In perceiving the need for political control of the economy, Hegel did not seek to get the populace to identify completely and unreflectively with the state's priorities by a mixture of force and propaganda, as those critics who accuse him of totalitarianism maintain. The transition from civil society to the state does not entail the complete subordination of the one to the other. As always, Hegel does not seek to deny either particularity or individuality, but merely to provide the possibilities for mediating between the two by appealing to universal values necessary for the expression of both. Personal and property rights are not sacrificed upon entering the state. The state exists to uphold them; it represents the entire complex of rights necessary for the self-development of each member of society:

> ... it is the end immanent within them, and its strength lies in the unity of its own universal end and aim with the particular interest of individuals, in the fact that individuals have duties to the state in proportion as they have rights against it. (para. 261)

Society provides the medium for the realization of our individual projects and the source of our co-operation with each other. To become conscious of this requires politics, the explicit recognition of a public dimension to our seemingly purely private concerns. Far from imposing the state's authority upon society, Hegel regards it as emerging from our social activities. He remarks that the formation of sub-groups within the system of needs, particularly of the professional associations or corporations, provide key institutions for the development of social awareness and combatting the subjectivism encouraged by the capitalist mode of industrial production (para. 264). They educate us to take the needs of others into account and to co-operate with them (para. 253 R). They provide a means for the individual to go beyond his particular interest and perceive the validity of an allegiance to the common good. Thus poverty sheds its degrading aspect, for

> Within the corporation the help which poverty receives loses its accidental character and the humiliation wrongfully associated with it. The wealthy perform their duties to their fellow associates and thus riches cease to inspire either pride or envy . . . (para. 235 R)

Bernard Cullen has argued that because Hegel excludes the indigent and unskilled wage labourers from the corporations (para. 252 A) and estates, they remain outside society as an unintegrated rabble.[17] He correctly notes that Hegel's attitude reflects a common liberal fear of giving political rights to the property-less. Indeed, Hegel has well-articulated philosophical reasons for believing that property is a precondition for independent, responsible behaviour. Yet this observation neither logically commits Hegel to a restricted electorate, nor renders poverty an intractable problem for him. The dispossession of the labouring classes stems, on his analysis, from 'the luxury of the business classes and their passion for extravagance' (para. 253). But the corporations will overcome their particularity and hence modify their behaviour so that crises of overproduction will not occur. The solution to the problem of poverty stems less from the integration of the poor, so much as the modification of the attitudes of the rich. It was the lack of such institutions in England which motivated his attack on the English Reform Bill. Without social reform as well, the enfranchising of a penurious rabble would spell disaster. Hegel did not reject the objectives of the Reform Bill, but believed a very different institutional framework was needed to attain the desired aim of 'bringing justice and fairness into the allotment of the parts played by the different classes and divisions of the people in the election of members of Parliament'.[18]

Social atomism and rampant individualism are not inevitable features of capitalist systems. They only flourish when the lack of mediating institutions cuts individuals off from their fellow citizens and a perception of their obligations to the whole. Hegel's argument is closely related to his discussion of personal identity. For without a sense of others we can have only a very inadequate grasp of ourselves. We cannot understand the values which give meaning to life and provide us with personal goals without a knowledge of the needs and requirements of others, for we articulate our private aspirations through a public language. To separate out our private rights from our public duties can only return us to the *bellum omnium contra omnes* of the state of nature, where each person is a prey to his or her capricious desires for a disparate set of objects.

This observation lies behind Hegel's reasoning that people enter politics via the estates rather than directly. Hegel's *Stande* reflect the various economic and social functions people perform. The three main divisions comprise the (i) agrarian, (ii) the commercial and industrial, and (iii) the bureaucratic estates (para. 202). Although the *Pobel* or rabble have no place within the scheme (para. 244 A), skilled industrial workers belong to the second group (para. 204). Some critics have misconstrued Hegel's theory as advocating a system of functional representation, which reduces the individual to a mere cog in the machinery of the state. However, Hegel clearly intends these intermediary institutions to liberate the individual from the narrow perspective of his role within the productive process. His criticism of direct democracy merely echoes traditional liberal fears of the tyranny of the majority. Subdued by the conditions of industrial labour and isolated from their fellows by the atomism of modern social life, the people are a prey to the manipulation of any demagogue willing to appeal to the lowest common denominator. Fortunately 'this atomistic and abstract point of view' is mitigated by the circles of association in civil society.

> To picture these communities as once more breaking up into a mere conglomeration of individuals as soon as they enter the field of politics, i.e. the field of the highest concrete universality, is *eo ipso* to hold civil and political life apart from one another and as it were to hang the latter in the air, because the basis could then only be the abstract individuality of caprice and opinions, and hence it would be grounded on chance and not on what is absolutely stable and justified. (para. 303 R)

Hegel makes three main criticisms of direct democracy. First, he argues that because of the complexity of modern industrial society, ordinary voters lack the technical expertise to decide issues of public policy for themselves and perforce must rely on the opinions of specialists (paras 301 R and 308 R). Second, the atomism and diversity of contemporary social relations restrict the benefits of participation, which only obtain in a small, relatively homogeneous group (para. 303 R). Hegel anticipated recent arguments about voter rationality in situations where any one vote is unlikely to affect the outcome, commenting that popular suffrage in large states 'leads inevitably to electoral indifference' so that 'election actually falls into the power of a few, of a caucus' (para. 311 R).[19] More seriously, he maintained that these conditions, combined with the individualistic ethos they encouraged, militated against any consensual agreement on a general will. This requires voters to be both well disposed towards and well informed about each other – clearly problematical once the electorate goes above a certain size and a degree of social differentiation exists. Intense minorities are liable to develop who will be consistently outvoted by a majority either ignorant or uncomprehending of their needs. Finally, Hegel challenges the coherence of the Rousseauian/ Kantian doctrine of the universal will. As we noted in section one, he maintains that the criterion of universalizability is totally vacuous and cannot either provide us with moral axioms or adjudicate between existing ones. Rather, it has the deleterious effect of giving our individualistic wants and desires the force of a moral law, as in the case of religious and political fanatics. The anarchy of the French Revolution, which culminated in the forced imposition of the will of a particular group on the populace, and Fichte's advocacy of government by an enlightened elite, illustrated the likely repugnant outcome of attempting to derive social institutions and concrete duties from the abstract will of the individual subject (para. 258 R).

Hegel's two-tier system aims to counteract these defects of Rousseauian democracy. It is participatory at each level, within the corporations, estates and legislature, since within small bodies such as these the virtues of discussion prevail, based on a certain coherence of common interests. However, he does not regard the delegates sent by the various associations to the estates as bound to the particular interests of the group they represent. Quite the reverse, they are chosen 'on the strength of confidence felt in them . . . as having a better understanding of [public] affairs than their electors'. Moreover, 'their assembly is meant to be a living body in which all members deliberate in common and reciprocally instruct and convince each other'. Debates are not formal affairs, in which each participant knows his opinion from the start; rather, agreement is reached through collective discussions. Public involvement in national politics does not cease merely because their delegates decide these issues. 'Estates assemblies . . . are a great spectacle and an excellent education for the citizens, and it is from them that the people learns best how to recognize the character of its interests' (para. 315 A). By participating at the local levels of community life and watching the national assemblies, people become both better able to judge the quality of delegates and to accept the legitimacy of the public authority. Thus far from denigrating freedom of speech and association, Hegel had a Tocquevillian faith in their value and necessity for transforming the private seeker after personal satisfaction into a citizen concerned with the public weal (paras 317–19).

Hegel clearly repudiates the bureaucratic, totalitarian conception of the state, often attributed to him, since it would deny both particularity and individuality. Nor did he believe that a communal spirit could be artificially created by the state, as fascist interpretators sometimes maintained. He explicitly rejected the 'machine state', arguing that 'the government must leave to the freedom of the citizens whatever is not necessary for its appointed function of organizing and maintaining authority . . . This is true regardless of utility, because the freedom of the citizen is inherently sacrosant.'[20] Unless the state has the reflective allegiance of its members it 'hangs in the air' (para.

265). Freedom of speech and association, therefore, play a vital part in his theory, because they encourage the active participation in political processes necessary to generate the social bonds which mitigate the atomistic individualism of commerce (paras 260, 264 and 317–19).

The Hegelian state reconciles the two conceptions of individual freedom characteristic of liberalism, namely the Kantian view of following self-posited goals and the Hobbesian notion of instrumental action for the satisfaction of certain innate desires. Whilst the former aspiration belongs to our role as political actors within a democracy, the second characterizes our activity as producers and consumers in the market. Contemporary theorists have noted a lack of fit between the two, creating a legitimation crisis reflecting the tension between our two persona. For example, as democrats we may agree on the necessity of certain public utilities which we nevertheless resent paying for as individualistic members of society, when they conflict with our private interest.[21] Thus we may support state education but send our children to private schools, or object to paying for it if we are childless. Hegel seeks to modify such conflicts by fostering an awareness of how our own projects fit in with those of others, forming part of a complex web of universal values which together make human life worthwhile.[22] Liberal institutions derive their rationale from revealing the respects in which social cooperation is vital to the pursuit of our numerous private goals:

> The result is that the universal does not prevail or achieve completion except along with particular interests and through the cooperation of particular knowing and willing; and individuals likewise do not live as private persons for their own ends alone, but in the very act of willing these they will the universal in the light of the universal and their activity is consciously aimed at none but the universal end. The principle of modern states has prodigious strength and depth because it allows the principle of subjectivity to progress to its culmination in the extreme of self-subsistent personal particularity, and yet at the same time brings it back to the substantive unity and so maintains this unity in the principle of subjectivity itself. (para. 260)

Hegelian and Contemporary Liberalism

Hegel neither treats the community as a supra-individual entity above the individuals who compose it, nor adopts a conservative relativism which merely endorses social relations as they stand. As we have seen, he relies upon a theory of individuality to provide criteria by which different social arrangements can be evaluated. However, despite the fact that Hegel addresses the problem of differentiation in industrial society, a critic could still object that this process has gone so far that we are no longer capable of sharing the common system of values required by his theory. The divisions in Western democracies derive as much, if not more, from ideological, ethnic or religious differences than from conflicts between various economic groups. This fact has induced many contemporary liberals to deny that one can ground liberalism in a concept of the good – it must rather remain neutral between different conceptions.[23] They argue that equality of respect demands that the rights of individuals to pursue their own view of the good takes precedence over a putative common good. If correct, neutralist liberalism would undermine Hegelian ethical liberalism. In this last section I shall briefly show how if their diagnosis of the atomization of modern society is true, it challenges their own theory as much as, if not more than, his.

Neutralist liberals' agnosticism concerning the possibility of a shared political morality leads them to interpret the market and democracy as procedural mechanisms for co-ordinating personal preferences. They habitually emphasize one or other of these institutions and accordingly adopt one or other of the aforementioned ideal types of the liberal agent. Both versions ascribe a priority to the individual's right to pursue his or her life free from external interference deriving from a public conception of the good. This limitation also excludes an appeal to any aggregative principle, such as utilitarianism involves, which might have met a formal requirement of counting each individual's interests equally, on the grounds that it does not respect the incommensurable differences between the goods people desire. As we have seen, Hegel provides trenchant criticisms of the unrestricted adoption of either of these mechanisms and the model of human agency underlying them. His main complaint is that both separate out our rights to pursue our own interests from our duties to others. As a result, neither can generate even minimal public provision of goods.

For example, in libertarian defences of the market model of politics, government action may not impose coercive burdens on private initiatives. The only rationale of the state is, in Hobbesian/Lockean fashion, to protect the rights possessed by individuals in the state of nature.[24] But this creates an insoluble dilemma, since amongst these rights they accord pride of place to an inviolable right to property – the *raison d'être* of the market approach. The minimal state could only be financed by coercing individuals into paying for it. We noted earlier Hegel's argument that the unchecked pursuit of self-interest eventually produced recurrent market crises of overproduction, and that the self-regulatory mechanisms of the capitalist system were not infallible. Some government regulation would therefore be in the collective self-interest. But even assuming that all could rationally perceive this from a purely egoistical point of view, 'free-riding' by those who believed they were safe from ruin would remain an insuperable problem. The argument that this quandary can be overcome by introducing market incentives which harness material self-interest to promoting the common good merely introduces coercion by the back door, in the form of a manipulative and paternalistic government.

Dissatisfaction with the image of humans as rational egoists has led democrats to style them as autonomous choosers.[25] However, the second model suffers from analogous difficulties. Agreement on any policy will require near unanimous agreement. Without unanimity the minority could always claim to have been denied their freedom by the majority, and in societies as diverse and complex as our own there is both a technical and a logical limitation on reaching such agreement. Too many diverse decisions would be required for us to have the time or the knowledge to make them. As Hegel noted in his reflections on the French Revolution, the problem can only be overcome by a forced uniformity imposed by a terror which eliminates the outspoken dissidents and cowers the rest into submission.

Hegel aimed to avoid both these extremes, believing that intermediary bodies, such as the corporations, would enable individuals to connect their particular goals with those of the rest of society and generate certain shared political norms.[26] Neutralist liberals appear to believe that social differentiation and political pluralism are incompatible with a system of shared values. Hegel, in contrast, holds that the articulation of different interests can only occur in an uncoerced manner when there is agreement on general principles. A commitment to the common good does not restrict political disagreement to disputes over the correct means to realize agreed ends – for rival groups might well debate the bearing of their shared beliefs on a particular issue, and hence their import and meaning. Though they may have a common conceptual framework for describing these ends, discussion of their implementation will raise questions of their worth and value. There is therefore no warrant for the belief of either Hegel's detractors or some of his defenders that his theory entails our unreflective identification with the values of our community. However, at a deep metaphysical level, he shows how the claims of differentiation are underwritten by a fundamental unity. This is the challenge neutralist liberalism has to meet.

Hegel contends that Particularity and Individuality must be mediated by the Universal. In other words, that an awareness of our essential capacities and needs comes through social interaction with other people and the development of intersubjective norms and values. Contemporary liberals treat the market and democracy as neutral mechanisms for the pursuit of private goals. Hegel interprets them as public agencies for the socialization of individuals and the development of a common stock of norms. Whereas they adopt either instrumental or self-developmental views of human agency, or separate the two from each other by associating the market with the first and democracy with the second, Hegel explicitly unites these two accounts. This synthesis produces a very different description of the liberal institutional framework to theirs, and is arguably less fraught with internal contradictions.

Notes

This chapter is based on research funded by the ESRC under its Postdoctoral Research Fellowship Scheme. Its contents are the responsibility of the author and do not necessarily reflect the views of the ESRC. An earlier version was read to the seventh conference of the Hegel Society of Great Britain on the *Philosophy of Right*. I'm grateful to the participants for their helpful comments on that occasion, and to Raymond Plant, Z. A. Pelczynski and Howard Williams for their remarks on a later draft.

1. Criticisms of this sort abound in English commentaries, e.g. L. T. Hobhouse, *The Metaphysical Theory of the State: A Criticism* (London, 1918); and K. Popper, *The Open Society and its Enemies*, 2 vols, (London, 1945), Vol. II, pp. 25–76. Yet they appear even in intellectual traditions more sympathetic to Hegel, e.g. B. Croce, 'Hegel, Lo "Stato etico" ', *Etica e Politica*, 2nd edn, econ. (Bari, 1973), pp. 213–15; N. Bobbio, *Studi Hegeliani* (Turin, 1981), pp. 67, 74, 82 and 189; and F. Meinecke, *Die Idee der Staatsräson in der Problem der neuren Geschicte* (Munich and Berlin, 1924), pp. 427–60. Of course not only liberals make this point – the argument originates with Marx's (1843) 'Critique of Hegel's Doctrine of the State', in *Early Writings*, trans. R. Livingstone and G. Benton (Hardmondsworth, 1975), pp. 72–4.
2. The three most important recent English commentaries all adopt this view: S. Avineri, *Hegel's Theory of the Modern State* (Cambridge, 1972); Charles Taylor, *Hegel* (Cambridge, 1975); and Raymond Plant, *Hegel*, 2nd edn (Oxford, 1983).
3. As K. H. Ilting has pointed out: 'This picture of Hegel accords so well with the conceptions of conservative, liberal and even fascist authors that even today it is often accepted and transmitted without question.' 'Hegel's Concept of the State and Marx's Early Critique', in Z. A. Pelczynski (ed.), *The State and Civil Society: Studies in Hegel's Political Philosophy* (Cambridge, 1984), pp. 93–113. Like all other students of Hegel, I'm indebted to Ilting's work in rejecting this interpretation.
4. All paragraph numbers refer to *The Philosophy of Right*, trans. T. M. Knox (Oxford, 1952). R refers to the Remarks and A to the Additions, or the appended student notes, to Hegel's paragraphs.
5. J. Bentham, *An Introduction to the Principles of Morals and Legislation*, ed. J. H. Burns and H. L. A. Hart (London, 1970), p. 12.
6. My account draws inspiration from R. N. Berki, 'Political Freedom and Hegelian Metaphysics', *Political Studies*, XVI (1968), pp. 365–83; Charles Taylor, 'What is Human Agency?', in T. Michel (ed.), *The Self: Psychological and Philosophical Issues* (Oxford, 1977), pp. 103–35; Bernard Williams, 'Persons, Character and Morality', in *Moral Luck* (Cambridge, 1981), pp. 1–19; and A. S. Walton, 'Hegel: Individual Agency and Social Context', in L. S. Stepelevich and David Lamb (eds), *Hegel's Philosophy of Action* (Atlantic, Highlands, 1983), pp. 75–92.
7. G. W. F. Hegel, *Lectures on the Philosophy of World History: Introduction*, trans. H. B. Nisbet (Cambridge, 1975), p. 52.
8. *Ibid.*
9. *Hegel's Logic: Being Part One of the Encyclopaedia of the Philosophical Sciences (1830)*, trans. William Wallace, 3rd edn (Oxford, 1975), para. 187 zus. (amended translation R. B.). See also paras 6 and 181.
10. Important discussions of this topic appear in Joachim Ritter, 'Person and Eigentum', *Metaphysik und Politik* (Frankfurt am Main, 1969); Peter G. Shillman, 'Persons,

Property and Civil Society in the *Philosophy of Right*', in D. P. Verene (ed.), *Hegel's Social and Political Thought* (New Jersey and Sussex, 1980), pp. 103–18; and Alan Ryan, *Property and Political Theory* (Oxford, 1985), pp. 118–41. Hegel's interest in property as embodying the personality of the labourer goes back to a study of Locke whilst in Tübingen; see Paul Chamley, 'Les origines de la penseé économique de Hegel', *Hegel Studies*, III, 1965, p. 226.

11. The centrality of classical political economy to Hegel's social philosophy has been stressed by many recent commentators. The following works are of particular importance: Paul Chamley, *Économie Politique et Philosophie chez Stuart et Hegel* (Paris, 1963); Manfred Reidel, *Bürgerliche Gesellschaft und Staat bei Hegel* (Neuwied and Berlin, 1970); and Raymond Plant, 'Hegel and Political Economy', *New Left Review*, 103–4 (1977), pp. 79–93, 103–13.

12. Hegel made detailed notes of Sir James Steuart's *An Inquiry into the Principles of Political Economy* (1767) from February–May 1799 according to K. Rosenkranz, *Hegels Leben* (Berlin, 1844), p. 86. Apparently he probably also knew Smith's work then, since he possessed a copy of the Basel edition of the 1791 text. See Norbert Waszek, 'The Origins of Hegel's Knowledge of English', *The Bulletin of the Hegel Society of Great Britain*, VII (1983), pp. 8–27 for details of his acquisition of these texts.

13. Rosenkranz comments that in his notes on Steuart 'Hegel fought against what was dead with noble feeling ... as he strove to save the *Gemut* of man amidst the competition and mechanical interaction of labour and commerce' (*Hegels Leben*, p. 86). Plant illustrates how Hegel's theory of alienation goes back to Schiller's *Letters on the Aesthetic Education of Man*, and that he applied these insights in a criticism of Smith's description of a pin factory in the *Jenenser Realphilosophie*, I, ed. Lasson (Leipzig, 1932), p. 328. See R. Plant, 'Economic and Social Integration in Hegel's Political Philosophy', in D. P. Verene (ed.), *Hegel's Social and Political Thought*, p. 79.

14. Hegel's concern with this problem, as all the commentators cited in n.15 have shown, is even more explicit in the *Jenenser Realphilosophie* and the Griesheim notes. Whilst not ignoring the important scholarly work of Ilting and Riedel on the intellectual development of Hegel's views, for my purposes it is sufficient to examine the texts he chose to publish. Suffice it to say, his critique of classical political economy is absolutely clear from these earlier versions.

15. Plant, 'Hegel and Political Economy', pp. 111–13; Avineri, *Hegel's Theory of the Modern State*, pp. 147–54; and Bernard Cullen, *Hegel's Social and Political Thought: An Introduction* (Dublin, 1979), pp. 85–116. I find all three overstate their case as to the degree Hegel is *logically* incapable of resolving this dilemma. For a corrective to these views see A. S. Walton, 'Economy, Utility and Community in Hegel's Theory of Civil Society', in Z. A. Pelczynski (ed.), *The State and Civil Society*, pp. 244–61. I'm grateful to Raymond Plant and Tony Walton for useful discussions on this point.

16. Marx, 'Critique of Hegel's Doctrine of the State', p. 61. For important criticism see K. H. Ilting, 'The Dialectic of Civil Society', in Z. A. Pelczynski, *The State and Civil Society*, pp. 211–26.

17. Cullen, *Hegel's Social and Political Thought*, pp. 97–116. Cullen's error, I believe, is to mistake Hegel's contingent political conservatism for the philosophical logic of his argument. Although easily done, one should remember Hegel's warning that philosophy is limited by positive right, and must recognize the contingent as such even whilst 'overcoming' it.

18. 'The English Reform Bill' (1831), *Political Writings*, trans. T. M. Knox (Oxford, 1964), p. 295.
19. See also 'English Reform Bill', p. 320.
20. 'The German Constitution', *Political Writings*, pp. 161–2. The 1818 text of the *PhR* reveals Hegel to have been even more adamant about the need for political participation. Censorship following the Karlsbad Decrees led to a sometimes contradictory toning down of these passages (paras 260–5) in the published version of 1820. See Ilting, 'Hegel's Concept of the State', pp. 98–104.
21. The thesis originates with J. Habermas, who claims to find the origins of this problem within Hegel's account of modern society, e.g. 'On Social Identity', *Telos*, 19 (1974), pp. 97–8.
22. The themes are more fully addressed in my 'Hegel's Conception of the State and Political Philosophy in a Post-Hegelian world', *Political Science*, 38 (1986), pp. 99–112.
23. This thesis is shared by such diverse thinkers as J. Rawls, *A Theory of Justice* (Oxford, 1971); R. Nozick, *Anarchy, State and Utopia* (Oxford, 1974); and R. Dworkin, *Taking Rights Seriously*, 2nd edn (London, 1978); but only B. Ackerman, *Social Justice in the Liberal State* (New Haven, 1980) makes neutrality *per se* his starting point.
24. This is the notorious argument of Nozick, *Anarchy, State and Utopia*.
25. Rawls's arguments potentially lead in this direction.
26. For the importance of Hegel's notion of the corporation for contemporary politics, see G. A. Kelly, 'Hegel's America', *Philosophy and Public Affairs*, 2 (1972–3), pp. 3–36.

CHAPTER 2

J. S. Mill, T. H. Green and Isaiah Berlin on the Nature of Liberty and Liberalism

In his seminal lecture, 'Two Concepts of Liberty', Isaiah Berlin examines the work of Mill and Green as exponents of the concepts of negative and positive liberty respectively.[1] Berlin regards the two accounts of liberty as incompatible and opposed to each other. He charges Green with adopting the two cardinal errors of positive liberty: (i) the use of a notion of self-realization which confuses 'freedom from' with 'ability to do'; and (ii) the identification of liberty with equality. Mill, in contrast, is praised as an exponent of the 'negative' definition of liberty as freedom from constraints.[2] This chapter criticizes Berlin's interpretation by maintaining that the core idea of Mill's *On Liberty* is a defence of that very notion of individual autonomy, as something which society should foster equally for all its members, which Berlin attacks. Moreover, Green believes his political theory is consistent with Mill's. He does not criticize the concept of liberty espoused by Mill so much as the utilitarian terms in which it is framed.[3]

The inadequacy of Berlin's treatment of both Mill and Green puts in doubt the validity of his negative/positive liberty distinction, at least as it is applied to them. To establish the unsatisfactory nature of Berlin's view of liberty will be the task of the first section of this chapter. The second and third sections examine the concept of liberty in the writings of Mill and Green respectively. Again, the argument will be that Green's account complements and completes Mill's version. I shall argue that individual freedom presupposes certain moral commitments on the part of all members of society to the fostering of a particular quality of life – one which values autonomy. An analysis of Mill's writings reveals this thesis to be an implicit component of his utilitarian doctrine. Green's theory, however, makes the social and moral basis of freedom explicit, thereby providing liberalism with solider foundations – a claim defended in the conclusion.

Two Concepts of Liberty

Berlin describes positive and negative liberty respectively as '[t]he freedom which consists in being one's own master and the freedom which consists in not being prevented from choosing as I do by other men'.[4] These definitions suggest that the difference between the two concepts rests upon a distinction between internal and external constraints on freedom. Negative liberty consists in freedom from the external hindrances placed in the way of my satisfying my desires. Positive liberty includes the removal of restrictions on my conceiving those desires in the first place. As Berlin concedes, they 'seem concepts at no great logical distance from each other'.[5] Indeed, earlier in the essay he clearly combines the two when arguing that negative liberty is asserted in '[e]very protest against exploitation and humiliation, against the encroachment of public authority, or the mass hypnosis of custom or organised propaganda'.[6] The first three cases are examples of external constraints on individual liberty, but the last two are surely internal.

It is not clear that mixing the two notions of constraints does involve any logical confusion of two different concepts of liberty. Rather, the concentration on purely external constraints makes the concept of negative liberty unacceptably narrow. For if liberty is simply not to be prevented by others from doing what you want, then you could increase your freedom by trimming your desires. The paradigm case is the contented slave, who is conditioned to accept his slavery as natural and whose desires and expectations therefore match the opportunities available to him. Berlin admits committing this error in his reply to his critics, but as he points out this strengthens rather than weakens the concept of negative liberty. If, for example, my agoraphobia (internal constraint) is removed by psychoanalysis I am not thereby obliged to walk about in open spaces. I merely have the choice to do so or not. This broadening of the concept of freedom to include the removal of internal constraints is entirely consistent with Berlin's view of negative liberty as 'the absence of obstacles not merely to my actual, but to my potential choices . . . due to the closing of such doors or failure to open them, as a result, intended or unintended, of alterable human practices . . .(CA)'.[7]

This notion of liberty as the ability to make an autonomous choice without the hindrance of removable internal or external constraints on possible life-plans has become accepted in most recent accounts of freedom. It is distinguished from positive freedom on the grounds that there is 'no requirement that an agent actually realize an end for him to be free from all constraints to realize that end'.[8] However, it is not certain that the concept of freedom can be emptied of all normative import. Benn and Weinstein, whose classic article expounds the above notion of liberty as autonomy, remark that 'there is something paradoxical about saying that a person is either free or not free to starve, [or] cut off his ears . . . on account of the standard association between "being free" and experiences or activities normally regarded as worthwhile'. As a result, they suggest that one can only be free to do something 'if it is a possible object of reasonable choice'.[9] Baldwin makes a similar point when he argues that the removal of inhibitions or complexes by psychoanalysis is consistent with his revised account of negative liberty. For the therapy aims 'not to determine the patient's life for him but to make it possible for him to determine it for himself'. According to Baldwin, this example centres on the 'central phenomenon' of negative liberty, namely that an agent's choices be 'carried out in the light of all his reasonable beliefs and desires', a condition he describes as 'weakly normative'.[10] On this account, the difference between negative and positive liberty arises from the belief of the proponents of the latter conception that it would be irrational, and hence not an object of freedom, not to pursue one's real interests once one was free in the negative sense to choose to do so. To employ Charles Taylor's terminology, freedom is not simply an opportunity concept, it is also an exercise concept.[11] The proponents of both negative and positive liberty can agree that individual freedom depends not simply on the quantity of options open to an agent but also the quality of choice available. However, for the advocates of positive liberty it is only a necessary but not a sufficient condition of freedom to be able to choose in a reasonable manner from a number of worthwhile options. They require that we use this freedom in a way consistent with our status as rational moral agents. This injunction arises from the contention, examined below, that individual freedom can only exist in a certain sort of commununity — namely, one orientated towards the common good.

Berlin's original formulation sought to avoid this conflation of freedom with rationality. He believed that self-consciousness could only be taken so far if the danger of replacing the natural, unplanned web of human needs and desires by a crude, rationalist set of rules, which the individual was obliged to obey, was to be avoided.[12] Those who adopt the autonomy view of negative liberty argue that reason could not determine action in the manner feared by Berlin because the range of possible rational choices is infinitely large. One is always faced with numerous alternatives of equal reasonableness. This plurality of acceptable rational choices, as Baldwin notes, leaves negative libertarians 'with a profound antinomy', and he appositely quotes Sidgwick's conclusion that 'unless we assume or prove a moral order of the world, there is a conflict between rational convictions'.[13] Berlin appears to accept this dilemma as a 'permanent characteristic of the human predicament'.[14] However, even if the problem proves irresolvable at a meta-ethical level, practically one cannot ignore it — particularly in those cases where individual rationality seems to conflict with freedom.[15]

An instance of such a conflict is that posed by the 'Prisoners' Dilemma'. Two prisoners are separately faced with the alternatives of confessing to a major crime or of being convicted for a minor one. If both confess they get a reduced sentence of ten years; if neither do they will be sentenced for only two years for the minor crime; if only one confesses he will go free and the other will be sent down for the full penalty of twenty years. If both are rational self-seekers then both will confess rather than risk their partner doing so and go down for ten rather than two years, thereby rendering themselves less free. The dilemma is particularly relevant to the negative/positive liberty distinction because it is related to an atomistic model of society which characteristically underlies the negative liberty thesis. According to this model, society is made up of self-regarding individuals who act rationally by seeking to maximize their want-satisfaction. Individual liberty is assessed in a social and moral vacuum. But our choices and preferences cannot be treated in abstract isolation from those of other people. In a celebrated article, Sen and Runciman have suggested a solution to the Prisoners' Dilemma in terms of Rousseau's conception of the 'general will'.[16] They argue that a prior commitment to a given moral ordering, honour amongst thieves for example, modifies the individualistic assumptions of the game to produce a better overall result.

Whilst Green's positive conception of liberty encompasses such a social theory, Mill's negative version of liberty does not. Both define liberty in terms of individual autonomy and the possibilities it opens up for self-realization in the pursuit of worthwhile ends.[17] However, Green sees individual behaviour as socially and morally orientated. This orientation produces an ordering but not, I shall argue, an imposition of human goals, thereby removing a chief objection to positive liberty – that it defines our 'real interests' for us. Mill, in contrast, attempts to adopt the classic negative libertarian atomistic model of society and treats collective choices as identical with a neutral utilitarian summation of individual preferences. Although Mill invokes a richer concept of liberty than the classical liberal notion of an absence of impediments to an individual's express wants, he remains perfectly orthodox in seeking to adjudicate between conflicting plans of life on grounds independent of any particular conception of the good life. It will be shown that this thesis is only possible because his utilitarianism presupposes his own moral preferences.

The combination of a rich theory of individuality with the claim that a liberal theory of justice must foster all lifestyles, and hence remain neutral between different concepts of the good, is shared by many modern liberal theorists.[18] The example of Mill will reveal this stance to be ambiguous and ultimately untenable. For the commitment to the central liberal value of autonomy presupposes a particular moral and social context which fosters individual liberty as a collective project. Without this context, freedom neither has meaning nor is possible for individuals.[19] The examination of Green's theory is intended to show that liberalism therefore requires a concept of the good as its foundation.

Mill's Concept of Liberty

Mill's objections to what we called the 'narrow reading' of negative liberty, as simply the absence of external constraints, are revealed in his criticisms of Bentham. Mill believes that Bentham's definition of freedom, as the absence of obstacles to the fulfilment of human desires, is open to the distortion noted above. It suggests that there is a theoretical limit to human freedom in the satisfaction of a fixed number of wants. As a result, our freedom could be increased by diminishing our desires. For Mill, the values of human freedom derive from the individual's capacity to increase and develop his wants in an infinite variety of ways. The human potential for self-expression is inexhaustible; any limitation of it is hence a restriction of human freedom.[20] This observation commits Mill to the definition of freedom as autonomy. As Berlin notes, Mill rejects Bentham's psychology because '[f]or him man differs from animals primarily . . . as a being capable of choice, . . . the seeker of ends, and not merely of means'.[21]

At the same time, Mill wants to retain utilitarianism as an objective standard capable of adjudicating between the conflicting desires of different individuals. He tries to bring the two together by amending Bentham's notion of happiness to include a distinction between those enjoyments which employ the 'higher faculties' and those which merely trade on the 'beast's pleasures'. He links this in *On Liberty* and *Utilitarianism* to a notion of self-realization which connects an increase in human happiness with the development of character in the sense of human capacities:

> A being of higher faculties requires more to make him happy, is capable probably of more acute suffering, and certainly accessible to it at more points, than one of an inferior type; but in spite of these liabilities, he can never really wish to sink into what he feels to be a lower grade of existence. We may give what explanation we please of this unwillingness; we may attribute it to pride, . . . , to the love of liberty and personal independence, . . . , to the love of power, or to the love of excitement, . . . , but its most appropriate appellation is a sense of dignity, which all human beings possess in one form or another, and in some, though by no means in exact, proportion to their higher faculties; and which is so essential a part of the happiness of those in whom it is strong, that nothing which conflicts with it could be, otherwise than momentarily, an object of desire to them.[22]

As Green, who quotes this passage *in extenso*, points out, Mill has done much more than amend Bentham's conception of happiness.[23] He has called into question the whole project of deriving moral axioms from his revised account of human psychology. He has done this in two ways. First, he has destroyed the notion of pleasure as a simple unitary concept, which can act as a criterion for making our choices without calling the status of our desires into question. Mill seems to want to suggest that in choosing some immediate pleasure over another higher pleasure an individual may not be making the best of himself. Yet this suggestion is just what Berlin, in criticizing Green, regards as repugnant. The pertinent question to ask in such a case is, then, as Berlin points out, 'in whose view' is such a pleasure better that another?[24] Different pleasures are largely incommensurable. The enjoyment to be derived from having a drink is simply different from that of reading a book or going for a walk. Comparing them can only make sense when we discriminate between motivations and do not take our desires as fixed and all-determining in relation to the goals and objects which we pursue. Berlin's first question, 'in whose view?', is logically related to his second, 'what self?'. The sort of discrimination between pleasures which Mill's revised utilitarianism pre-supposes cannot simply be a matter of doing what you want. It must also be related to your basic purposes or self-realization – a notion Mill slips in under the heading of human dignity. This concession, as Green comments, reveals that 'the real ground ... of Mill's departure from the stricter utilitarian doctrine, that the worth of pleasure depends simply on its amount, is his virtual surrender of the doctrine that all desire is for pleasure' (para. 167).

Mill's 'sense of dignity' is a moral term in the traditional sense. To quote Green: 'he regards it as a counter motive to desires for animal pleasure' (para. 166). What is involved is a distinction between human beings as we find them, subject to animal desires, and human beings as they could be if all their capacities were realized – a distinction which the language of morals seeks to bridge. Mill has reintroduced this distinction by arguing that some goals are more significant than others, but failed to alter his psychology accordingly. For Mill (formally at least) what is at stake is simply the desirability of different pleasures as defined by de facto desires. But the evaluative language he uses to distinguish between these different pleasures goes further, examin-ing the different possible modes of being of the individual. In this latter instance, motivations and desires do not count simply in relation to the attractiveness of the pleasures we expect from their fulfilment; in which case, 'in whose view?', but also in virtue of the kind of life or person that we are or want to be, precisely 'what self?'. Berlin does not regard these as legitimate questions to ask. It will be argued below that whilst Mill's solution has many of the dangers Berlin fears, Green's does not.

Mill plays upon the ambiguity of moral language in order to derive a theory of autonomy and self-realization from false psychological premises. He incorporates the ideals of positive liberty into his utilitarianism in order to maintain the appearance of being a negative libertarian. This comes out very clearly in the famous passage of *On Liberty* where he quotes from Von Humboldt that

'the end of man, or that which is prescribed by the eternal or immutable dictates of reason, and not suggested by vague and transient desires, is the highest and most harmonious development of his powers to a complete and consistent whole'; that, therefore, the object 'towards which every human being must ceaselessly direct his efforts, and on which especially those who design to influence their fellow-men must ever keep their eyes, is the individuality of power and development'; that for this there are two requisites, 'freedom, and variety of situations', and that from the union of these arise 'individual vigour and manifold diversity', which combine themselves in 'originality'.[25]

Mill has, however, immeasurably impoverished this notion of self-development to mean simply the second-order desire to satisfy the first-order desires. Calculating reason, given the opportunity to experience sufficient pleasures, will work out which most satisfy human desires and the individual will progressively move up the hierarchy of pleasure from a base animal happiness to the higher happiness of a civilized being. However, there are both internal and external obstacles to human progress which might inhibit our possibility to experience or conceive of fresh pleasures. This leads Mill's interpretation of self-realization into the two problems associated with negative accounts of liberty noted earlier. Mill argues that want-satisfaction is intrinsically good. But desires are reason-dependent – people would not want particular objects unless they believed they were desirable. Mill cannot avoid, as he does, the question of what are to count as 'reasonable beliefs and desires'.

Resolving this issue is a necessary preliminary for tackling the second problem of how to mediate between conflicting desires. Bentham believed that the world could be so arranged that the psychological mechanism underlying human action could be allowed free play to establish a natural order amongst human beings. Such a view is, of course, something Mill is seeking to avoid. It is significant that he did not pursue his plans for a science of ethology and harshly criticized the excesses of Comte's positivism. Instead, he sees the development of the state in terms of a *modus vivendi* which allows, in so far as this is consistent with the liberty of others, individuals to pursue their own goals. He appeals to the necessary moderation which individuals have to practise in pursuing their own desires, seeing this restraint as a product of human sympathy and the experience which a mature society has acquired. Some such assumption was necessary, as Sidgwick was to point out, since both the abnegation exercised by individuals involved in pursuing their own personal happiness and the injunction to cultivate the greatest happiness of the greatest number are logically independent and not derivable from the psychological premises of utilitarianism.[26] But, as Green remarked, Sidgwick's conclusion that 'As rational beings we are manifestly bound to aim at good generally, not merely at this or that part of it' (a very similar claim to that of Mill in quoting the passage from Von Humboldt cited above) plainly involves a more radical rejection of utilitarianism than he allows.[27] Reason in the utilitarian tradition prescribes means not ends. Sidgwick breaks with this in making a distinction between pleasure as defined by de facto desires, and the greatest pleasure of the greatest number as something which as rational beings we can see as desirable. Mill admits a similar distinction when he quotes Von Humboldt as saying that 'the end of man' is prescribed by 'immutable dictates of reason', not 'vague transient desires'. Yet he cannot consistently hold on to this position without bringing the utility principle into conflict with the negative view of liberty as independent from a notion of what is morally best for human beings on the whole.

John Gray has argued that Mill adopts an indirect form of utilitarianism.[28] The utility principle, according to Gray, is an axiological principle defining the end of human conduct, namely 'that pleasure and freedom from pain are the only things desirable as ends', not a moral axiom that we maximize happiness.[29] The individuality of self-development, which Mill praises so much in *On Liberty*, does not conflict with his utilitarianism, since Mill is not suggesting that we seek to maximize happiness directly. Rather, this is the end product of the process of character formation, which is so central to his doctrine of liberty. Utility is only maximized, therefore, by allowing individuals the possibility for experimentation and hence self-development.[30]

Whilst Gray's view undoubtedly absolves Mill from the traditional charge of inconsistency, it also reveals the circularity of Mill's solution to the classic utilitarian problem of moving from the pursuit of one's own happiness to the pursuit of the general happiness. For his conclusion is contained in his contentious premise that we are Millian utilitarians by nature. Thus, Mill argues that human nature must be allowed to develop 'according to the tendency of the inward forces which make it a living thing'. Character formation is the development of an 'authentic' self. Only a 'person whose desires and impulses are his own – are the expression of his own nature, as it has been developed and modified by his own culture – is said to have a character'.[31] But he also claims that, given sufficient experience, the rational satisfaction of wants will lead the individual from a 'lower' to a 'higher' self.[32] In this way he is able to dovetail his conception of individual psychological progress, expressed in terms of the increase of individual autonomy, with his moral ideal, as encapsulated in the principle of utility.

At the very least Mill invites the corruption of his liberalism as a result of the poverty of this ethical theory. For his account of human development misses the point that character formation is not a matter of satisfying desires by giving them free play, but of identifying those objects which are desirable. Mill's unwillingness, on liberal grounds, to engage in the identification of human goods, because he believes we should be free to choose, makes the construction of any plan of life highly arbitrary. Once the investigation of the appropriate objects of human action has been laid to one side, then the distinction between higher and lower satisfactions, central to Mill's notion of a worthwhile life, is also undermined. Why shouldn't we be satisfied with the lowest type of experience when there is no motivation to change? The nature of human flourishing can only be elicited by the study of the objects of human action, not by the mechanics, biology or psychology of human impulses and desires.[33] Mill avoids such questions because his revised utilitarianism is but a rationalization of his view of human goods. Mill smuggles into his liberal theory a teleological conception of human fulfilment, framing it in utilitarian terms so that what people desire is identified with the end of humanity which reason enjoins us to realize.

Some interpreters argue that Mill's essay contains two logically distinct doctrines of liberty. The first, encapsulated in Mill's 'very simple principle', limits the reasons which can be adduced to interfere with individual liberty to the prevention of harm to others. The second, the notion of autonomy or individuality outlined above, is a metaphysical doctrine defining what liberty consists in.[34] However, by including 'the moral coercion of public opinion' amongst his list of impediments to 'liberty of action',[35] Mill invokes his fuller notion of freedom when he formulates his principle. This is not surprising, since Mill believes the major threat to freedom in modern societies comes from the pressure to conform arising from the power of majority opinion in democracies and the enervating effects of industrial labour. A society of contented slaves is too real a prospect for Mill to limit political liberty to the narrow negative version Rees and others attribute to him.

The issue of social conformism poses a particularly difficult problem for Mill because of his empiricist theory of personal identity. As we saw, he regards the development of character as deriving from the provision of opportunities to experience new pleasures, not from a willed desire on the part of the individual. As he put it in the *Logic*: 'the will to alter our own character is given us, not by any effort of ours, but by circumstances we cannot help: it comes to us from external causes, or not at all.'[36] Mill is able to counter Owen's fatalistic belief that we are necessarily products of our social environment, only by assuming that we have a natural desire for self-development.[37] This optimistic view of human nature allows him to pass as a conventional liberal in most circumstances. But a difficulty arises should social conditions inhibit our desire for self-improvement. Mill admits that the

> Capacity for the nobler feelings is in most natures a very tender plant, easily killed, not only by hostile influences, but by the mere want of sustenance; and in the majority of young persons it speedily dies away if the occupations to which their position in life has devoted them, and the society into which it has thrown them, are not favourable to keeping that higher capacity in existence.[38]

Such circumstances, Mill argues, require the state to intervene to provide the conditions suitable for human self-development or freedom. This argument could still be consistent with the broader definition of negative liberty outlined in the first section. For he need not impose a set of interests upon the individual to place him in a position to choose between higher and lower pleasures. The difficulties begin when conflicts between different conceptions of the good life arise. Mill appears to resolve this question without imposing any 'real' will upon the actual preferences of individuals. He maintains that social legislation simply provides the necessary co-ordination of different individual wants and preferences commensurate with their maximum satisfaction. I shall argue below that Mill achieves this solution by a sleight of hand. He can only provide a coherent ordering of different individuals' preferences because he assumes a hierarchy of pleasures within the individual. For a calculation on the part of various agents as to how to satisfy a number of contingently arrived at wants can provide no rules by which to arrive at a common interest – their preferences would be too unstable to allow a consistent ranking. His concept of a common interest is therefore parasitic upon a theory of the good. The pursuit of certain objects, of poetry rather than pushpin, constitutes our true freedom because it realizes our capacities, giving us 'power over our character' and hence rendering us 'morally free'. Only 'a person of confirmed virtue is completely free',[39] because the virtuous alone have the stamina and conviction to resist the temptations and enervating effects of industrial society.

Mill's position is clearest in the *Principles of Political Economy*. Here liberty is viewed in a classically negative manner, as 'acting according to one's own judgement of what is desirable', but is subject to numerous limiting conditions. Some, like the bar on entering into irrevocable contracts (including marriage), are against external constraints on autonomy – viz. the ability to enter into new relationships in the future.[40] Others, concerning the care of lunatics or children, reflect internal restraints.[41] However, the most interesting example, as Martin Hollis has shown, focuses on Mill's own version of the Prisoners' Dilemma discussed in section one.[42] According to Mill, 'the practical principle of non-interference', that 'individuals are the best judges of their own interests',[43] is undercut by the observation that '[i]n the particular circumstances of a given age and nation, there is scarcely anything really important to the general interest, which it may not be desirable, or even necessary, that the government should take upon itself, not because private individuals cannot effectively perform it, but because they will not'.[44]

Mill realizes that there are certain forms of collective action, analogous to the type examined earlier, which are unlikely to be performed without a prior commitment on the part of all concerned to the goal it seeks to achieve. Thus, to quote Mill's example, the reduction of factory hours from ten to nine would be for the advantage of all working people, but 'will not be adopted unless the body of operatives bind themselves to one another to abide by it'.[45] A worker who refused to work ten hours when others continued to do so would be sacked. Moreover, without the sanction of law it might always be in the immediate interest of the single individual to increase his or her wages by working an extra hour, thereby eroding the long-term advantage of the reduction of hours since all would be again obliged to work the tenth hour to be on a par with everyone else. The fact that in such a situation the individual's immediate self-seeking will ultimately make things worse for everybody (the blackleg included) gives, as Sen and Runciman have shown, 'an immediately and plausible sense to Rousseau's notion of the members of a society being "forced to be free" '.[46] Agreement between individuals is only to be achieved by a prior commitment. Formally, Mill rejects the positive libertarian solution of a common good shared by all individuals. Instead, he deploys his theory of self-development and argues that such agreement would naturally develop as an ontogenetic process. Whilst this solution enables him to remain in form a negative libertarian, it has the potential for just the sort of tyrannical manipulation Berlin fears from Green.

In *Utilitarianism* Mill argues 'that the happiness which forms the utilitarian standard of what is right in conduct, is not the agent's own happiness, but that of all concerned'. He implies that this is necessarily true for purely procedural reasons requiring that you 'do as you would be done by'. But he ends his discussion by considering what would be needed to make 'the nearest approach to this ideal'. The principle of utility, he believes,

> ... would enjoin, first, that laws and social arrangements should place the happiness, or (as speaking practically it may be called) the interest, of every individual, as nearly as possible in harmony with the interest of the whole; and secondly, that education and opinion, which have so vast a power over human character, should so use that power as to establish in the mind of every individual an indissoluble association between his own happiness and the good of the whole ... [47]

The identification of what these interests are, however, is extremely difficult for Mill without subverting the individual's freedom of choice. Neither utility nor social norms are particularly attractive candidates, since both could be used to override individual life-plans on grounds Mill seeks to avoid. More recently Gray and Wollheim have argued that Mill's account of interests is similar to Rawls's 'thin' theory of primary goods.[48] Mill can argue on these grounds, for example, against an individual voluntarily choosing to become a slave, since this would necessarily deprive him or her of the opportunity to frame and execute any plan of life. Yet even if this reading is correct, it still leaves Mill with the intractable problem of how to decide between conflicting interests without appealing to a strong theory of the good.

Mill's harm principle, for example, cannot mediate between conflicting freedoms in a neutral manner. The exclusion of moral offence alone provides proof of its value-laden nature. In general, Mill seems to avoid the problem by assuming that the higher pleasures are essentially complementary. His view of marriage as the union of male reason and female intuition provides a particularly striking instance of his social ideal in this respect.[49] He never appears to have contemplated that different liberties might clash. In any case, his indirect utilitarianism saves him from attempting to weigh incommensurable freedoms, such as the right to free speech and the right to privacy, against each other in order to show which combination produces less harm on balance. Rather, he assumes that the refinement of human pleasures brings with it 'the better development of the social part of [the individual's] nature' with the result that society becomes increasingly consensual – a view curiously at odds with his praise of diversity![50]

In the *Principles* Mill apparently rejects the notion of a natural harmony of interests between rational actors, in all circumstances at least. As we saw, this conclusion led to a justification of state intervention which would certainly infringe a prima facie reading of his defence of liberty. However, Mill resolves this problem in *On Liberty* by assuming the revised account of individuality given above, in which our wants and the 'true' interests of humanity are identified. This strategem is evident in the manner in which he refers both to 'higher' and 'lower' pleasures and the consequences and effects of our acts in the same breath as he talks of human interests. Unless he can prove humans to be Millian utilitarians by nature, this commits him to trying to rank within a common system of values goods which are strictly speaking incommensurable. It is this difficulty which Mill's progressivism seeks to obviate. In the passage quoted above, for instance, he achieves this result by identifying interest and happiness. The interest of the individual and society are united in a common desire to maximize happiness. Since this goal might be interpreted differently by different people, Mill defines it in terms of self-realization. To avoid the philistine Benthamite utopia of contented pigs, he appeals to 'utility in the largest sense, grounded on the permanent interests of man as a progressive being'[51] – just the sort of 'objective' concept of human ends Berlin explicitly attacks. Thus Mill neatly resolves the conflict between liberty and utility by asserting that our true freedom inheres in our maximizing utility. Whilst liberal in spirit and inspiration, Mill's theory is therefore based on the assumption 'that in some ultimate, all-reconciling, yet realizable synthesis duty is interest', a doctrine Berlin equates with positive liberty.[52] Although Mill begins from premises not inconsistent with negative liberty, he ends up by smuggling in a supposedly objective notion of human flourishing which is the trademark of theories of positive liberty. He supplements his principle of liberty with a doctrine of individuality or self-realization framed in utilitarian terms. Individual and social liberty are thereby identified by just the sort of imposition of a 'real' interest upon an individual's empirical interest Berlin most fears. This does not mean that all conceptions of liberty which invoke a theory of self-development, and in particular Green's, need involve such a 'monstrous impersonation' as Mill's requires to render them coherent.[53]

Green's Concept of Liberty

Green begins his *Prolegomena* by noticing a disjunction in the minds of his contemporaries between the high aspirations for humanity, which they acknowledge when reading poetry or engaging in religious worship, and the base view of human nature which had emerged from the developing natural science of humanity (para. 1). Mill, as we have seen, tries to reconstruct the former in terms of the latter. Green's first task is to submit this whole enterprise, and naturalism generally, to a harshly critical assault. In these theories actions are conceived as deriving partly from natural impulses and wants, partly from experienced pleasures and pains. Human development is a natural sequence of events in which reason, acting on the basis of antecedent pleasures and pains, seeks ever more complex forms of happiness by satisfying de facto desires. Green, however, notes that human desire is quite different in quality to animal impulse or appetite. Human beings have a capacity to evaluate desires which is in turn related to their power of self-evaluation. Such judgement is impossible in naturalistic terms, since 'it is obvious that to a being who is simply a result of natural forces an injunction to conform to their laws is unmeaning' (para. 7).

It is not sufficient to regard knowledge as the outgrowth of a process of natural evolution, for how would it be possible for a being which is merely a product of natural forces to form a theory of those forces? (para. 8). Knowledge must rather presuppose the presence in humans 'of a principle not natural, and a specific function of this principle in rendering knowledge possible' (para. 8). Green argues, in Kantian manner, that the view of the world, essential to science, as a related series of objects and events, is not a product but a presupposition of knowledge. But he goes beyond Kant to regard the relation of objects in the manifold of experience not simply 'as fictions of our combining intelligence', but as explicable only on the assumption of the existence of a divine consciousness present both in mind and nature and guaranteeing their ultimate unity. 'Consciousness is therefore not just the basis of our knowledge of uniform relations between phenomena, but of there being those uniform relations' (para. 33).

Green links this account of the metaphysical basis of knowledge to his criticism of naturalist ethics. To see actions as the product of antecedent impulses and desires, explicable by natural laws analogous to those of physics, is to make morality redundant. But, Green argues, natural laws are themselves a product of human consciousness, which in turn reproduces the divine consciousness. Morality is to be accounted for in a similar manner. Calling into question our animal wants and passions is to relate the idea of the object of desire to the self, which in turn presupposes Green's theory of knowledge and of consciousness. Desire, intellect and will interact in the framing of motives for actions. Natural instincts and impulses are transformed into desires for self-satisfaction through the relation of consciousness of the object of desire to a possible self. Thus:

> Even those desires of man ... which originate in animal want or
> susceptibility to animal pleasures in the sense that without such want or
> susceptibility they would not be, yet become what they are in man, as
> desires consciously directed to objects, through the self-consciousness
> which is the condition of those objects or any objects being presented.
> (para. 125)

Self-realization or self-development, even of the most minimal kind, involves
the individual in conceiving his or her life as an end in itself and framing goals
for which s/he seeks to live. This is only possible for beings who can
distinguish themselves from the manifold of their experience, actual and
possible. Moral experience is thus only conceivable for a self-conscious subject,
capable of acting in an autonomous manner as outlined in section one.
Morality and freedom are inextricably linked. By freedom Green means 'the
primary or juristic sense of power to act according to choice or preference',
without internal or external constraints. He then extends the argument and
maintains that 'such freedom is precious to [us] because it is an achievement
of the self-seeking principle'. We can only attain freedom in the 'juristic' sense
if we have overcome our conflicting desires and natural conditioning by
seeking moral freedom. Virtue similarly implies the ability to act in an
uncoerced manner, to freely choose to behave morally.[54]

We are now in a position to assess Berlin's criticisms of Green's notion of
positive liberty.[55] Berlin's comments carry some force, for Green appears to
place a transcendent self over and above an empirical self and this is only
possible if one accepts his metaphysics. The first part of this paper discussed
the similarities between positive and negative liberty ignored by Berlin's
distinction. Both concepts relate the freedom of agents to the ends they
choose. For Green, and most advocates of positive liberty, choosing between
ends implicitly prescribes certain types of self-satisfaction as being more
important for humans than others. However, this reasoning does not entail the
imposition of a 'real' self upon an 'empirical' self, but forms part of the process
of critical evaluation which we all employ when seeking to choose between
possible courses of action. Green asks us to seek the realization of a telos within
humankind, not that we substitute a new 'higher' self for an old base self. The
language of morals is precisely the language of this transition from 'is' to
'ought'. It is not imposed upon the individual, but emerges out of common
human practices.

As a result, Green's positive conception of liberty is compatible with many
of the attributes of individual liberty praised by Mill and his admirers. In *On
Liberty* Mill attacks a world in which custom turns human thoughts and action
into 'ape-like imitation':

> The human faculties of perception, judgement, discriminative feeling,

mental activity, and even moral preference, are exercised only in making a choice. He who does anything because it is the custom makes no choice. He gains no practice either in discerning or in desiring what is best. The mental and moral, like the muscular powers, are improved only by being used.[56]

It is just such a conception of the exercise of human faculties which Green is attempting to articulate. But what is 'best' can only arise from individuals challenging the satisfaction of their desires in the circumstances in which they find themselves and seeking higher forms of satisfaction which, to refer back to an earlier quote from Mill, fulfil their 'higher faculties'. This end Green describes as a higher realization of our moral capabilities. This sort of reasoning leaves open the question of what these capabilities are. As Green points out, we have no picture of the fully developed human being before us, nor can we ever have. Yet in engaging in any activity we are forced to ask 'How can I carry this practice out in such a manner that I do it well?' This inquiry involves the further question 'What does this activity develop in me?' In other words our 'mental and moral ... powers' are 'exercised'. What both these questions imply is a conception of the common good of humankind. The search for the good is what gives human practices their unity with respect to the 'end of man'. For, to quote Von Humboldt once more, this goal is not 'suggested by vague and transient desires' but is 'the highest and most harmonious development of [man's] powers to a complete and consistent whole'. Accordingly, as Green writes, it is 'the practical struggle after the Better, of which the idea of there being a Best has been the spring' (para. 172) which generates human self-realization. This process, as has already been shown, cannot be explained naturalistically as an evolution of self-regarding desires. Rather, it is by virtue of consciousness that 'man ... is determined, not simply by natural wants according to natural laws, but by the thought of himself as existing under certain conditions, and as having ends that may be attained and capabilities that may be realized under those conditions' – a way of thinking Green describes as the manifestation of a 'self-objectifying principle' within the moral agent (para. 175). What is all important, there-fore, is the will to contribute in some form or other towards human fulfilment. That will cannot by its very nature be imposed upon people. Its development is made possible only by an openness to the idea of human self-realization, which is the operative ideal in any liberal society.

Green grounds his theory of knowledge, and by extension his theory of morals, in a conception of God. A 'divine principle' is said to realize itself in human beings through their consciousness and will, leading humanity to perfection and harmonizing conflicting human wills. There would appear, then, to be some basis for Berlin's fear that a single 'real' self can be imposed upon independent 'empirical' selves by conceiving of the 'true' self as some entity, such as spirit or the state or the notion of humanity as a collective subject, which realizes the potential of its members. Green, however, explicitly counters such a perversion of his doctrine:

> Our ultimate standard of worth is an ideal of *personal* worth. All other values are relative to value for, of, or in a person. To speak of any progress or improvement of a nation or society or mankind, except as relative to some greater worth of persons, is to use words without meaning. (para. 184)

For Green, individual self-development is necessarily something one does for oneself. It involves conceiving oneself as an end to be realized. Green's denial of naturalism implies this human ability to act autonomously by being conscious of the forces affecting us, and to transcend them as far as possible. But such acts are not without purpose, since they involve the development of those specific capabilities which define what we are. Self-realization involves recognizing that there is a hierarchy amongst human satisfactions, that we value some more than others. This does not mean that individuals transcend their animal selves to become totally spiritual beings, or that there is a 'higher' self dictating continuously to a 'lower' self within each of us. Human beings live on several layers of existence and the lower imply, but are not cancelled out by, the higher.[57] Personal identity is constituted by the choices made at all levels of one's existence: from a liking for a particular type of food, to religious or political beliefs. Personal freedom consists of being an autonomous agent that all levels of existence, as far as that is possible for a finite being such as humankind. Yet there is an implicit telos in such activity too, implied in the very notion that we have capabilities which are refined through being exercised in specific practices. For the activities which an individual engages in cannot be separated off from his or her personality and explained either by external factors, internal impulses or a combination of both. For it is precisely through such activity that we realize ourselves. Our different acts are no longer to be regarded as disparate and unconnected events, but have a unity in the self which defines them. Self-realization is thus the development of human capacities through engaging in activity. In so doing, individuals are seeking a personal good, bettering themselves by conceiving what their best self could be like.

The above might be accepted as having established the ideal-regarding nature of desire, that to have wants requires some notion of human fulfilment. It need not imply that there can be any agreement on what those ends are. This point is obviously central to a doctrine of positive liberty, and needs to be justified if Berlin's accusation of its tyrannical implications is to be countered. Green's answer is that we never realize ourselves solely as individuals, but in the context of society. Part of my identity is constituted by the social role I adopt, a role which has many facets to it: involving my membership of a particular professional group, my friends and family, the city and country I live in, and so on. There is a certain contingency about many aspects of this identity. I frame my plan of life within limits. But the essential point is that my effort of identification, or seeking a personal good, will inevitably be expressed in social terms. I am not, as in the negative libertarian theory, an abstract individual, defined simply by a number of psychological features which determine my behaviour. Instead I find my self involved in a society which inevitably defines an aspect of what I am and want to be. A community consists of a number of shared ways of experiencing and interpreting the world, from which we cannot cut ourselves off without ceasing to engage in relationships with other people. Even if we did so we would necessarily retain part of this cultural baggage to think and act at all – Robinson Crusoe is very much an eighteenth-century English gentleman even on his island. Thus, as Green puts it: 'The individual's conscience is reason in him as informed by the work of reason without him in the structure and controlling sentiments of society' (para. 216).

These shared concepts and practices involve a socially embodied pursuit of the good life analogous to that which we have described in isolation for the individual. Indeed, the individual's search for a personal good is both constituted by, and creates, the wider search by society as a whole of which he or she necessarily forms a part. All societies, to some extent, conceive themselves as realizing an idea of the good life to which all their members, to some greater or lesser degree, participate in promoting. It provides the necessary framework behind all individual actions, given that they occur within a social context. Negative libertarians deny this, noting that theories of negative liberty evolved when social cohesion had broken down to a radical degree, and the clash of opinion demanded that large areas of life be defended from political or religious fanatics. But in defending a pluralist view of the world, the negative libertarian must nevertheless trade on just the sort of framework which he denies in principle. As we saw, Mill treats each individual as naturally unique and regards custom and tradition as a block on our individuality. Green, in contrast, appreciates that the liberal commitment to autonomy is a product of Western civilization. Mill's value-laden utilitarianism enabled him to neglect the vital role social conventions play both in shaping our identity and in enabling individuals to co-exist without a constant resort to coecion. However, without the assumptions built into his theory of self-development, a Millian society of rational experimenters would quickly degenerate into a Hobbesian state of nature. For Green, pluralism involves an equality of respect for individuals to realize themselves. This self-realization of autonomous individuals is necessarily done in conjunction with others on the basis of a conception of what is best for human beings which is held in common by virtue of membership of a given society, rather than a mutual interest to protect one's neighbours' safety lest someone invades one's own. This conception of the good is not a static ideal or custom which individuals mechanically obey. It is the living force within all communities, stimulating and being stimulated by the activities of their members. It is not an ideal completely relative to the particular society you find yourself in, for it is grounded on a notion of the fully realized individual. That is an eternal ideal, not fully realized in any particular society, but which all societies in history attempt to make real.

Green illustrates this thesis by tracing the development of the Western moral tradition from its Greek and Judaeo-Christian origins to the present day. He does not see history as a process of inevitable development, or as an endless series of events, but as the realization of the ideal as it has appeared in human history. It is thus possible for societies to vary in the extent they embody the ideal of human perfection. It is not a unilinear development since there can be a regression away from the ideal, such as Green believed to be happening in his own day. But it is a tradition capable of surviving even the dark ages. For it lives eternally in human minds as the foundation for all meaningful activity in society. There are three components of positive liberty:

1   that it involves self-development towards a personal good,
2   that this personal good is inextricably linked with a social good,
3   that the notion of the fully-realized individual – of society as 'the individual writ large' – is the operative ideal throughout history.

All three are inextricably linked and lead human beings to call into question their desire for satisfaction in an immediately attractive pleasure in the first place (para. 232).

The common good, which is logically connected with Green's idea of freedom, has often been misinterpreted as a number of particular goods which individuals desire in common. This interpretation is obviously a misrepresentation. Rather, the 'common good' is the common pursuit of the self-realization of human capabilities by members of a given society. Society is not therefore the fully realized individual in the sense Berlin claims – 'the "true" self which, by imposing its collective (or "organic") single will upon its recalcitrant "members", achieves its own, and therefore their, "higher" freedom'.[58] Instead, it represents – as an ideal, not as empirical fact – the universal development of all human capabilities of which the individual is a unique and particular synthesis. Individuals contribute to the common good in seeking their own personal good whilst at the same time asking what is good for humankind as a whole, that is, what all searches similar to their own must have in common. Society is the expression of this dual search as embodied in its laws, customs, morals and institutions.

It is important to stress the tripartite nature of this enterprise, for it prevents anyone taking any single individual will or collective entity or religious belief and imposing it as the fully realized self on others. Green's theory entails not only having equality of respect for other individuals pursuing their own personal good but also, what is perhaps more important, some notion of what this requires of us as members of a particular society. Equality of respect involves enabling all members of society to participate in it on equal terms.

This is both a relative and an absolute doctrine of equality. It is relative to the particular community individuals find themselves in, but it is absolute with regard to both the integrity of the individual as a unique synthesis of human capacities and faculties – as an end in him or herself – and in the sense that it is grounded in an ideal of the ultimate good as what is good for human beings on the whole. It is the equal right of each individual to realize his or her potential via participation in the goods basic to human fulfilment.[59]

Whilst Green's view of liberty is not incompatible with individual liberty, it is not personal freedom in Berlin's negative sense of simply doing what you want to do at any particular time. Baldwin believes that Green's definition of 'freedom in the positive sense', as 'the liberation of the powers of all men equally for contributions to a common good',[60] 'surely requires that the subject of this freedom be a society and not an individual person'.[61] But Green's argument, as we saw, is that individual freedom requires that society recognizes an equal freedom for all. Liberty and equality go together because my opportunities for self-development are a product of society as a whole, and not simply my individual will. They are not confused therefore, but stand together in the creation of a society providing the optimal conditions for self-development.

Weinstein suggests that Green's interpretation of freedom can be taken as relating to the conditions under which liberty can be exercised, rather than as a positive definition of what liberty is.[62] These conditions, as we have seen, involve the absence of both internal constraints, such as being of sane mind, and external constraints, such as a number of basic material resources. The distinction between negative and positive liberty would then disappear, since both define liberty in terms of the removal of constraints on freedom rather than the goals achieved. This aim is clearly part of Green's argument when, in his famous 'Lecture on Liberal legislation and freedom of contract', he claims that the regulation of hours of work is not incompatible with *laissez-faire* liberalism. But Green goes further to equate being free with being virtuous. As he points out: 'Moral freedom is not the same thing as a control over the outward circumstances and appliances of life. It is the end to which such control is a generally necessary means, and which gives it its value.'[63]

Individual freedom has moral value only to the extent that it is orientated by the common good. Whilst the possession of certain material goods and capacities are necessary for human action, Green specifically excludes the possibility of identifying the common good with a particular set of such goods – the sort of argument favoured by welfare rights theorists for example (para. 245). The common good provides the basis for a common morality. It offers criteria for deciding what constitutes a rational or reasonable choice. Namely, that it must necessarily be a moral choice taking the tripartite form suggested above. Such reasoning produces:

. . . on the one hand an ever widening conception of the range of persons

40

between whom the common good is common, on the other a conception of the nature of the common good itself, consistent with its being the object of a universal society co-extensive with mankind. The good has come to be conceived with increasing clearness, not as anything which one man or set of men can gain or enjoy to the exclusion of others, but as a spiritual activity in which all may partake, and in which all must partake, if it is to amount to a full realization of the faculties of the human soul. (para. 286)

Hence, Green's theory of liberty is undeniably 'positive', requiring us to uphold the common good and acknowledge our duties to others as a condition of being free. It remains for us to see whether this preserves freedom, or is a metaphysical ruse to destroy it, as Berlin claims.

Conclusion

The distinction between positive and negative liberty hinges on the former's insistence that an autonomous life is only possible under social conditions provided by a collective allegiance to the common good. Negative libertarians, like Berlin, argue that such agreement is incompatible with individual liberty. It is inconsistent with offering people the possibility to choose how they should live. We cannot oblige people to pursue a given course, because we cannot know what is truly best for people beyond what they express a preference for. For Green, however, the social nature of human life means that an absolute moral individualism, of the sort Berlin espouses, ultimately undermines freedom. It can provide no grounds for going beyond the *bellum omnium contra omnes* except the 'force of the sword' of Hobbes's *Leviathan*. Green argues that the exercise of freedom presupposes the existence of certain options, and these can only be provided by a respect for the common good which furnishes the social morality necessary to mediate between conflicting individual plans.

Green's notion of the 'common good' is similar to what Joseph Raz has called an 'inherent public good'.[64] That is a good the benefits of which are under the sole control of each potential beneficiary and which by their nature could not be voluntarily controlled and distributed by any single agency. Raz's example is tolerance, which benefits all to the extent that their behaviour warrants it but which cannot, like friendship, be controlled by anyone but the individuals themselves. Such a good cannot be regarded as instrumentally, as opposed to intrinsically, beneficial, because its existence is constitutive of the ultimate good of the quality of life derived from living in a tolerant society. If tolerance was interpreted as instrumentally beneficial, then an individual could justify being intolerant in order to gain a personal advantage (e.g. when racialists claim that expelling coloured immigrants increases job opportunities). It might be argued that such intrinsic common goods nevertheless infringe human liberty, since they ascribe value to something independently from the interest particular individuals have in it. However, it was noted in section one that liberty, defined as freedom from constraints, entails a number of normative conditions. These include internal states of mind, that the individual can make rational decisions, and external circumstances, that a reasonable number of options are open. If autonomy is intrinsically valuable, which it is presumed most liberals believe to be the case, then so are the goods which provide the necessary options for it to be a workable ideal. Some of these conditions will be social rather than purely individual in character. For key opportunities can only be provided by certain 'inherent public goods' like tolerance. Take the earlier example of factory hours. It was noted that the collective action needed to obtain the reduction from ten to nine hours required a sense of worker solidarity to be achieved. Without such shared feelings the common interest could always be undermined by short-term individual gain. The instrumental reasons for combining with others are not in themselves sufficient to oblige each person to do so. The other elements turn on a deeper commitment to the ideal of freedom itself and the possibilities for others to enjoy the increased opportunities that will come from working less for the same pay. The commitment within Green's schema stems from the requirement to pursue those goods necessary in a given society for human fulfilment generally, and not simply my own.

What these goods are will of course reflect our view of human nature and society. Green does not commit the error, usually associated with positive liberty, of asserting that our 'real interests' reside in certain specified goods. His point is that goods are not identified, pursued and distributed, in a social and moral vacuum. As Michael Walzer points out, even staple goods – bread for example – take on different meanings in different contexts, as the body of Christ, the staff of life, and so on.[65] The 'common good' consists of a set of common meanings about what are worthwhile goals of freedom and of how they should be shared. These objectives cannot be separated from the goods people actually do desire but, Green argues, through being desired by individuals in communities, rather than in isolation, they take on a definite normative structure. Goods are common because they are rooted in shared practices. This contention forms the real contrast between Green and Mill. Green attempts to provide a framework within which we may equally and freely debate the moral commitments involved in acting in an autonomous manner as real individuals, with the tastes, desires and beliefs that we achieve through living in society. This debate takes the triadic form outlined above. Mill, on the other hand, assumes a narrowly conceived and excessively individualistic human agent who perforce must live in an 'iron cage' of rational rules derived from an assumed set of humanity's 'real interests'.

Mill and Green agree that freedom can only be exercised on the basis of reasonable choices. Since the definition of what is reasonable implies some notion of the end of human endeavour, their differences derive from divergent conceptions of human nature. Whilst for Green human beings seek the good, Mill believes they desire happiness. Yet in Mill's theory individuals think they are only pursuing their own interest and self-development. It is this element which provides grounds for Berlin's view of Mill as the champion of negative liberty. But since Mill relates this process to the development of both an 'authentic' and a social self he, rather than Green, is guilty of covering 'self-deceit' under a 'metaphysical blanket'.[66] Green, in contrast, regards the agent as consciously framing a plan of life which contributes to the common good in its three aspects and as such fulfils the requirements of practical reason.

If liberalism was simply a set of procedures for maximizing the want satisfaction of self-seeking individuals, then a neutral method for aggregating preferences akin to utilitarianism would provide its most adequate defence.[67] But we have already disputed the possibility of generating either coherent preference orderings or the institutional arrangements necessary to secure optimal satisfaction from self-interest alone. Nor can a narrow individualism provide the motivation for agents to act in a socially responsible manner. Mill could only resolve these problems by imposing a putative real interest upon the conflicting empirical interests both within and between different individuals. He appreciated, no less than Green and Berlin, that the rationale of liberal institutions stems from their fostering a particular lifestyle – that of the self-developing and morally responsible individual. But he was wrong to suppose that a commitment to it could be derived from an individualistic, interest-based conception of society. Respect for autonomy, which I take to be the central value of liberalism, emerges from a process through which each person relates to others in the course of developing his or her personality. They value their goals and purposes as part of a number of common goods which, taken as a whole, make for a valuable social life. Relations with others depend on shared meanings and upholding those goods necessary for self-development generally, regardless of whether one has the taste or ability to pursue them all personally. For the availability and mutual respect for such goods provide the social conditions necessary for liberty. To cut liberalism off from the common good, therefore, is to deprive it of its foundations.

Notes

This chapter is based on research funded by the ESRC under its Postdoctoral Research Fellowship Scheme. Its contents are the responsibility of the author and do not necessarily reflect the views of the ESRC. I am very grateful for the written or verbal comments, often on successive versions of this chapter, of Tom Baldwin, Isaiah Berlin, Keith Dowding, Richard Flathman, Caroline Forder, John Gray, David Miller, Ross Harrison, John Morrow, Peter Nicholson, Raymond Plant, Quentin Skinner and Andrew Williams.

1. Isaiah Berlin, 'Two Concepts of Liberty', in *Four Essays on Liberty*, Oxford: Oxford University Press, 1969, pp. 118–72.

2. Berlin, *Four Essays*, pp. xlix (n.), lxi, 133 (n.), 150. The view has been very influential, e.g. in the otherwise excellent book by Melvin Richter, *The Politics of Conscience – T. H. Green and his Age*, London: Routledge, 1964, p. 24.

3. On the political and philosophical influence of Mill on Green see: R. L. Nettleship, 'Memoir of Green', in *Works of T. H. Green*, ed. R. L. Nettleship, London: Longman, 1888, III, p. xliv; and Christopher Harvie, *The Lights of Liberalism*, London: Allen Lane, 1976, pp. 151, 303 n. 35.

4. Berlin, 'Two Concepts', p. 131.

5. Berlin, 'Two Concepts', p. 131.

6. Berlin, 'Two Concepts', p. 128.

7. Berlin, 'Introduction' to *Four Essays*, pp. xxxvii–xl.

8. Tom Baldwin, 'MacCallum and the Two Concepts of Freedom', *Ratio*, XXVI (1984): 130. A similar point is made by William E. Connolly, *The Terms of Political Discourse*, 2nd edn, Oxford: Blackwell, 1983, pp. 143–6.

9. S. I. Benn and W. L. Weinstein, 'Being Free to Act and Being a Free Man', *Mind*, 80 (1971): p. 195.

10. Baldwin, 'MacCallum and the Two Concepts', pp. 131–3.

11. Charles Taylor, 'What's Wrong with Negative Liberty?', in A. Ryan (ed.), *The Idea of Freedom*, Oxford: Clarendon Press, 1979, pp. 253–70.

12. John Gray, 'On Negative and Positive Liberty', *Political Studies*, 28, (1980): 518–21, also argues, against Berlin, that even negative freedom requires some notion of self-determination if 'internal' restraints on freedom are to be avoided. But this, despite Gray's disclaimer, must involve conflating acting freely with acting rationally, a view strongly resisted by Berlin in 'From Fear and Hope Set Free', *Concepts and Categories*, Oxford: Oxford University Press, 1978, pp. 173–98.

13. Baldwin, 'MacCallum and the Two Concepts', p. 140, quoting Henry Sidgwick, *Lectures on Green, Spencer and Martineau*, London: Macmillan, 1902, p. 168 n. 58. A similar dilemma faces Connolly's ideal of autonomy in *Political Discourse*, p. 157.

14. Berlin, *Four Essays*, p. li.

15. On this point, see B. Williams, 'Conflicts of Values', in Ryan (ed.), *Idea of Freedom*, pp. 221–32.

16. W. G. Runciman and A. K. Sen, 'Games, Justice and the General Will', *Mind*, 74 (1965): 554–62.

17. I discuss the source of these common assumptions in a shared Victorian moral and political language which went beyond their epistemological and conceptual differences in my *Liberalism and Modern Society*, Cambridge: Polity, 1992, Ch. 2.

18. E.g. J. Rawls, *A Theory of Justice*, Oxford: Clarendon Press, 1971; R. Dworkin, 'Liberalism'; in S. Hampshire (ed.), *Public and Private Morality*, Cambridge: Cambridge University Press, 1978, pp. 113–43. I examine these theories in detail in my, 'Defining Liberalism: Neutralist, Ethical or Political?', in R. Bellamy (ed.), *Liberalism and Recent Legal and Social Philosophy, Archiv für Rechts- Und Sozialphilosophie*, Beiheft Nr. 36 (1989), pp. 23–43.

19. My argument in this respect runs parallel to that of J. Raz, *The Morality of Freedom*, Oxford: Clarendon Press, 1986.

20. J. S. Mill, *Autobiography*, in J. M. Robson and J. Shillinger (eds), *Autobiography and Literary Essays, Collected Works I*, Toronto: University of Toronto, 1969, p. 139.

21. I. Berlin, 'John Stuart Mill and the Ends of Life', in *Four Essays*, p. 178.

22. J. S. Mill, *Utilitarianism, On Liberty and Considerations on Representative Government*,

London: Dent, 1972, pp. 8–9. (NB References to pp. 1–6 are to *Utilitarianism* and pp. 63–170 to *On Liberty*.)

23. T. H. Green, *Prolegomena to Ethics*, ed. A. C. Bradley, Oxford: Clarendon Press, 1883, para. 167. All references to paragraph numbers in the text are to this work. Mill's position is arguably more complicated than Green suggests, in that strictly speaking he eschews moral axioms as such for moral guidelines, e.g. his debate with Spencer on this point in *Utilitarianism*, pp. 58–9.

24. See Berlin, 'Two Concepts', p. 133 (n.):

> 'The ideal of true freedom is the maximum of power for all members of human society alike to make the best of themselves' said T. H. Green in 1881. Apart from the confusion of freedom with equality, this entails that if a man choose some immediate pleasure – which (in whose view?) would not enable him to make the best of himself (what self?) – what he was exercising was not 'true' freedom; and if deprived of it would not lose anything that mattered. Green was a genuine liberal; but many a tyrant could use this formula to justify his worst acts of oppression.

25. Mill, *On Liberty*, pp. 115–16.

26. H. Sidgwick, *Methods of Ethics*, 6th edn, London: Macmillan, 1901, esp. concluding chapter.

27. Green quoting Sidgwick, *Methods of Ethics*, III, xiv, 2, in *Prolegomena*, para. 365.

28. John Gray, *Mill on Liberty: A Defence*, London: Routledge, 1983. For a similar view see Richard Wollheim, 'John Stuart Mill and Isaiah Berlin – The Ends of Life and the Preliminaries of Morality', in Ryan (ed.), *The Idea of Freedom*, pp. 253–70.

29. Mill, *Utilitarianism*, p. 6; Gray, *Mill on Liberty*, pp. 19–28.

30. A good recent restatement of the sort of view Gray and Wollheim are attacking is Ted Honderich, 'The Worth of J. S. Mill on Liberty', *Political Studies*, 22 (1974): 463–70. My own account owes much to the able survey of C. L. Ten, *Mill on Liberty*, Oxford: Oxford University Press, 1980, Chs 2 and 3.

31. Mill, *On Liberty*, pp. 117–18.

32. Mill, *Utilitarianism*, p. 16.

33. In developing my criticisms of Mill I am indebted to the work of Charles Taylor, especially his essays 'What's Wrong with Negative Liberty', in Ryan (ed.), *The Idea of Freedom*, pp. 175–94 and 'What is Human Agency?', in T. Michel (ed.), *The Self: Psychological and Philosophical Issues*, Oxford: Clarendon Press, 1977, pp. 103–35.

34. J. C. Rees, *Mill and his Early Critics*, Leicester: Leicester University Press, 1956, pp. 48–9.

35. Mill, *On Liberty*, p. 72.

36. J. S. Mill, *System of Logic* ed. J. M. Robson, *Collected Works*, VIII, Toronto: University of Toronto, 1974, p. 840.

37. Mill, *Logic*, pp. 836–43. For a fine analysis of this passage see G. W. Smith, 'The Logic of J. S. Mill on Freedom', *Political Studies*, XXVIII (1980): 238–52.

38. Mill, *Utilitarianism*, pp. 9–10.

39. Mill, *Logic*, p. 841.

40. J. S. Mill, *Principles of Political Economy*, ed. J. M. Robson, *Collected Works*, III, Toronto: University of Toronto, 1965, V, xi, 2, p. 938, 10, p. 953.

41. Mill, *Principles of Political Economy*, V, xi, 9, p. 951.

42. Martin Hollis, 'The Social Liberty Game', in A. Phillips Griffiths (ed.), *Of Liberty*, Cambridge: Cambridge University Press, 1983, pp. 31–44.
43. Mill, *Principles*, V, xi, 9, p. 951, V, xi, 10, p. 953. Mill adopts this formulation in most sections of this chapter.
44. Mill, *Principles*, V, xi, 16, p. 970.
45. Mill, *Principles*, V, xi, 12, p. 957.
46. Runciman and Sen, 'Games, Justice', pp. 556–7.
47. Mill, *Utilitarianism*, p. 16.
48. Gray, *Mill on Liberty*, p. 88; Richard Wollheim, 'John Stuart Mill and the Limits of State Action', *Social Research*, 40 (1973): 12; and Wollheim, 'Mill and Berlin', p. 267.
49. J. S. Mill, *Subjection of Women*, in *Essays on Equality, Law and Education, Collected Works*, XXI, Toronto: University of Toronto, 1984, pp. 306, 336.
50. Mill, *On Liberty*, p.121.
51. Mill, *On Liberty*, p. 74.
52. Berlin, 'Two Concepts', p. 171.
53. The phrase is from Berlin, 'Two Concepts', p. 133, and is used against doctrines of positive liberty generally, rather than Mill's theory.
54. T. H. Green, 'On the Different Senses of Freedom as Applied to Will and to the Moral Progress of Man', in *Works*, II, paras 17–18.
55. For a parallel defence of Green to my own, see Peter Nicholson, *The Political Philosophy of the British Idealists: Selected Studies*, Cambridge: Cambridge University Press, 1990, Study IV. I provide a more historical account of Green's political theory as a whole in 'T. H. Green and the Morality of Victorian Liberalism', in Richard Bellamy (ed.), *Victorian Liberalism: Nineteenth Century Political Thought and Practice*, London: Routledge, 1990.
56. Mill, *On Liberty*, pp. 116–17.
57. T. H. Green, *Lectures on the Principles of Political Obligation*, in *Works* II, paras 134, 141.
58. Berlin, 'Two Concepts', p. 132.
59. A similar concept of equality is to be found in Bernard Williams, 'The Idea of Equality', in P. Laslett and W. G. Runciman (eds), *Philosophy, Politics and Society*, second series, Oxford: Blackwell, 1967, pp. 110–31.
60. T. H. Green, 'Lectures on Liberal Legislation and Freedom of Contract', *Works*, III, p. 372.
61. Baldwin, 'MacCallum and the Two Concepts', p. 133.
62. W. L. Weinstein, 'The Concept of Liberty in Nineteenth Century British Political Thought', *Political Studies*, 13 (1965): 146, 151.
63. Green, *Political Obligation*, para. 219.
64. J. Raz, 'Right-based Moralities', in J. Waldron (ed.), *Theories of Rights*, Oxford: Oxford University Press, 1984, p. 187.
65. M. Walzer, *Spheres of Justice*, Oxford: Martin Robertson, 1983, p. 8.
66. Berlin on positive liberty in 'Two Concepts', p. 171.
67. As advocated, for example, by R. Dworkin, *Taking Rights Seriously*, 2nd edn, London: Duckworth, 1978, p. 276.

CHAPTER 3

An Italian 'New Liberal' Theorist – Guido De Ruggiero's History of European Liberalism and the Crisis of Idealist Liberalism

Idealism as a respectable liberal metaphysic is generally regarded as having died a none too dignified death with the First World War and the rise of authoritarian regimes in the 1920s and 1930s with which, in many people's eyes, it was deeply and damningly ideologically involved.[1] This makes it rather curious that Guido De Ruggiero's *History of European Liberalism* – a work written from a definite idealist standpoint – should have become (and maintained its position as) a standard text of the subject.[2] Much more than a timeless statement of liberal ideals, however, its value inheres in its analysis of the crisis of liberalism in the interwar period. Written in 1924, it became a manifesto of the liberal (i.e. non-communist) anti-fascist movement, being a response both to the end of the cosy bourgeois world of nineteenth-century Europe, with which both Idealism and liberalism are usually identified, and the desertion of large sections of the liberal political class to either fascism or socialism. The book's worth as liberal theory can only be appreciated, therefore, if it is seen as an attempt to redefine the tenets and traditions of liberalism in the light of the highly charged political situation of the 1920s.

Idealism and the Risorgimento Liberalism of the Italian Hegelian Tradition

Born in Naples on the 23 March 1888, De Ruggiero's cultural formation was entirely within the Southern Italian Hegelian tradition and his political philosophy can only be understood with reference to it.[3] The Neapolitan Hegelians – Francesco De Sanctis and Silvio and Bertrando Spaventa – sought to interpret the *Risorgimento* – the movement of national unification – in terms of the Hegelian ethical state. They justified their activities against the largely foreign-backed monarchical regimes of the time and in favour of a united Italian state by reference to the collective will of the Italian people.[4] As Silvio Spaventa wrote:

> The end of our revolution, as of every revolution was precisely that of making possible the unfolding of that new life which we felt within us and which was closed within our thoughts, destroying the obstacles and impediments which restricted it to this august sphere of the individual conscience, and to put it into action in the universal conscience of society.

The true state – its ethical force – lay in the people constituted as a nation: 'It is nationality which restores this living consciousness of the State, because it is the intimate reflexion of its own material in which human association is brought about, that is to say the complex of the universal and distinctive characteristics of a people.'[5]

The resulting Italian state, however, was far from reflecting the fully rational Hegelian constitution. For a start, Italy lacked the cultural cohesiveness implied by the Hegelian *Volksgeist* – those shared practices and cultural values which makes the transition from civil society to the ethical state a possibility. The problem was twofold: first, cultural divisiveness existed both between the educated classes and the largely uneducated majority and between the different Italian territories; and second, economic divisiveness existed both between the industrial north and the agricultural south and between large landowners, small proprietors, the big industrialists and the workers. The state was thus fragmented into different groups each locked, in Hegelian terms, in their own particularity through the lack of a common culture to mediate between them. In a famous phrase the Italian state existed, it remained to create the Italians.[6]

This catalogue of problems which bedevilled the new Italian nation was epitomized in the 'southern question' and hence unavoidably at the centre of the Neapolitan Hegelian's thinking. They were disdainful of the solutions proferred by the 'meridionalisti' – men such as Pasquale Villari, Giustino Fortunato and Gaetano Salvemini – who came from the positivist tradition and looked for a solution via the extension of the franchise, a federal system of government and a redistribution of resources towards the south.[7] They rejected such initiatives as fundamentally unsound because they were based on an atomistic view of society which reduces the individual to an empirical unit governed by a particular set of needs and desires and egoistically seeking their satisfaction. They saw the studies of Mosca and Pareto as providing confirmation from within the positivist camp of their own view that this programme would leave ordinary people at the mercy of elite groups who could manipulate their perception of their interests through control of the organs of power.[8] The Hegelians credited this approach with the descent of modern Italian politics into the sort of political brokerage later identified with

Giolitti's policy of *trasformismo*. By contrast, they advocated the Hegelian notion of individuality as dependent upon a shared moral and cultural tradition capable of embodying both individual and collective goals. The difficulty was how this could be created in a society in which cultural and economic divisions seemed to close the individual within a liberal individualist ethos, cutting him off from his fellow men.

The problem was one of political identity, and two strategies developed to solve it, represented respectively by the two main philosophers of the second generation of Italian Hegelians – Benedetto Croce and Giovanni Gentile.[9] They took it upon themselves to revise Hegel in a radical manner in an attempt to create at one and the same time an Italian culture and an Italian people. Both, in their different ways, sought to provide via their philosophical and historical studies a cultural tradition capable of reintegrating man's practical activity into his search and need for a framework of meaning, value and certainty. However, whereas Croce's philosophy largely continues the Hegelian project of reconciliation to the world, seeing man in the last instance as the servant of Providence, Gentile sought to appropriate the power of Spirit to man.[10] It is to this latter development of the Italian Hegelian tradition that De Ruggiero – Gentile's star pupil – belongs, though he took it in a liberal rather than the fascist direction of his mentor.

The First World War

In the years prior to and including the First World War De Ruggiero's thinking more or less converged with that of Gentile.[11] Gentile's 'actualism' represents the subjective extreme of Idealism in that the present activity of reflective awareness is regarded as the absolute foundation on which all else depends. The act of thinking is the 'pure act' which creates the world of human experience.[12] As De Ruggiero expressed it in his first major book, *Contemporary Philosophy* of 1912:

> The world of thought is actuality, concreteness, search and achievement, aspiration and attainment. This new conception of the world as the world of our struggle and labour must supplant the old conception of the world as a natural whole which is simply the creation of our imagination, arising from the accumulation of our past experiences and the expectation of new experiences.[13]

Man's thought exists only in his acts and the social world he creates with others through the transformation of reality. Consciousness of self emerges from the practical activity of the will, of human *praxis*, as it shapes the natural world. In common with Hegel, he sees the most concrete example of this as being a sense of nationality – the cultural baggage we necessarily carry around with us to have any sense of personal identity at all.[14] But De Ruggiero went beyond Hegel and turned actualism into a philosophy of radical liberation and his liberalism must be seen in the light of it. Two themes dominate De Ruggiero's definition of liberalism: first, the view of liberty as the individual's capacity for unfettered development and self-expression; and second, the need to situate human freedom in the institutions and culture of liberal society conceived of as the embodiment of human will.[15] De Ruggiero believed that a community could evolve spontaneously out of human activity if only it was given the opportunity to freely develop. It was the vision of a society built on human will and involving the participation of all its members. This was the attraction of the First World War for it seemed to obviate the need for a mediating, pre-existing culture to focus and define the individual's actions. It met the dual end of a total mobilization of the people on the one hand and centring their action upon the core concept of the nation on the other. It was, in the words of practically everyone advocating entry into the war in Italy at the time, to be the completion of the *Risorgimento*, giving the nation a spiritual unity to complement its political unity.

De Ruggiero put these ideas together in a long article of 1916 on 'Italian Thought and the War'.[16] He began with a declaration of the central tenet of actualism, that 'the understanding of life can and must make itself felt in its turn as life, and no longer as the mirror image of life'. The war he saw as the embodiment of this ideal. Everyone, whether they had wanted the war or not and whatever their reasons for becoming involved, was equally engaged in the practical exigencies of fighting. This gave their particular actions a higher significance as contributions to the national war effort. He attacked the view, made popular by Croce, that the war was the war of historical materialism. The ideologies of the pre-war world, he argued, democratic, nationalist, socialist and liberal had indeed been dominated by the narrow sphere of self-interest. But the war had changed that and had revived man's sense of his ability to act as an autonomous agent rather than in service to certain set desires which the system of production was designed to satisfy. The ethic of the war was the 'idealism of action', endowing such values as heroism, nobility, patriotism and fellowship with a force they had lost. They were no longer parts of an outmoded rhetoric to cover up essentially selfish motives but derived their meaning from a common struggle: 'the individual is reborn, no longer in the contingencies of his egoism, but in the universality of his being, in the purity of his humanity, in the unity of his race.' De Ruggiero's nationalism was therefore far from being based on an uncomplicated allegiance to an already existing community or political unit; indeed he largely despised the run-of-the-mill nationalists such as Enrico Corradini. His argument was that participation in the war created national feeling. In the very different circumstances of the post-war world, however, this was revealed as being largely contingent on the special circumstances engendered by armed struggle and he was forced to examine what made such a commitment unlikely under the liberal democratic regime of modern Italy.[17] This analysis was carried out in the role of political commentator for a number of newspapers – in particular *Il Resto del Carlino* and later *Il Paese* – and in two books on English politics which resulted from his stay there from late 1920 to mid-1921 and motivated his shift to a new liberalism.[18]

The Two Red Years (1919–20)

The war clearly had not produced anything like the national, to say nothing of the moral, unity sought for by Gentile and De Ruggiero. Officially victors, the defeat at Caporetto was far from redeemed by the Vittoria Veneto. The war had been far beyond Italy's means as a nation, and the years 1919–20 were probably, with the exception of 1943, the period of greatest social and political agitation in modern Italian history. Industrial expansion had been totally sustained by the state's war effort which could little afford it in the first place, so that the post-war period witnessed a sharp decrease in demand and concomitant industrial unrest. This though was better organized than ever before, union membership having dramatically increased. At the same time, there was a widespread agrarian unrest amongst agricultural workers and small proprietors, again better organized than before by associations formed amongst ex-combatants. Yet if these different groups achieved a modicum of success in their own areas their efforts were far from being co-ordinated. The introduction of proportional representation in the 1919 elections had greatly increased the number of seats of socialists and the Catholic 'Popular Party', but neither group had what could be called a coherent political line. For a start, the socialists alienated a large section of the peasant class eager to buy land by committing themselves to land nationalization, whilst the *popolari* were an extremely heterogeneous group held together by the tenuous bonds of religion. The only attempt to give this unrest a decidedly political orientation – the factory council movement organized by Gramsci and *L'Ordine Nuovo* in Turin – had failed miserably due to its isolation from any similar action. For De Ruggiero the pressing problem was how to organize these different groupings.

The war had seemed to unite two seemingly antithetical demands – the spontaneity of action, as a free creative liberation from the past, and the spirit of order, of doing one's duty in the post assigned to you by the needs of the war whether as officer or common soldier.[19] In the post-war crisis spontaneous action seemed to exist in plenty but there was nothing which could be called a common conception of society to give it direction and purpose. But De Ruggiero – in contrast to Gentile – looked upon these different movements as signs of health, believing that 'liberalism is ... spirit and therefore an eminently organising force'. He saw no need therefore 'to counter the liberal political mentality with an organic and organising mentality'.[20] The war he believed had proved this, and he contrasted as examples of what he meant the concept of economic co-operation and a trust. A trust is a protectionist arrangement whereby a more powerful element dominates the others, depriving the system of the stimulus of competition and innovation. This was organization in a bad sense as represented by Germany during the war. Co-operation, however, was a libertarian concept which conserves the smaller forces enabling them to participate freely in the system – an organic unity.[21] He saw the industrial unrest in a favourable light as a move away from the organization of the trust imposed by the big industrialists to a new type of organization emerging out of the nascent workers' movement. It was not just a protest against bad pay and working conditions but something more positive:

> an affirmation of conscience, of personality. The great modern industrial movement has created the new physiognomy of work, has given to work a conscience adequate to itself. But the material conditions in which work is carried out are inappropriate to the development of this conscience.

The labour of the workers was nullified by the weight of the accumulated labour of the past concentrated in capital, that of the peasant by landed property, the work of the clerk by an impersonal bureaucracy. Wage labour alienated the worker from the products of his labour. The war had aggravated the situation by increasing the concentration of capital in the hands of 'a small brigade of a few great financiers and a few great industrialists'. The workers were simply seeking 'to leave the amorphous state of a mass and to acquire their own personality by virtue of their productive activity'. What was required was a new synthesis of labour and capital, which must lighten the weight of the latter on the former by attacking monopolies and involving these new forces. He sought:

> A daring programme of industrial and agrarian legislation; which looks beyond the already constituted particular interests, to where these fuse with other new ones, in a supreme interest in the conservation of social life, which would be equally to the advantage of all.[22]

De Ruggiero's interpretation of this movement hinges on an essentially Hegelian view of the nature of modern society. Labour is crucial in De Ruggiero's actualist philosophy for the development of human self-consciousness and personality. It involves the objectifying of the human agent's will, giving substance to his material and spiritual needs. Indeed it creates them, since they are not biologically determined givens but formed and organized through the domination of nature. As this control increases and society develops, no single individual can satisfy all his needs and we are forced to co-operate with others. A network of mutually beneficial productive relationships develops which forms the basis for a new harmony in modern society. The growth of individuality is frustrated, though, when the products of our labour are alienated to someone else. This is exacerbated by factory conditions in which one's relation to the productive process as a whole is difficult to perceive. The individual in capitalist society still works to satisfy his own needs and desires and is thus enclosed in the sphere of self-interest. As a result, there had been an unfair accumulation of capital in the hands of a few and the consequent enervation of the labour of the mass of the workers. But the workers' movement, in De Ruggiero's appraisal, was not simply moti- vated by need – in fact living conditions had improved greatly since unification. Its importance was that it went beyond need, was an organized expression of the individual worker's solidarity with others and thus repre- sented a concomitant diminishing of individual particularity. The influence of George Sorel's interpretation of contemporary proletarian movements in the light of early Christian millenarianism is important here, for it helped Italian intellectuals to regard the industrial struggle in semi-religious terms as 'taking up the revolutionary movement of the Risorgimento', thereby creat- ing a link to the earlier problematic of the Neapolitan Hegelians.[23]

De Ruggiero's thinking in this respect has obvious affinities to that of Gramsci and in particular the 'revolutionary liberal' Piero Gobetti – both ideologues of the Turin factory council movement.[24] But he accused them of substituting a narrow class interest – that of the workers – for that of society as a whole, and in the case of the Communists of imposing it on the workers themselves via the party bureaucracy. For De Ruggiero an unbridgeable divide existed between human free will and 'scientific' laws of social and economic development which Marxism inevitably resolved via the party in the direction of the latter. He believed the workers' movement, allowed freely to develop, would transcend class and lead to identification with membership of the whole national (and ultimately international) community.[25] What he was proposing was a new work ethic of human brotherhood which would in the long run contain and triumph over every struggle:

> It would be pointless, he was to write in 1940, to speak of the economic subject of work, as spontaneous, inventive and constructive activity if this subject was not understood as moral personality, as the autonomous source of energy. Similarly it would be empty to speak of the solidarity of work if man does not grasp in his moral conscience the more profound and intimate sense of the bonds which bind him to other men.[26]

The problem for practical politics was thus to secure the conditions for this ethic to develop, a programme which had more in common with Gramsci's proposals for a new hegemony than he would have cared to admit. His distinctive contribution to the contemporary debate derived however from the influence of English new liberalism and the philosophy of Hobhouse on his thought.

New Liberalism Italian Style and the Struggle against Fascism

The appeal of Hobhouse's philosophy for De Ruggiero was the manner in which he built his reconceptualization of a liberal society on the basis of a new concept of the individual.[27] Hobhouse follows Mill and Green in seeing individuality not as the cultivation of self-interest but the development of character or personality. Now if, he argues, man's end is not the pursuit of pleasure *per se* but the realization of his nature, then society can be seen not as the arena of competing individuals but as a co-operative pursuit of self-realization. Liberalism, as Hobhouse redefined it, is thus 'the belief that society can safely be founded on [the] self-directing power of personality [and] that it is only on this foundation that a true community can be built'. It was the vision of a society based on the possibility for the spontaneous fulfilment of the capacities of all its members. Liberty, however, is not 'impulse', but 'rational self-determination' towards the good. He brushes aside a potential conflict between different individuals' freedom for self-development by seeing self-realization as a rational process implicity oriented towards the common good. Following T. H. Green he argues that 'full development of personality is practically possible not for one man only but for all members of the community'.[28]

Man is a social animal and his conception of the good is necessarily defined in and through the practices he engages in with others and which embody the development of reason in both the individual and humanity as a whole. Now Hobhouse, famous for his attack on Hegel and Bosanquet in *The Metaphysical Theory of the State*, is clearly not interpreting this process in conventional Idealist terms.[29] The essence of his criticism of the Hegelian doctrine of the state is that a putative real will of the individual is identified with the customs and practices (the general will) of an actual state. Hobhouse liberalizes Idealism by arguing that our freedom is prior to any particular set of social arrangements and consists in our ability to chose and frame them for our own ends. The basis for community is thus the rational perception that my self-development is intimately related to that of my fellows, that each individual's particular good is found in the common good.[30] Hobhouse argued that the existing distribution of wealth and power prevented the development of such a consciousness. By not just redistributing wealth but power as well, so that individuals participated in the management of their place of work, the local community and central government, he hoped to foster an organic conception of society based on co-operation and mutual aid. He thus appears to invert the Hegelian concept of the state as the unfolding of reason downwards from Spirit to man, to see it as the rational perception of common human goals amongst individuals. The teleology however is implicitly the same, being based on the belief that there is a natural 'line of development' which mediates and harmonizes individual wills.[31] As I shall argue below, his position is therefore difficult to sustain without some of those self-same presuppositions concerning the nature of actual communities which he so attacked in Hegel and Bosanquet.[32]

'New liberalism' so defined had obvious attractions for De Ruggiero though. It seemed to provide a revision of the Idealist conception of community in the direction he was seeking, namely as the product of individual effort, and a legislative programme adequate to his interpretation of the workers' movement. As we saw, he regarded the accumulation of wealth and power in the hands of a few industrialists and landowners as the principal bar to the development of a new political consciousness amongst workers.[33] Hobhouse argued that since any particular action in the productive process is necessarily done in co-operation with others, it is wrong to award any single individual a disproportionate amount of the social product. Thus a minimum wage was required for any individual contribution which could only be increased by personal effort to the maximum 'industrial value of the individual'. This in turn becomes an argument for the co-operative ownership and management of industry by workers and capitalists. Hobhouse's argument develops out of his notion of the common good as the combination of individual and social goals, and its feasibility was dependent on this perception being actually present in the minds of members of society. In this way, he strongly distinguished his 'liberal socialism' from the bureaucratic 'official' socialism of the Fabians on the one hand and vulgar Marxist 'mechanical' socialism on the other: 'It must come from below, not from above, . . . it must emerge from the efforts of society as a whole to secure a fuller measure of justice and a better organization of mutual aid . . . '[34]

It was precisely in these terms that De Ruggiero wished to see the social unrest of the early 1920s and hence justify 'new liberal' policies in Italy. There was some irony in this – Hobhouse's tract of 1911 had been written in the wake of 'the People's Budget' with the progressives in the liberal party in the ascendant. The war and the coalition government seemed to present a very different spectacle and De Ruggiero was reduced to singling out Asquith's *Paisley Policy* of 1920 for the dubious role of the post-war 'Summa' of new liberal politics. He approved in particular of Asquith's rejection of 'state socialism' aiming at direct public management of industry for the 'liberal socialist' programme of 'public control':

> the formation of mixed commissions of capitalists, technocrats and workers with the remit to examine not simply questions of pay, but be responsible for the overall supervision of the industry. The State would also be represented as curator of the interests of the consumers.

This programme constituted 'a real co-partnership of capital and labour'.[35] Marx was correct in seeing capital as accumulated labour, but wrong to seek to abolish it altogether. If the nineteenth century had seen the concentration of capital in a few hands so that workers were justified to see the war of capital and labour as part and parcel of class struggle, the logic of labour was itself undermining this opposition via the development of worker co-operatives and limited companies.[36] He distinguished his attitude on this issue both before and after the Second World War from the 'liberal socialism' (*liberalsocialismo*) of Carlo Rosselli and Guido Calogero. His own doctrine of 'social liberalism' (*liberalismo sociale*) was not the liberalizing of a socialist economy but the establishment of the social conditions for liberalism to flourish.[37] The core of new liberalism as he interpreted it was thus Hobhouse's fleshing out of Green's notion of the common good in the organic conception of society. The essential element was that individuals should be free to rationally frame their life-plans – 'What the English designate with the expression: equality of opportunity' – and that a certain amount of state regulation was necessary to secure this. Once achieved this by itself would issue in mutuality of respect and social harmony. Thus liberalism in England had broken out of the old individualist formulas 'to reaffirm its spiritual worth':

> Which is not in the atomistic opposition of individual to individual but the full organic unfolding of a superior spiritual individuality ... The principle of the State, of the organic nature of life, is not therefore repugnant to liberalism, rather it constitutes its most evolved expression.

This higher unity was a spiritual rather than a naturalistic or material entity, 'an affirmation of self':

> From this fact issues not just the positive and constructive work, but also the critical role of liberalism, which in the face of the danger of an oppressive servility threatened both from top and bottom, before the brutal mechanism of economic forces which attempt to nullify all the dignity and nobility of human labour, critically reaffirms the autonomy of spiritual values, the sense of human personality, the self-same rights of individualism, which are not crushed, but realised in its organic conception.[38]

In De Ruggiero's opinion the post-war crisis in Italy was primarily the result of the operation of 'classical liberalism'. Classical liberalism saw man as an individual producer whose co-operation with others was freely entered into by all parties and open to renegotiation. Freedom of contract, it was held, ensured the responsiveness of society to its members. De Ruggiero criticized this view both because he believed the freedom it claimed necessary for it to work did not exist and because it put forward a theory of the individual he found repugnant. A society which conceives itself as essentially a mechanism for the satisfaction of individual interests would be spiritually empty and have no basis on which conflicting interests could be reconciled. As a result it was likely to become polarized between rich and poor and the inherent tensions flare up once economic growth could no longer be maintained to make such a conception of society a going concern.[39] This, for De Ruggiero, was precisely what had happened in post-war Italy and he found proof of it in the sectional division of society between fascism and socialism. In a number of articles written on his return to Italy he bitterly attacked the desertion of the liberal cause.[40] Luigi Einaudi, the leading advocate of *laissez-faire* liberal economics in Italy, was a special target of his criticism. He is amazed by Einaudi's interpretation of the fights between fascist and socialist organizations in Bologna as a struggle between the freedom of the worker to choose his own work and state socialism. The apparent liberty held out by Einaudi was little less than slavery for the workers who were only demanding

> One of the fundamental postulates of liberalism: equality before the owning classes ... For the sake of a purely formal liberalism, for a merely decorative nationalism, by breaking up the workers organizations, we are squandering the richest national energies, dissipating its solidest capital, we are sacrificing the most real liberty which is the liberty of all men to make themselves fully men.[41]

On the other hand those liberals who appeared to make overtures in the direction of the socialists were simply seeking to pacify an incipient workers' revolt. 'Filo-socialism', as he called it, 'was nothing but the vulgar effect of fear' which revealed its true colours in the wholesale desertion of previously self-styled liberals to fascism in 1922.[42]

Fascism, far from being the solution to the contemporary crisis, was symptomatic of it. The problem was one of authority, not in the sense of law and order, but of self-government:

> The force of the State is but the resultant of the forces which converge in it. Give to the great masses the clear concrete sensation, that the State is not outside or against them, and that they obey the State, because they feel they are obeying their own law, [and] they feel in being governed, not servitude, but an autonomous act, a means of self-government.[43]

Of course it was in precisely such terms that Gentile justified fascism – what distinguished De Ruggiero from his doctrine? Gentile argued that fascism was the true liberal party, continuing the tradition of the Neapolitan Hegelians and completing the *Risorgimento*. The *squadristi* carried on the process of regeneration begun during the war by combining moral and material force, theory and action, in revolutionary violence. The liberal state had failed to unite will and power, fascism had filled the vacuum with the moral force of the cudgel (*manganello*). This was the genuine expression of liberalism, the achievement of complete freedom via the subjection of nature to man's will making it an instrument of his ends and thus spiritualizing it. The revolution over, the fascist corporate state organized the moral will of the people within the political force of the state. The unions or 'syndicates' represented the corporate personality of the worker which together with the employers' organizations were in turn to be organized within the framework of the national personality

– the state. As a result the individual pursuing his private interest came via the corporation to a consciousness of the general interest.[44] Gentile's argument here seems to be little more than a mechanical exposition of the Hegelian state in which men do not enter the political arena directly but via associations, corporations, and so on. Hegel had believed that the classes of society were so sharply differentiated from each other that the notion of direct participation in politics was a non-starter since self-interest could never generate a sense of general interest. It was necessary therefore to have a degree of corporate autonomy in public life in which the groups would regulate their own particular forms of life. He believed, however, that at a higher level the individual would become aware of the interrelatedness of the 'system of needs', that all labour is social as well as individual, and that consciousness of this fact would promote the development of a community awareness within civil society.[45] This was a perception open to the representatives and bureaucrats who formed a universal class through their direct allegiance to the state, rather than all members of society. For De Ruggiero, Gentile had obviously trivialized the Hegelian analysis by simply creating the differentiation which Hegel believed existed in his day and by identifying the will of the individual somewhat arbitrarily with that of the fascist state. The individual under totalitarianism has no will of his own at all. Gentile restricts the individual to seeking his private interest in that of his group since there is no incentive for him to transcend it. This is the function of the state authority. Thus the corporate state can in no sense be called a higher form of self-government since individual interests are manipulated rather than allowed to develop freely.[46]

De Ruggiero regarded the corporate state as the logical development of classical liberalism's image of man and society. The mechanical reduction of human individuality to a number of self-referential desires was plausible enough whilst the ideological hegemony of bourgeois values made the belief in a homogeneity of interest in capitalist society a workable ideal. But the ultimate legacy of the industrial revolution had not been the simple domination of a particular class and set of ideas over all others. When the political viability of capitalist society was called into doubt then liberal individualism came to create a very different style of politics, the very reverse of liberal values. Respect for the value of the individual could not be sustained on the basis of the model of man it proposed. Since all that was required was the satisfaction of certain narrowly defined interests this could be achieved just as well via the technical or bureaucratic state. The fascist corporate state was thus little more than the institutionalization of Giolittian *trasformismo* – the control of political life by a mixture of intimidation and bribery by a number of *clientele*.[47] But the problem of how to develop a sense of common interest in a society deeply imbued with an ethic of possessive individualism remains as intractable for De Ruggiero as it was for Gentile – he surely has simply chosen to ignore it. De Ruggiero's naive belief in the natural supremacy of liberal values is in marked contrast to Gramsci's contemporary reflections in the

Prison Notebooks on the difficulty of mobilizing revolutionary consciousness within the proletariat, the relationship of consciousness to social structure and the consequent role of the party and intellectuals in organizing the masses. In the place of analysis De Ruggiero simply exhorted intellectuals to perform, to adopt Gramscian terms, the 'traditional' role of keeping liberal ideals alive and remain open to the overtures of the working class.

The History of European Liberalism

These, then, are the themes which get their fullest elaboration in *The History of European Liberalism* of 1924. The book is divided into a historical treatment of liberalism in the main European countries and a theoretical examination of liberalism in the light of this. The most telling of the historical sections is undoubtedly that on Italy. He begins by attacking the legacy of the liberal Hegelians – the 'Historical Right' who ruled Italy in the years immediately following the *Risorgimento* and who had been claimed by Gentile as precursors of fascism. Because Italian unity had not been the creation of a genuine national movement the state had become highly authoritarian in character:

> Raised to power not through a spontaneous development of liberal ideas in the minds of individuals, but by a virtual act of conquest sanctioned by a merely nominal plebiscite, this party confined liberty to the narrow political caste which took actual part in public life, and even, in its highest theoretical expressions, came to identify liberty with the State itself.

The goal of liberalism though is not any state 'but the State as the organization of liberty'. Italian politics had, unfortunately, failed to move in this direction and continued under the 'left' who took over the government to be a system used by the ruling class for their own restricted ends. This process culminated in the political management of Giolitti and was made worse rather than better by the extension of democracy:

> The fault of this art of government was that behind an impressive facade of liberalism and democracy it concealed a decadent governing class and a non-political populace. The social convulsions that followed the war revealed the illusion, stripping off the pretence and laying bare what had previously been papered over. It then appeared how far the Italian people were from having assimilated modern liberalism, with its opposed but complimentary elements, individual liberty and State organization.[48]

De Ruggiero's analysis of the situation is in marked contrast to his fellow liberal idealist and anti-fascist Benedetto Croce. His *History of Italy* was a veritable panegyric to Giolitti's political acumen, whose hated policy of *trasformismo* is praised by Croce as proof of his talent at uniting the country. He too laments the divisions in society resulting from the materialization of spiritual values but sees no possibility for mediating between these groups besides political prudence. The class divisions consequent upon industrialization had weakened the value system of traditional society in which man's place in society derived its meaning by reference to a cosmic order inherent in the nature of things. The adoption of compromise and tinkering with the political system was consequent upon the impossibility – after the initial success of bourgeois individualism – for any one section of society to universalize its claims to form a common community of values. Hegelian philosophy had been the supreme modern attempt to provide such a structure in seeking to interpret the differentiation of society as an emanation of *Geist* in history. Croce somewhat stubbornly sought to hold on to this notion, perversely interpreting whatever disasters history threw up as the workings of Providence and exhorting his countrymen to do likewise. But, as De Ruggiero pointed out, such a view was tantamount to utter passivity and resignation to one's lot. Reviewing Croce's book he blamed his philosophy for the separation of culture and politics which had in his view precipitated the current crisis. Having turned politics into 'mere administrative techniques, not fed by the springs of conscience and knowledge', Croce's moral condemnation of fascism lacked all conviction. It was rather the mouthing of 'common places of a not totally forgotten rhetoric'.[49] The rise of fascism had shown that the pragmatic approach of compromise, co-operation and fairness had been insufficient to cope with the rival claims of different groups. De Ruggiero sought to fill this lacuna via an appeal to a new liberalism based, as in Hobhouse, on the personality of man: 'The energy which the Italians will in the future bring to their reaffirmation of human personality will be the measure of their ability to participate in the entire life of modern liberalism.'

De Ruggiero shares with traditional liberalism the belief in the all-importance of individual autonomy. The social and cultural worlds are products of human creativity rather than emanations from antecedent conditions independent of man's will and desire. At the same time he did not want to suggest that the set of practices which emerge at any one time is entirely arbitrary, a chance agglomeration. He was thus concerned to see the historical process as essentially rational, yet in a radically different perspective to Hegel. For the rationality is no longer that of Spirit, but of the conscious ends that men set themselves in making history. Yet this immediately set a problem for him. He argues in Kantian manner that man's freedom consists 'in the capacity and ability to pursue a moral end' and that liberalism presumes

> that this capacity belongs to every man as man and is not the privilege of a few. Every man must therefore have his opportunities through the removal, so far as possible, of obstacles to his development, yet without the substitution of another's work for his own.

But in so saying De Ruggiero is immediately faced with the classic problem of what is to count as development. In giving an account of what possible obstacles there might be, he falls foul of the usual moralizing associated with liberals turned righteous, fulminating against 'the caprice of individuals ... squandering their chances of a higher and worthier freedom; so that Society is right to intervene'. The difficulty was that De Ruggiero's own analysis had shown that the basis for the sort of moral agreement he presumed had broken down. He hoped that if industrial society allowed free development beyond class interest it would be able to produce a moral community based on a conscious interpretation of its own activities. The 'social environment' was to be freely fashioned to give full expression to human personality. He attacked the Marxist notion of laws of human development. Socialism had been but a stage in the worker's realization of his creative powers which liberalism overcame in a 'higher individualism' the complete spiritualizing of the world. But the complete liberalizing of De Ruggiero's Idealism has in the end rendered it completely vacuous. The stress on the individual as the source of all value is ultimately self-defeating. Personality is fashioned within society, in the forming of relationships and the solving of problems. Complete liberation is ultimately the negation rather than the affirmation of both self and the world, as is all too clear from the actions of the self-styled liberators of today. As he himself remarked: 'Freedom exists so far as it is exercised, so far as it faces the increasingly complex demands of life', so that 'without an inferior freedom, an elementary school of character, no truly free personality can ever emerge into the light'.[50]

As he noted on several occasions, it is the fact that man lives on several levels which renders the administrative solution ultimately unsatisfactory. The need to adjudicate between competing ends makes politics unavoidable. Yet, and here is the rub, it is in this lower stage that the unlikelihood of a solution arises, for they absorb individuals into the routines of everyday life, making it impossible to transcend present concerns for no basis exists to express common needs, hopes and fears that go beyond the immediacies of technique and social structure. De Ruggiero and Hobhouse sought to get around this difficulty by appealing to a subject which was prior to any such constitutive interests. Individual will, the realm of value, stands outside the existing world of fact so that a sense of community derives from the rational perception by the individual from a point which transcends his particular situation of the necessary harmony of individuals' wills. The Hegelian motto that 'What is rational is actual and what is actual is rational' did not mean the perception of reason in the world, as Croce had argued but, De Ruggiero's actualism reasserting itself, its 'actualization'.[51] Yet how is the individual in such a situation to have any basis for identification with the projects of his fellows, since these attachments are surely themselves socially produced?

In common with Hobhouse, he sees community arising from the comprehension of the interelatedness of all social activity, but he does not want to adopt the conservative stance of simply endorsing things as they stand and extolling the merits of 'our station and its duties'. Part of the problem was that the basis of such a conception even in its conservative form did not exist. The fragmentation of society into different occupational specialisms meant that individuals not only felt no direct contact between their role and that of others, but were often dissatisfied with them as well. A factory worker who has a dull and boring job to do is not necessarily going to be any more reconciled to it by having a share in management. A liberal individualist strategy of simply increasing his pay and reducing his hours to be left alone to do what he wants with his spare time may well appear to be the most rational course he can take. Withdrawal and protection from society – a liberalism based on rights, the *bête noir* of Idealist philosophers – are likely to appeal most once the constitutive bonds of community have broken down. Community cannot be created out of individual development alone without the ties of human interaction which sustain and develop it. Talk of the development of human capacities only makes sense in Idealist terms in the context of the shared practices of society which bring them forth. The activities people engage in, from forming friendships to eating and working, are not done indifferently but with a sense of meaning to the extent that societies embody a framework of values appropriate to each task – of, for example, loyalty, etiquette and application in the instances given above.[52] But De Ruggiero was seemingly trying to create this out of nothing – in such a situation the ethical state does indeed become the imposition of a presumed 'real will' on the existent wills of the people.

The years under fascism were spent pondering this problem, producing in 1946 a series of essays suitably entitled *The Return to Reason*, calling for a revival of the utopian tradition of political thought. What was required, he argued, was a language which transcends the present, enabling us to transform it. Man needs a framework of beliefs with the scope and function of religion but without falling into the error of substituting other-worldly for this-worldly goals. But 'the ideal needs of the human spirit' are rather difficult to define and not surprisingly De Ruggiero got little further than extolling their necessity. As it was, the post-war world looked little different to that before fascism. His revised liberalism had little success except amongst intellectuals within the 'Party of Action'. The politics of the day was divided to an even greater extent between the rival ideologies of capital and labour and more characterized by political jobbery than ever before.[53]

Conclusion

De Ruggiero's amalgam of Idealism and liberalism make a curious combination in the modern world, not because they are a hybrid mixture but because both belonged to a period and a moral consensus which had passed. Via Idealism De Ruggiero had attempted to revitalize liberalism as a theory capable of commanding our allegiance, but could only do so in terms of a cultural tradition which the social changes with which liberal theory was associated had largely undermined. The philosophy of liberation he espoused was itself the product of liberal individualism, though in radical form. Far from offering an Idealist solution to the crisis of liberalism his political philosophy was itself a product of it. This does not, however, in any way vitiate the larger project of providing a new moral community adequate to the problems of the contemporary world. So if his book does not provide the fundamental critique of liberalism necessary for such a social philosophy to emerge, it at least has the merit of telling us where not to begin – namely within liberalism itself.[54]

Notes

This chapter is based on research funded by the ESRC under its Postdoctoral Research Fellowship Scheme. Its contents are the responsibility of the author and do not necessarily reflect the views of the ESRC. I am grateful to Raymond Plant, Quentin Skinner and Jonathan Steinberg for their comments on an earlier version of this chapter.

1. The classic statement of this view is L. T. Hobhouse, *The Metaphysical Theory of the State*, London, 1918. A similar opinion expressed by J. B. Baillie in *Studies in Human Nature*, London, 1921, p. vii aroused the wrath of De Ruggiero in *Filosofi del Novecento*, 3rd edn, Bari, 1946, p. 3.

2. References are to the Collingwood translation *The History of European Liberalism*, Oxford, 1927. Described by him as 'a great book', he believed 'no book known to me since T. H. Green has, I think, made so fine a theoretical contribution to liberal doctrine, and this is far more complete and far more highly organized than anything of Green's' (letter of Collingwood to De Ruggiero, 18 November 1926, Collingwood MSS, Bodleian Library, Oxford, Folder 27). His fear that its Idealism would limit its market in the English-speaking world appears to have been unfounded, as it seems to have a place in the bibliography of any treatment of the subject.

3. For biographical information see E. Garin, *Intellectuali Italiani del XX Secolo*, Roma, 1974, pp. 105–36 and G. Calo and L. Salvatorelli, 'Guido de Ruggiero', in *Accademia Nazionale dei Lincei*, Quaderno 13, Rome, 1949.

4. See S. Landucci, 'L'hegelismo in Italia nell'età del Risorgimento', *Studi Storici*, 7 (1965), 597–628 and S. Onufrio, 'Lo "Stato etico" e gli hegliani di Napoli', *Nuovi Quaderni del Meridione*, 5 (1967), 76–90, 171–88, 436–57. The rest of this paragraph summarizes my 'Croce, Gentile and Hegel and the Doctrine of the Ethical State', *Rivista di Studi Crociani*, 20 (1983), 263–81; 21 (1984), 67–73.

5. Silvio Spaventa, *Dal 1845 al 1861, lettere, scritti. documenti*, ed. B. Croce, 2nd edn, Bari, 1923, pp. 20, 149.

6. I explore this central theme of Italian thought in my *Modern Italian Social Theory: Ideology and Politics from Pareto to the Present*, Cambridge, 1987.

7. For a history of the whole southern movement see R. Villari, *Mezzogiorno e democrazia*, Bari, 1979.

8. E.g. B. Croce's articles 'È necessaria una democrazia?' and 'Il partito come giudizio e

come prejiudizio', in *Unità* I (1912), reprinted in *Cultura e vita morale – intermezzi polemici*, 2nd edn, Bari, 1925 which gives a comprehensive account of the Idealist view of politics in this period.

9. On Croce see my 'Liberalism and Historicism – Benedetto Croce and the Political Role of Idealism in Italy c.1890–1952', in A. Moulakis (ed.), *The Promise of History*, Berlin/New York, 1985 and E. E. Jacobitti, *Revolutionary Humanism and Historicism in Modern Italy*, Yale, 1981. On Gentile see H. S. Harris, *The Social Philosophy of Giovanni Gentile*, Urbana, 1960, whose account I largely follow.

10. The best record of their differences was the early debate begun by Croce in *La Voce* of 1913 reprinted in *La Voce 1905–14*, ed. A. Romano, *La cultura italiana del '900 attraverso le riviste*, Vol. 3, Turin, 1960, pp. 595–605, 608–25, 630–8. See my *Modern Italian Social Theory*, Ch. 5 for an extended discussion of the debate drawing on the Gentile–Croce correspondence, and H. S. Harris, *The Social Philosophy of G. Gentile*, pp. 19–22 for an account more sympathetic to Gentile.

11. See G. Sasso, 'Considerazioni sulla filosofia di De Ruggiero', in *De Homine*, XXI (1967), pp. 23–70 for a comparison of Gentile and De Ruggiero's philosophy showing the substantial influence of Gentile throughout all De Ruggiero's writings. De Ruggiero's paper 'La scienza come esperienza assoluta', in *Annuario della Biblioteca Filosofica of Palermo*, II (1912), pp. 229–339 essentially reproduces the themes of Gentile's first outline of his actualism in 'L'atto del pensare come atto puro', in *Annuario*, I (1912), pp. 27–42.

12. H. S. Harris, 'Gentile', *Encyclopaedia of Philosophy*, III, New York, 1967, pp. 281–5.

13. *Contemporary Philosophy*, trans. R. G. Collingwood and A. Howard Hannay, London, 1921, pp. 375.

14. *Contemporary Philosophy*, pp. 16–18.

15. *European Liberalism*, pp. 357–63. *Idem*, 'Liberalism', in *Encyclopaedia of the Social Sciences*, Vol. 9, London, 1933, pp. 435–41.

16. 'La pensée italienne et la guerre', *Revue de Metaphysique et de morale*, 23 (1916), pp. 748–85.

17. 'La pensée italienne', pp. 751, 762, 764, 756–61, 769, 760–1.

18. The articles are almost completely collected in Guido de Ruggiero, *Scritti Politici 1912–26*, ed. Renzo de Felice, Bologna, 1969. De Felice's long introduction pp. 1–76 is the best analysis of De Ruggiero's political thought, but see too Francesco de Aloysio, 'Note su Guido de Ruggiero politico nel periodo della nascita e dellavvento del fascismo', *Rivista storica del socialism*, 23 (1960), 725–45 which is an important corrective to E. Garin, *Intellettuali*, pp. 105–36. The two books are *L'Impero britannico dopo la guerra*, Florence, 1921 and 'La formazione dellimpero britannico', in *L' Europa nel Secolo XIX*, Vol. I. *Storia Politica*, ed. D. Donati and F. Carli, Padua, 1925, pp. 477–513.

19. 'La pensée italienne', pp. 770–1. For the constrasting views of Croce and Gentile see G. Gentile, *Guerra e fede. Frammenti politici*, Naples, 1919 and B. Croce, *Pagine sulla guerra*, 2nd edn, Bari, 1928. Croce recorded his dissent from De Ruggiero's (and Gentile's) opinions in a review of his article in *La Critica*, 15 (1917), pp. 130–2, which, as he explained in a letter to Gentile, he regarded as expressing the dangers of actualism (*Lettere a Gentile*, ed. A. Croce, Milan, 1981, No. 770, 10 January 1917, pp. 533–4).

20. 'Il tramonto del liberalism', *Il Resto del Carlino*, February 1917, *Scritti*, p. 174.

21. 'Il trionfo del liberalismo', *Il Tempo*, 23 January, 1919; *Scritti*, pp. 196–200.

22. 'Tendenze', *Il Resto del Carlino*, 28 April 1919, *Scritti*, pp. 236–9.
23. On Hegel see *Philosophy of Right*, paras 189–208 and R. Plant, *Hegel: An Introduction*, 2nd edn, Oxford, 1983, Ch. 9. For De Ruggiero's ideas see his *Problemi della vita Morale*, Catania, 1914, pp. 55–60.
24. On this point I agree with de Aloyisio's criticism of Garin's view that De Ruggiero was a follower of Salandra at this time – a position held by Croce if anyone ('Note su G de Ruggiero', pp. 727–8). On Gobetti see G. De Caro, 'Da *Energie Nove* a *La Rivoluzione Liberale*', *Nuova Rivista Storica* (1961), pp. 568–82. De Ruggiero contributed three articles to Gobetti's *Rivoluzione Liberale*, examined below, from 1922–4. For Gramsci's attitude see the fine analysis of J. Femia in his *Gramsci's Political Thought*, Oxford, 1981, pp. 139–51.
25. See 'Discussioni socialiste', *Il Resto Carlino*, 17 July 1919 and 'Lo Stato socialista', *Il Paese*, 2 August 1921, *Scritti*, pp. 274–8, 380–4.
26. *Il concetto del lavoro nella sua genesi storica*, Il filo di arianna, n. 20, Rome, 1947, p. 42.
27. I am here more or less paraphrasing De Ruggiero's own account of Hobhouse in *European Liberalism*, pp. 155–7, where he passes his famous judgement on the work as 'the best formulation of the new English Liberalism of the twentieth century' combining 'the teaching of Mill and Green in a modernised form' (p. 155). Justification for an idealist reading of *Liberalism* is provided by Stefan Collini, *Liberalism and Sociology – L. T. Hobhouse and Political Argument in England 1880–1914*, Cambridge, 1979, Ch. 4.
28. L. T. Hobhouse, *Liberalism* (1911), Oxford, 1964, pp. 66, 80–1, 69, 67–8.
29. See Stefan Collini, 'Hobhouse, Bosanquet and the State: Philosophical Idealism and Political Argument in England 1880–1918', *Past and Present*, 72 (1976), pp. 86–111.
30. *The Metaphysical Theory of the State*, pp. 71, 60–1.
31. *Liberalism*, pp. 70, 69.
32. Stefan Collini, *Liberalism and Sociology*, pp. 147–70, 235–40 shows how Hobhouse's argument is based on his account of progress and that after the First World War this becomes more idealist in nature than otherwise.
33. See *Il concetto del lavoro*, 'Capitale e lavoro'.
34. *Liberalism*, pp. 88–109.
35. *L'Impero britannico dopo la guerra*, pp. 59–62.
36. 'I presupposti economici del liberalismo', *La Rivoluzione Liberale*, I (1922), n. 2, 19 February, pp. 6–8; 'La politica inglese in Italia', *Il Paese*, 2 March 1922; 'In tema di collaborazione', *Il Paese*, 17 June 1922. All in *Scritti*, pp. 472–6, 521–5.
37. 'La lotta politica – liberali e laburisti', *La Rivoluzione liberale*, III (1924), n. 13–14, 25 March–1 April, p. 51 and 'Liberalismo sociale e liberal-socialismo', in *Il ritorno alla ragione*, Bari, 1946, pp. 240–5.
38. *L'Impero britannico dopo la guerra*, pp. 57–8.
39. 'I presupposti economici del liberalismo', 'Orientamenti', *Il Paese*, 30 July 1922; 'Il trionfo della tecnica', *Il Resto del Carlino*, 19 December 1922, in *Scritti*, pp. 535–9, 595–600.
40. 'Il concetto liberale', *La nostra scuola*, 16–31 March 1921, in *Scritti*, pp. 365–71. (Prefaced to his book on English politics as a statement of his ideas on liberalism, it earned the book sequestration by the authorities.) 'Decalogo Spicciolo', *Il Paese*, 2 April 1922; 'Servitù o libertà', *Il Paese*, 13 June 1922, 'Krumiraggio liberale', *Il Paese*,

20 June 1922; 'Liberali!', *Il Paese*, 15 October 1922, in *Scritti*, pp. 482–6, 510–14, 526–30, 585–7.

41. 'Servitù o libertà', *Il Paese*, 13 June 1922, in *Scritti*, p. 511.
42. 'Il concetto liberale', p. 367. The liberal party, he argued, was the continuation of the liberalism of the nineteenth century only in the same sense that 'a deposit of coal is the continuation of a forest': 'Liberali!', p. 586.
43. 'Il problema dell'autorità', *Il Paese*, 8 December 1921, in *Scritti*, p. 423.
44. *Che cosa è il fascismo. Discorsi e polemiche*, Florence, 1925, pp. 29–33, 41–63, 65–94, and H. S. Harris, *The Social Philosophy of G. Gentile*, pp. 167–82.
45. *Philosophy of Right*, paras 189, 260, 301, 302; Charles Taylor, *Hegel and Modern Society*, Cambridge, 1975, pp. 438–49; Plant, *Hegel*, Ch. 7.
46. 'La dialettica del camaleonte', *Il Paese*, 8 October 1922; 'Nuova letteratura Cavouriana', *Pagine Critiche*, 1 August 1926, in *Scritti*, pp. 572–5, 658–67.
47. 'Intorno al Fascismo', *Il Resto del Carlino*, 14 February 1922; 'L'avenire del Fascismo', *Il Paese*, 13 September 1921; 'Il Fascismo e la lotta agraria', *Il Paese*, 5 November 1921; 'Memorie inutile', *Le Battaglie del Mezzogiorno*: all in *Scritti*, pp. 450–4, 389–92, 402–6, 615–19. 'Il liberalismo e le masse', *La Rivoluzione Liberale*, II (1923), n. 12, 1 May 1923, p. 49.
48. *European Liberalism*, pp. 326, 327, 329, 339, 342.
49. Review of B. Croce, *Storia d'Italia Rivista Storica Italiana*, XIVI (1929), p. 312. See too Croce's review of *European Liberalism* in *La Critica*, XXIII (1925), pp. 305–6.
50. *European Liberalism*, pp. 343, 350–7, 358, 388–9, 393–5, 355.
51. G. De Ruggiero, *Il ritorno alla ragione*, Bari, 1946, pp. 14, 29.
52. Similar points with regard to Kant, Rawls and Hobhouse are made by Michael Sandel, *Liberalism and the Limits of Justice*, Cambridge, 1982, pp. 133–74 and Gerald F. Gaus, *The Modern Liberal Theory of Man*, Beckenham, 1983, pp. 257–61, 270–4.
53. *European Liberalism* was reprinted in 1941, leading to him losing his chair at Rome and his arrest in 1943 for his activities in the 'Party of Action'. *Il ritorno alla ragione* of 1946 consists of articles written during this period, developing the arguments of *European Liberalism* (pp. vi–viii and preface to third edn of *European Liberalism*, 1943). In 1943 he became Rector of Rome University and was Minister of Education in the Bonomi adminstration (June–December 1944). He died in Rome on 29 December 1948.
54. See Stefan Collini, *Liberalism and Sociology*, pp. 245–53 and A. MacIntyre, *After Virtue*, London, 1981, pp. 1–6, 238–45.

CHAPTER 4

Carl Schmitt and the Contradictions of Liberal Democracy[1]

The current revival of interest in Carl Schmitt seems, superficially at least, somewhat baffling – particularly as most of the recent work has come from scholars on the left of the ideological spectrum.[2] Condemned to relative obscurity for his compromises with the Nazi regime, the present attempts to disinter his works have appeared to some commentators as distasteful as they are unnecessary.[3] However, though undeniably disturbing, Schmitt's writings remain of pressing relevance for contemporary political theorists. Schmitt rose to prominence during the Weimar period as one of Germany's leading jurists. Through a prodigious number of books and articles, he became the foremost analyst of the regime and its ultimately fatal crisis. In the process, he was led into a provocative examination of the relationship between liberalism and democracy. He argued that within modern mass industrial societies the first risked being undermined by the second. As a result, many of the central concepts of liberal democracy, such as popular sovereignty, representation, public opinion, consensus and constitutionality, had become detached from the values and practices that gave them their meaning.

This critique of liberal democracy remains challenging. At present, liberal democratic principles have practically eclipsed all other modes of political argument. Yet the reality is frequently inconsistent with the ideals. Often, liberal democratic rhetoric is simply used to provide a spurious legitimacy for politicians and the institutions to which they owe their power. New Right liberals such as Hayek on the one hand, and social democratic liberals such as Rawls and Dworkin on the other, have both pointed to these discrepancies between theory and practice. What neither group has questioned is the continued relevance of doctrines fashioned in the very different circumstances of the nineteenth century to the large-scale states, complex societies and international economies of today. What follows explores the resources Schmitt's writings offer for a rethinking of liberal democracy. The first three sections will examine respectively Schmitt's account of liberalism, his views on the clash between liberalism and democracy, and his resulting reconceptualization of politics. The final section will draw on this analysis in an attempt to reconceive liberal democracy in a manner that meets Schmitt's challenge.

Liberalism

For analytical purposes, it is convenient to break down liberalism into its philosophical, social and political elements and consider each in turn, though Schmitt himself insisted that all were aspects of a 'consistent, comprehensive metaphysical system'.[4] It was Schmitt's contention that the social assumptions and politics of liberalism were seriously flawed within modern societies, thereby weakening the force of its philosophical principles.

At the philosophical level, liberals have affirmed a commitment to the concepts of equality, liberty, individuality and rationality. They have been egalitarians in the sense of denying that anyone is naturally the subordinate of anyone else. This view does not entail regarding everyone as the same, merely that all human beings are of equal moral worth. Rather than seeking to guarantee an equality of outcome in the manner of socialists and democrats, liberals desire that everyone should have an equal opportunity to deploy what talents they do possess on the same basis as everyone else. Their attachment to liberty goes together with this interpretation of equality, for liberals have traditionally attempted to achieve the most extensive individual liberty compatible with the assertion of an equal degree of liberty for all other members of society. Similarly, their egalitarianism also informs their insistence on the moral primacy of the individual person against any social collectivity. Finally, and in Schmitt's view most crucially, as rationalists they contend that views in the public domain at least have to be open to critical scrutiny and amendment so their validity can be tested and affirmed.

As the above exposition indicates, liberals see these four concepts as hanging together in a particular way. The coherence of this interpretation does not lie in any special affinity between the concepts themselves, however. Not only have adherents of other ideologies understood this particular conceptual complex in very different ways, there have also been profound differences of opinion amongst liberals themselves as to why at a philosophical level these concepts fit together as they do, and what political consequences follow from them. Philosophically, the liberal canon includes methodological individualists and holists, materialists and idealists, determinists and voluntarists, utilitarians and adherents of natural rights, whilst politically it extends from libertarian upholders of the free market to social liberal defenders of the welfare state. In Schmitt's view, what links these different versions is a common belief in the moral significance of the individual within any social order, and the importance of competition between individuals in all spheres of life as a means of arriving at truth and happiness. These are the commitments which give liberal ideology its distinctiveness.

These core notions can be traced to the social forces which liberalism both reflects and helped to shape. Historically, the most important social influences on the formation of liberal individualism were the wars of religion and the rise of modern science in the sixteenth and seventeenth centuries, and the passage from feudalism to capitalism from the same period through to the nineteenth century. The first fuelled the demand for religious toleration which lies behind much of the liberal commitment to rationalism and the moral equality of individuals. Liberalism's general concern with protecting each individual's ability to pursue his or her own conception of the good, to the extent that this does not illegitimately interfere with a similar pursuit by others, can in large part be traced to this source. Hence, the traditional liberal defence of those civil and personal liberties necessary for individuals to live in accordance with their own beliefs, free of victimization for unorthodox religious, political or sexual views and practices. The second – the transformation from feudalism to capitalism – went hand in hand with the liberal attack on ascribed status and its commitment to equality of opportunity. The closed feudal order of inherited rights, with its hierarchical system of aristocratic privileges, was to give way to an open and egalitarian capitalist order, in which an individual's social position and success supposedly mirror his or her ability and effort – a way of life best realized in a free market economy.

Some contemporary liberals and many of liberalism's critics regard the ethos resulting from such social origins as essentially sceptical, subjectivist, materialistic and egoistic. Traditionally, however, liberals have been extremely wary of such attitudes and sought to avoid them. Indeed, Schmitt observed that liberals have characteristically held an optimistic and perfectionist rather than a pessimistic view of human nature.[5] Although liberals insist on the individual's right to pursue his or her own conception of the good, this does not mean that they treat all beliefs or ways of life as equally valuable. Drawing on the experimental method in modern science and the Protestant defence of freedom of conscience, liberals merely contend that we have a right to find out the worth (or worthlessness) of our opinions for ourselves – indeed, this is the only way for truth and morality to emerge. According to this thesis, the validity of ideas and practices can only be asserted if individuals are allowed to experiment, calling into question accepted doctrines and trying out new and occasionally eccentric or potentially offensive pursuits. A way of life or belief that cannot withstand the light of public scrutiny is not worth saving in the first place. Similarly, liberals maintain that personal virtue is only realized through taking responsibility for our lives. For the state or any group to paternalistically impose its views on the rest of society is to risk falling into dogmatic error, demoralizes the population and produces stagnation. Individuals must be able to make mistakes so that they can learn from them.

Much the same mixture of ethical and instrumental reasoning lies behind the liberal adherence to the economic individualism of the market. This aspect of the liberal social vision emerged from the experience of the entrepreneurs, traders, shopkeepers and artisans of early capitalism, and invokes the image of an idealized market order in which rewards are closely linked to effort and desert. This linkage was codified in the labour theory of value and, in British and American culture at least, drew additional force from the religious beliefs of certain Protestant sects which encouraged industriousness as a mark of salvation. As we noted, liberals have tended to praise the market to the extent that it acts as a stimulus to individual initiative and discovery which brings about the progress of society. In this respect, the virtues of a free market in labour and commodities parallel those of a free market in ideas – they promote the good and weed out the bad. When these advantages are missing, liberals have often proved less enthusiastic about *laissez-faire*. As Schmitt commented, the 'economic line of reasoning that social harmony and the maximisation of wealth follow from the free economic competition of individuals, from freedom of contract, freedom of trade, free enterprise' is 'only an application of a general liberal principle ... : that the truth can be found through an unrestrained clash of opinion and that competition will produce harmony'.[6]

The political face of liberalism follows on from the philosophical and social elements outlined above. For the demand to construct the state on liberal principles grew out of the political struggles caused by the wars of religion and the erosion of feudalism. As the social structures based on status gave way to contractual relationships between civil equals, so the feudal hierarchical political structures were undermined. The state, like society as a whole, came to be seen as a voluntary association held together by the mutual consent of its members rather than by ties of deference to social superiors – a conception of the political order summed up in the theory of the social contract.

Schmitt singled out three basic components of the liberal political settlement: the separation of state and civil society, the rule of law and parliamentarism. A strict distinction of state and civil society lies at the heart of liberal politics. The purpose of the state is solely to regulate and facilitate social interaction, rather than to substitute for individual initiative through the state management of social institutions. The rule of law is designed to ensure the state keeps to its regulatory role and exercises it in a neutral manner that guarantees the fairness and openness of society. According to this notion, laws must reflect the impersonal authority of universal reason, rather than the particular whim of the ruler, as under an absolute monarchy. For Schmitt:

> The whole theory of the *Rechtstaat* rests on the contrast between law which is general and already promulgated, universally binding without exception, and valid in principle for all times, and a personal order

which varies case to case according to particular concrete circumstances.[7]

As a corollary of the universality of law, all laws are to be applied impartially and equally. There must be no special exemptions for particular groups, such as nobles or clerics, as there had been in the past. Finally, the laws aim to guarantee to the greatest extent possible the equal right of each individual to pursue his or her own plan of life. The most basic rights in this respect are traditionally the rights to private property and freedom of belief, for these rights are essential to the liberal understanding of toleration and the market mechanism.

Schmitt regarded liberal political institutions as parliamentarist rather than democratic. Whereas democracy ultimately leads to a form of social self-government that destroys (as we shall see) both the state–civil society divide and the rule of law, parliamentarism assumes and upholds them. Schmitt maintained that for liberals the legitimacy of parliamentary accords derives from their truth and justice rather than the mere authority of parliament to command. Reversing the Hobbesian formulation of sovereignty, for liberals *veritas* rather than *authoritas* underpins the law.[8] The rationale of parliament follows from the general liberal belief in competition and criticism. 'The essence of parliament', on Schmitt's account, 'is public deliberation of argument and counterargument, public debate and public discussion, parley'. For liberals contend that out of this 'process of confrontation of differences and opinions' a 'real political will results'.[9] As he appositely quoted from Bentham: 'In Parliament ideas meet, and the contact between ideas gives off sparks and leads to evidence.'[10]

The parliamentary system incorporates two main features intended to achieve this goal. First, parliamentary proceedings should be open, public and free rather than secret, private and restricted. Corruption and falsehood are supposedly dissolved by exposing all political life to the light of reason. 'Freedom of speech, freedom of the press, freedom of assembly and parliamentary immunities mean freedom of opinion in liberal thought' and are intrinsic to a system based upon a 'competition of opinions in which the best opinion wins'.[11] Second, parliamentarism involves the division and balance of powers. The separation of the executive, legislative and judicial branches of government supposedly preserves the impartiality and universality of law. By distinguishing the framing of legislation from its implementation and interpretation, liberals hope to ensure that no group or individual has an incentive to make laws that suit their particular ends and interests. The idea of a balance of powers within the legislative chamber reinforces this end, for it promotes competition and discussion by forcing a multiplicity of differing opinions and interests to debate with each other by preventing any group having the ability to impose its view upon others.[12] Both these devices aspire to maintain parliament as a deliberative rather than a commanding chamber, concerned with general laws rather than with particular policies or decisions – the prerogative not of the legislature but of the executive and judiciary respectively – for 'only a universally applicable law, not a concrete order, can unite truth and justice through the balance of negotiations and public discussion'.[13] Democracy, in contrast, abolishes these distinctions within a unitary system of popular government in which norms give way to decisions, a point we shall return to in the next section.

According to Schmitt, the conceptual, socio-economic and political elements of liberal doctrine are inextricably interconnected, forming part of a single historical process. Liberalism corresponds in large part to the self-image and aspirations of the emergent middle classes, and operated in the eighteenth and nineteenth centuries as a creed whereby they sought to oust the aristocratic and agrarian elite and fashion a new environment suited to the needs of commerce, industry and the professions. Against the aristocratic ideal of a hierarchical and static society, it presents a social vision of an association of self-reliant and responsible citizens, co-operating in pursuit of material and moral improvement and progress.

These social assumptions may have had a certain plausibility in the eighteenth and early nineteenth centuries, but in the twentieth century they are highly questionable. As Schmitt's older contemporary Max Weber observed, in a mass industrial society dominated by large-scale corporations and other administrative organizations on the one hand and increased functional differentiation on the other, the type of free individual agency assumed by liberals appears in jeopardy. The first process has gradually enveloped individuals into the rule-bound and hierarchical structures of bureaucratic agencies, replacing the entrepreneur with the administrator and professional director and deskilling a large portion of the workforce. The second has so enhanced the complexity of industrial societies that our ability rationally to encompass the resulting social diversity within a single moral and cognitive framework has been considerably reduced. The more individuals become trapped in the logic of their various and occasionally conflicting social roles and functions, and bombarded by a growing mass of often contradictory information and sources of persuasion, the more their capacity for autonomous orientation in the world becomes undermined. These developments have distorted the liberal ideals of the market and parliamentarism. Moreover, they are inextricably linked to the rise of organized labour, which in threatening the socio-economic and political domination of the middle classes potentially poses the greatest challenge to liberal hegemony.

As we saw, in liberal eyes the free market does not produce social conflict – it resolves it. The invisible hand mechanism of the laws of supply and demand allegedly promotes the harmonization of individual life plans. For analogous reasons liberals advocate free trade between states as the best means for achieving international peace. However, perfect competition and the smooth operation of the price mechanism assume that consumers are both fully informed about their needs and the available services on offer to meet them, and that they are equally able to make their demands felt. But in reality, the size of markets, the inequitable division of wealth, the control exercised by large corporations and labour organizations over the supply of goods, services and information in a particular area, all mean that individuals rarely possess such knowledge and can only very imperfectly influence the economy even when they do. Such factors have meant that in practice the market economy has given rise not to a co-operative society of mutually improving individuals, but to a world of conflicting group interests. In Schmitt's view, the same causes have radically altered the nature of democracy and invalidated the balance between the liberal and the democratic elements of the parliamentary system.

Liberalism and Democracy

Schmitt argued that liberalism and democracy are only contingently related, and that in fact they rest on opposed principles of equality. Liberalism rests on a principle of formal equality. According to this doctrine, all individuals are to be treated equally by virtue of their common humanity. Our status is not given to us at birth; it has to be achieved through a fair competition in which everyone has an equal chance of working his or her way to the top (or falling to the bottom) of society. Equality on this interpretation goes together with difference and produces differential outcomes. Democracy, in contrast, rests on a principle of substantive equality. Citizenship, Schmitt believed, assumes 'a substantial equality within the circle of equals', for equal rights only 'make good sense where homogeneity exists'.[14] It had been this reasoning that had led to restrictions on democratic participation within both ancient Athens and the British Empire.

Liberal democracy falsely conflates these two conceptions of equality. Taking Rousseau's radical model of liberal democracy as an example, Schmitt remarked on how Rousseau had subsumed the liberal conception of a contract embodying general, universalizable laws under the democratic conception of a homogeneous citizenry united by a common good. Schmitt maintained that 'a contract assumes differences and oppositions': it represents an agreement between the diverse groups and individuals of civil society on a common framework. Rousseau's general will, however, requires the homogeneity of the common good for its realization. Schmitt contended that therefore the idea of a contract or constitution is redundant in Rousseau's theory. Instead, it relies on the 'democratic identity of governed and governing' in which the unanimity of citizens 'must go so far that the laws come into existence *sans discussion*'.[15]

The incompatibility of liberalism and democracy went unnoticed so long as the franchise was limited, as it had been during the early stages of capitalism.

In the past, liberals linked political citizenship to the possession of certain educational and propertied preconditions necessary for making 'independent' decisions. According to this line of thinking, those lacking a certain level of intellectual and economic independence are unable to appreciate the liberal attachment to rational enquiry and the pursuit of the good because they depend on others for their opinions and livelihood. As such, they have no interest in the liberal way of life with its emphasis on individual autonomy. Workers and women formed the main categories of the excluded. Liberals hoped that universal education and the discipline of the market would enable them eventually to enfranchise all adults, but the circumstances of mass industrial society came to drive a wedge between liberalism and democracy. The extension of the suffrage to all on the basis of the liberal notion of a universal formal equality of persons detracts from the substantive equality involved in democracy. 'In concreto the masses are sociologically and psychologically heterogeneous',[16] so that democratic institutions become flooded by conflicting interests and passions that cannot be reconciled through rational debate. Parliament and government risk paralysis as a result, a phenomenon Schmitt knew all too well from the polarized pluralism of the Weimar period. In this situation, the liberal notion of each party and group having an 'equal chance' threatens the state with dissolution. The only coherent liberal response is Mill's and de Tocqueville's fear of the 'tyranny of the majority', of democracy as enforced conformity to the lowest common denominator.[17]

Mass democracy and modern industrial economies threaten the three main features of the liberal political settlement examined above. First, they promote the absorption of civil society into the bureaucratic structures of the 'total state'. Mass politics and a more complex economic system generate increasing demands on the state from a variety of organized groups and interests. As a result, society and economy become politicized, and the classical role of the state as the mere regulator of a 'private sphere' proves untenable. The state is forced to intervene and take on a broader public service and administrative role – from promoting investment and maintaining the infrastructure, to providing welfare and education. Second, these developments in turn undercut the ideal of the rule of law. The promulgation of universal norms no longer suffices. Within a complex system requiring detailed economic and social regulation to meet a variety of purposes, specific decisions reflecting compromises between competing claims on resources necessarily take their place.

Finally, both these processes destroy the viability of parliament. For a start, the democratic goal of achieving an identity between rulers and ruled renders parliament redundant. 'Against the will of the people', Schmitt remarked, 'an institution based on discussion by independent representatives has no autonomous justification for its existence.'[18] Hence the call by anarcho-syndicalists, council communists and other advocates of direct democracy for its replacement by a network of self-governing bodies. That such schemes are largely utopian offers little solace to liberals, since the very aspects of modern societies that make them implausible prove just as damaging to liberal democratic institutions. As parties replace individual notables as the main political actors, discussion gives way to a contest between organized interests. Electoral debate is orchestrated by these parties, which set the agenda and manipulate the electorate. Echoing the sentiments of elite theorists such as Michels and Mosca, Schmitt observed that 'the masses are won over through a propaganda apparatus whose maximum effect relies in an appeal to immediate interests and passions. Argument in the real sense that is characteristic for genuine discussion ceases. ... the parties ... do not face each other today discussing opinions, but as social or economic power-groups calculating their mutual interests and opportunities for power.' Thus, the formation of public opinion 'is no longer a question of persuading one's opponent of the truth or justice of an opinion but rather of winning a majority in order to govern with it'. Party dominance makes a mockery of liberal notions of popular sovereignty, representation and the division of powers. Representatives lose their independence and become mere lobby fodder. Parliament ceases to be an open chamber of debate and turns into an ante-chamber to the closed committees and bureaux of 'invisible rulers' that is almost totally controlled by the executive. Parliamentary procedure degenerates into 'a superfluous decoration, useless and even embarrassing', 'a mere facade' with 'argumentative public discussion an empty formality'.[19] Schmitt even doubted whether parliament can serve the rather debased function Weber (and later Schumpeter) accorded it, of selecting and training an elite. Nor did he believe that the competition between parties worked in trusted liberal fashion to ensure a high quality of leadership. Rather:

> What numerous parliaments in various European and non-European states have produced in the way of a political elite of hundreds of successive ministers justifies no great optimism. But worse, in destroying almost every hope, in a few states, parliamentarism has already produced a situation in which all public business has become an object of spoils and compromise for the parties and their followers, and politics, far from being the concern of an elite, has become the despised business of a rather dubious class of persons.[20]

In Schmitt's view, therefore, mass democracy deforms rather than reinforces liberalism. Instead of spreading the liberal virtues of discussion within a heterogeneous population, democracy subverts rational debate and replaces it with a putative homogeneous popular will. So long as the demos remains relatively circumscribed, the contradiction between the two goes unnoticed. However, the complexity and diversity of modern industrial societies have undermined the basis for a common good on which the rational formation of a general will depends. The processes of functional differentiation have enhanced both cognitive and moral pluralism. Individuals not only rationally desire diverse and often incommensurable goods, they also frequently adopt distinct and occasionally contradictory kinds of reasoning in the different contexts within which they operate. In these circumstances, no such collective agent as 'the people' operating with a single will exists. Rather, it becomes a construction of various elite groups who act in its name towards the creation and shaping of a popular will through propaganda, 'education' and organized manipulation. Jacobins, Bolsheviks and radical liberal democrats have all been confronted by this problem and been forced towards various forms of democratic dictatorship.[21] Concluding his analysis, Schmitt remarked that the popular acclamation of a ruler, produced through various Caesarist methods involving psychological and non-rational forms of persuasion, offers the only plausible expression of democracy within a mass society. Only this procedure can provide a 'direct expression of democratic substance and power'. At the same time, such a practice runs counter to the whole rationale of liberalism and destroys it.[22]

The Concept of the Political

Schmitt blamed the failure of liberalism to appreciate or resist the challenge posed by democracy on its lack of an adequate conception of the political and hence of the state. Schmitt based his concept of the political around the distinction between 'friend' and 'enemy'. He argued that all forms of human thought and action demarcate their sphere of influence via certain fundamental distinctions. Thus, 'in the realm of morality the final distinctions are between good and evil, in aesthetics beautiful and ugly, in economics profitable and unprofitable'.[23] The political concepts of 'friend' and 'enemy' are autonomous from these conceptions and unlike them 'are neither normative nor spiritual antitheses'. Rather, they reflect respectively the 'concrete', 'existential' reality of the intensity of union or conflict, between opinions, groups or individuals.[24]

Schmitt's thesis has sometimes been misrepresented as a typically Teutonic glorification of power that identifies politics with war and even advocates war as good in itself.[25] In fact, he carefully avoided both these pitfalls. He flatly rejected Clausewitz's affirmation that 'war is nothing but the continuation of political intercourse with a mixture of other means', insisting that 'war is neither the aim nor the purpose nor even the very content of politics'. War was an extreme case and should not be seen as 'common, normal, something ideal or desirable'. It was almost always politically prudent to seek to avoid war.[26] Indeed, Schmitt went so far as to deny that there existed any normative justification for people killing others apart from the actual possibility of those others killing them.[27] However, Schmitt maintained that it was an ineliminable aspect of the human condition that threats to our security arise from the actions of others and that hostilities between rival modes of living might break out. It was these possibilities that gave rise to a specifically political form of behaviour.[28] For he contended that resolving or seeking to avoid such dangers and disputes could only be achieved through political decision as opposed to normative agreement.

According to Schmitt, the liberal ethos denies the concept of the 'enemy' which defines the need for politics, for 'the essence of liberalism is negotiation, a cautious half measure, in the hope that the definitive dispute, the decisive bloody battle, can be transformed into a parliamentary debate and permit the decision to be suspended forever in an everlasting discussion'.[29] As he sarcastically remarked, the liberal responds to 'the question: Christ or Barabbas?, with a proposal to adjourn or appoint a commission of investigation'.[30] Liberalism seeks to depoliticize and neutralize all potential sources of conflict by turning 'the enemy from the viewpoint of economics into a competitor and from the intellectual perspective into a debating adversary'. The prospect of warring factions is dissipated by 'perpetual competition, perpetual discussion'.[31]

Such thinking assumes a metaphysics deriving from the Enlightenment faith in human perfectibility through reason that Schmitt rejected.[32] Leo Strauss has pointed out that Schmitt was not as clear as he might have been on this point.[33] He wanted to defend the objective reality of the political within human relations. As a result, he thought it necessary to assert the total autonomy of politics from economic, ethical or aesthetic considerations. Thus, he noted how 'the morally evil, aesthetically ugly or economically damaging need not necessarily be the enemy; the morally good, aesthetically beautiful or economically profitable need not necessarily become the friend', although 'emotionally the enemy is easily treated as being evil and ugly, because every distinction, most of all the political, as the strongest and most intense of the categorisations, draws upon other distinctions for support'.[34] However, elsewhere he indicated that politics cannot be completely separated from these other spheres and distinctions either. For it is the tensions arising between incommensurable and incompatible values and options that render politics necessary. A world without politics would be 'a completely pacified globe' in which culture and civilization had been reduced to the bland level of 'entertainment' and 'there would not be a meaningful antithesis whereby men could be required to sacrifice life'.[35] Moreover, it would have necessarily entailed the most terrible use of force to bring about. Remarking on the contemporary attempt to introduce a new world order through the League of Nations, Schmitt shrewdly observed how the rhetoric had changed but not the logic of the political. On the contrary, a universal peace implies the most horrific and total of wars, the war to end all wars against all the so-called enemies of an idealized humanity.[36] Thus, Schmitt did not detach politics from morals as completely as it might seem. Rather, as Strauss saw, 'Schmitt's ... affirmation of the political rests on the affirmation of morality', on taking moral convictions seriously enough to dispute the liberal humanitarian belief that they could all be treated as mere individual preferences and reconciled in some grand synthesis.[37]

Schmitt's assertion of the necessity of politics derives from his acknowledgement of the fact of pluralism within modern societies. In Schmitt's phrase, 'the political world is a pluriverse, not a universe'.[38] Like Weber, Schmitt contested the liberal rationalist's faith in the ultimate ethical harmony of the world. Good consequences do not always follow from good acts, or evil from evil ones; similarly, truth, beauty and goodness are not necessarily linked. Most important, he recognized that we are often faced with difficult or tragic choices between conflicting but equally valuable ends – for no social world can avoid excluding certain fundamental values. In this situation, as Weber insisted, we cannot escape the responsibility of choosing which gods we shall serve and by implication deciding what are to count as demons.[39] Both Weber and Schmitt have been accused by critics of adopting a subjectivist and nihilistic standpoint which subordinates norms to the will to power. However, their insistence on the inescapability of making political decisions between conflicting moral views involves no such stance. They are merely committed to an ethical and epistemological pluralism which resists the possibility of unifying all rationally acceptable forms of life within a single framework. From this perspective, the resolution between hard cases cannot be decided as a matter of principle.[40] In this sense politics and morals are distinct, for no universal norm or disinterested and neutral third party exists to mediate such conflicts.[41] They can only be resolved politically, through decision, not metaphysically, through rational discussion.

The locus of political decision making is the state. Schmitt feared that the authority and power of the state are threatened by certain internal centrifugal forces to which liberalism gives free reign. As we saw, Schmitt appreciated that the pluralism which is the source of political conflict had been greatly enhanced within modern societies. The division of labour results in individuals belonging to an increasing number of associations that compete with the state for their loyalty and undermine its sovereignty. In his view, liberal doctrine could not cope with this process. Because it lacks a conception of the political, liberalism has no adequate theorization of the state. Although liberals stop short of the anarchist's complete denial of the state, they advance no positive theory of the state either. Rather, they offer a concerted critique of state power and seek 'only to tie the political to the ethical' through the concept of the rule of law, and 'to subjugate it to economics' by subordinating the state to the demands of civil society. Both these moves misunderstand and weaken the state's function.

Schmitt argued that the legalistic liberal conception of the state overlooks the fact that states and the rule of law are the end products of political struggle. The raison d'etre of the state is the stabilization of internal conflict and resistance to encroachment from hostile external powers, for the orderly administration of a state's territory rests on its monopoly of force and its ability to defend the 'friends' of a political order from its 'enemies'. Three consequences follow from this analysis. First, it reveals that liberalism rests on a constitutive political 'moment' which establishes the rule of law. Liberal constitutionalism is founded not on a basic principle or norm – as Kelsen famously argued – but a politically established normal situation.[42] In Schmitt's words:

> Every general norm demands a normal, everyday frame of life to which it can be factually applied and which is subjected to its regulations. The norm requires a homogeneous medium. This effective normal situation is not a mere 'superficial presupposition' that a jurist can ignore; that situation belongs to its immanent validity. There exists no norm that is applicable to chaos.[43]

The provision of this normal situation belongs to the state: 'The endeavour of a normal state consists above all in assuring total peace within the state and its territory. To create tranquillity, security and order and thereby establish the normal situation is the prerequisite for legal norms to be valid.'[44] Second, it follows that sovereignty is a political act that lies outside the law. If 'for a legal order to make sense, a normal situation must exist', then 'he is sovereign who definitely decides whether this normal situation exists'.[45] Most constitutions and bills of rights contain provisions for their suspension or overriding in emergency situations which threaten public safety. Such regulations implicitly acknowledge the degree to which the legal order requires stable political conditions for its existence. However, the law cannot spell out the precise details of what constitutes such an emergency nor how it is to be resolved. 'The most guidance the constitution can give is to indicate who can act in such a case.'[46] Whoever holds this power is the sovereign, or as Schmitt concisely put it: 'sovereign is he who decides on the exception.'[47] In Schmitt's view, the liberal constitutionalist attempt to deny the need for a sovereign in this sense ignores the political basis of law itself. This position is only coherent when the circumstances of politics have ceased to exist. At any other time, it jeopardizes the constitutional settlement by depriving it of any form of defence. Third, as a result the preservation of legitimate government rests on the state's ability to act politically and forestall antagonisms. No amount of discussion can resolve what Schmitt regards as a true political conflict – one between enemies; only a decisive decision can.

Schmitt's conception of the political and the resulting role of the state informs his account of the undermining of liberalism by democracy. Liberalism presupposes the depoliticization of large areas of social and economic life. The rule of law provides a framework which enables social and economic activities to be freely pursued without them degenerating into political conflict. As we saw, this situation assumes the separation of state and civil society. What liberal constitutionalists conveniently or naively forget is that in concrete terms this separation depends on the political capacity of the state to uphold the norms of bourgeois hegemony; that 'in the concrete reality of the political no abstract orders or norms but always real human groupings and associations rule over the other human groupings and associations'.[48] Definitions alone cannot prevent economic, ethical or aesthetic differences turning into political antagonisms. An economic system based on exchange and mutual contracts, for example, 'by no means precludes the possibility that one of the contractors experiences disadvantage . . . and finally deteriorates into a system of the worst exploitation and repression'.[49] In such a situation, the exploited and repressed cannot defend themselves by economic means alone and will regard any attempt to maintain such domination under the guise of 'pure economics' as 'a terrible deception'. Hence the notion of a 'free economy' governed by principles of justice will not survive without the backing of a strong state which can effectively neutralize political conflict within the economic sphere.[50]

Democracy weakens the ability of the state to maintain the neutralizations and depoliticizations of the various domains of human life which are central to liberalism. It enables hitherto 'social' and 'economic' demands of the masses to become legitimately politicized as they seek public redress of their grievances. As a result, 'state and society penetrate each other'.[51] Once sovereignty becomes vested in the will of the people or (more realistically) its representatives, the notion of a constitutional order upheld by the state loses any meaning. In a situation where a putative popular will and the rule of law are one and the same, the latter offers no check on the former but is rather formulated by it. Consequently, it becomes constitutionally possible to undo the constitution.[52]

Writing during the last days of the Weimar Republic, it was precisely this danger that Schmitt feared and sought to prevent.[53] Legalistic interpretations of the Weimar constitution by liberal jurists, such as Richard Thoma, defended the right of parties like the Nazis to exploit their legal freedoms to challenge the constitution itself. They also sought to limit the power of the Reich President under Article 48 to forestall such moves by declaring an emergency and outlawing certain activities. Schmitt, by contrast, argued that a distinction must be made between legality and legitimacy. In his view, the legalists' 'value-neutral' and 'purely functional' interpretation of the constitution, as guaranteeing all parties an 'equal chance' to acquire power through the normal processes, only makes sense for those groups that accept the constitution's legitimacy and underlying principles. Otherwise the majority party ceases to be a mere component of the constitutional order, it becomes the state itself possessing the legal power to overturn the whole system.[54] Moreover, Schmitt maintained that the decision over what is legitimate activity or not can only be made politically, not by a court on the basis of legal norms. He believed that the courts have neither the will nor the authority to act in such circumstances. Their formalistic reasoning is unsuited to decisiveness in a complex situation and they lack the popular mandate necessary to take on a party or group claiming significant support. Those Weimar jurists who upheld the supreme court's legal position as the sole competent 'defender of the constitution' failed to appreciate the political foundation of constitutional norms, which in a democracy flow ultimately from the people. For this reason, he insisted on the President's entitlement as the sovereign power to restore 'normality' in exceptional circumstances. Unlike the supreme court, he saw the President as a political actor whose plebiscitary election gave him the authority to stand above the various party factions and to act in the name of the people as a whole. He saw the President as a 'commissarial dictator', encharged with the preservation of the legal order. As such, the President both belonged to the constitution by virtue of being its defender, and stood outside it in the sense that he could act in an extra-legal, political manner.[55] Unfortunately, the weakness of the Hindenberg Presidency combined with the prevarication of the court and the impotence of parliament resulted in Schmitt's worst fears being realized, with the Nazis filling the political vacuum. Once Hitler had become Chancellor, it took him less than a year to pass the Enabling Act and accomplish his pseudo-legal revolution setting up a dictatorial party state.

Given Schmitt's position, why did he join the Nazi party in 1933? Opportunism apart, his Hobbesian insistence that the rule of law rests on the power of the sword led him to the conclusion that we must obey whoever has the authority to command and provide us with protection. He soon learnt his mistake. His attempt to re-establish normality by providing a new constitutional order for the Nazi regime resulted in a sustained campaign against him by the SS after 1936, when even sham considerations of legality ceased to be of great importance. Schmitt had failed to see that for the Nazis, the exception was the norm.

Defending Democratic Liberalism

Schmitt's account of the weakness of parliament and liberal constitutionalism in the face of the democratic pressures of a system involving a mass electorate and competitive political parties has many contemporary resonances. In Britain, for example, the Conservative Party under Mrs Thatcher was able to use a regimented parliamentary majority obtained with around 43 per cent of the vote to change the structure of the British state in an often radical manner. Against considerable and frequently intense opposition, including some within its own ranks, the Conservative leadership consistently claimed that its electoral mandate and the absolute sovereignty of parliament gave it the legal authority to implement whatever policies it desired. Whenever this notion was challenged in the courts, the judiciary typically upheld the executive's conviction that the state and the government of the day are one and the same. When, as in the Ponting case, juries questioned this belief, the law revised to prevent such 'misinterpretations'. The election of a Labour government in 1997 raised expectations of changes to the constitutional and political system to prevent such abuses in the future. Schmitt's arguments have a great deal to offer in this context,[56] providing support for the reformers as well as a sober realism that ought to temper some of the movement's more idealistic elements. Nonetheless, some of his arguments are so radical that they risk throwing out the baby with the bath water. In what follows, we shall argue that it is possible to rethink the institutions and principles of liberalism in political terms in order to meet the challenges of modern mass democracy diagnosed by Schmitt.

Schmitt's definitional mode of argument led him to interpret parliamentary democracy too narrowly and hence to exclude the possibility for its positive transformation. Thus, Schmitt identified what he saw as the essential principles of parliament ('discussion and openness'[57]) and democracy ('homogeneity', itself dependent on substantive equality[58]). He then claimed to show how these principles contradict each other: the unanimity that democracy assumes makes the endless conversation of parliament irrelevant; the homogeneity of democracy clashes with liberalism's commitment to individualism. But, as John Keane has pointed out, there is no reason for us slavishly to subscribe to Schmitt's essentialist definitions or one-sided descriptions of either parliament or democracy. Hence, in respect of parliament, Schmitt's interpretation is a caricature: 'first, in its striking disregard of the pre-liberal history of parliament; in its failure, secondly, to spot the wide gulf between the liberal principles of openness and discussion and the actual functioning of nineteenth-century parliaments; and, finally, in its blind dismissal of the possibilities of democratically reforming parliament, of strengthening its power in opposition to the Total State.'[59] A closer examination of the key term in Schmitt's depiction of parliament, namely open (public) discussion, reveals a similarly partial analysis by the German theorist. Schmitt maintained that discussion 'means an exchange of opinion that is governed by the purpose of persuading one's opponent through argument of the truth or justice of something, or allowing oneself to be persuaded of something as true and just'.[60] Discussion is premised on 'discovering what is rationally correct'.[61]

Now while there is something in this description, it is certainly not exhaustive. Schmitt typically reduced open discussion to one core element: rational persuasion. But discussion is also oriented to *understanding*. On the basis of such understanding two or more parties might find that they have more in common than they realized, that compromise is more advantageous than aggression and that both can win in different ways. Coalition politics in parliamentary democracies is predicated on such understandings. Or such understanding may, through disclosing dissimulation and showing what a rival really thinks, lead to the conclusion that confrontation is inevitable. In that case discussion may still have been useful in revealing an adversary's tactics and strategy. Discussion oriented to understanding is thus one condition of informed political *calculation* about the most appropriate *decision* to take in the circumstances. Discussion and decision are thus (contingently) linked. But Schmitt could have none of this in his analysis of parliament. He ruled out calculation as a significant element of parliamentary discussion because 'there has been deliberation and compromise . . . everywhere in world history': 'it is not the principle of a specific kind of state or form of government.'[62] Here, definitional fiat is used to undergird an essentialist notion of parliament: first it is reduced to one central tenet, open discussion; then that tenet is itself reduced to one core element, rational persuasion. A more wide-ranging view of discussion, and a more historical view of parliament which examines its own complex anatomy and relationships with civil society, will want to take a different, multi-dimensional, approach. It was Schmitt himself who once remarked that 'every clear antithesis exercises a dangerous power of attraction over other distinctions that are not as clear'.[63] Ironically, his own antithesis – discussion or decision – has a similarly distorting effect.

The above argument should not be construed as an apology for the current state of parliamentary politics. As the British case amply demonstrates, modern parliaments have been increasingly marginalized by the executive, disciplined by the party machine, pressured by powerful interest groups in civil society. None of this proves, however, that parliament has no impact on these agencies; indeed, without parliament the influence of government, organized labour or transnational corporations would be even stronger than it is. Further, what body other than parliament has the capacity to represent the plural, heterogeneous demands of the type of fragmented society Schmitt described? Schmitt rightly criticized the pluralist theories of J. N. Figgis, H. J. Laski and G. D. H. Cole for denying the need for any central sovereign body,[64] though he acknowledged the possibility of a federal state.[65] In such a state, surely only a parliament can perform this very function of mediating between the interests of various socio-economic, cultural and ideological groups.

This possibility becomes all the more plausible once we realize the equally tendentious nature of Schmitt's definition of democracy. If we agree that democracy is an essentially unitarian notion and practice, we will be forced on to the tracks of his argument about the contradiction between democracy and parliament. But again there is no compelling reason to agree with his definition. Democracy is not reducible to a priori principles such as the 'general will'. It is as much an evolving practice as it is a metaphysic, allowing for competing conceptions of democracy, as the debate between theorists of direct democracy, democratic elitism, pluralism, corporatist democracy, Marxism and its variants readily shows.[66] Reform-minded liberals or socialists will seek to expand the democratic process by repairing the deficiencies in the working of parliament: for instance, by promoting measures to secure the accountability of parliament to society and the accountability of the executive to parliament; by supporting electoral, voting and other constitutional changes designed to protect the individual from the arbitrary state. Schmitt – committed neither to modern parliament nor democracy – had no interest in this. His notion of democracy implies dictatorship, since dictatorship represents the quintessential identity of ruler and ruled. But the identity is phoney. As Schmitt acknowledged, in reality there is no unitary community to represent. In that case, the dictator can only represent himself or herself, some doctrine, programme or constituency.

Where Schmitt's argument has more cogency is in respect of his critique of rationalism in politics, and the friend–enemy distinction. Let us take each in turn, and show how a more political liberalism might use them as a resource for its own practice. Schmitt is correct to argue against an over-rationalized conception of politics – as if political disagreements could be resolved, even hypothetically, by sustained discussion alone. Often they cannot, not primarily because some people refuse to be rational, but because rationality, like 'truth', is itself a situational norm – a product of social relations – not a universal attribute of abstract humanity or a property capable of being disclosed in an 'ideal speech situation'. More simply, people have different perceptions of what is rational for them, and those perceptions are dependent upon the culture and traditions to which they belong, the ideologies to which they subscribe, the ideal and material interests they wish to secure. This is another way of saying that what is deemed rational to a given group of people will depend upon their distinctive 'final vocabulary': terms that enshrine their presuppositional biases and commitments.[67] This vocabulary is 'final' in the sense that if doubt is cast on the worth of these words, their user has no non-circular argumentative recourse'.[68] Friends of liberalism, parliament and democracy employ a final vocabulary which includes such terms as individualism, discussion, openness, liberty, equality and progress. These terms represent the ultimate convictions of liberals, but there is no way they can be transcendentally vindicated (and even if they could this would be politically irrelevant). This does not matter so long as one is willing to offer a political rather than a simply philosophical defence of these principles. This defence can be consequentialist and pragmatic in form. Parliamentary democracy can be defended on a number of grounds: that it is less conducive to tyranny and terror, or the use of systematic and widespread torture of its citizens than the alternatives; that it represents the best way yet known of organizing and co-ordinating a complex modern society; that parliamentary democracy is a system amenable to peaceful reform and to expanding the circle of inclusiveness, that is, allowing more and more groups to partake in the conversation of democracy. Political liberals subscribe to these ideals either because they are the ones consistent with the kind of society they want, or/and because they are part of their own cultural formation.

It follows that a pragmatic, political defence of the institutions of liberalism has no need for the fallacy of universal rationality and for the view that everyone in politics is potentially a liberal; members of Hezbollah or Class

War are not. In this way, a political liberalism recognizes its own contingency and the need to identify and defend itself against its enemies, for it is not transcendental arguments that will be decisive in defending liberal institutions but politics. Those who threaten the kind of society liberals value are the enemies of liberalism, not because they are irrational or unenlightened but because they are illiberal. Liberals can learn from Schmitt about the 'friend-enemy' distinction.

On first encounter the notion of 'enemy' seems atavistic and vicious; in fact, it is a useful gauge for recognizing when politics is normal, and when it is becoming, or has become, pathological. In Schmittian terms an 'enemy' is a public entity, a grouping which threatens to negate in a very concrete manner one's way of life.[69] An enemy can either be domestic or international. Normally it is states that define who the enemy is; and war is the 'most extreme consequence of enmity'.[70] But Schmitt's analysis is broad enough to encompass a number of conflicts that fall short of war, for example ideological struggle, and which exist within civil society. For instance, in the Salman Rushdie case, the enemy of supporters of literary freedom are all those who would silence the author or ban his books. For ecological activists, the multinational polluters are the enemy. For radical feminists in the academy, the friends of the canon are the ones to be routed.

It is true that the friend-enemy distinction is less clear-cut than Schmitt often implies; it may be as issue centred as it is group centred, and hence a very unstable distinction. Often, too, enemies can be manufactured by powerful interests not because they are real enemies – a genuine threat – but because to treat them as such is expedient for purposes of power politics and imperial expansion. But Schmitt's main point remains valid. So long as society and the world consists of various groupings, with divergent interests and values, there will always be 'enemies'. This is a normal state of politics, and understanding of this point discourages barbaric utopian visions of a totally pacified world, or the inflation of one's own commitments and programmes to the status of universal doctrine. Schmitt pointed out both the hypocrisy behind, and the dangers in, 'pseudo-universalism'.[71] The hypocrisy lies in seeking to de-politicize what is inescapably political, disguising a local power claim or set of historically located values under the cloak of moral rectitude. The danger is that the invocation of universal categories such as Justice, Peace, Law, Humanity or New World Order threatens to create a category of political non-persons, since those who fall outside these delineations become not enemies but potentially 'foes'; they become, in other words, subject to a demonization which permits not simply their defeat, but their elimination; they are not antagonists or adversaries, but moral vermin.[72] America becomes 'the great Satan'; the former Soviet Union becomes 'the evil empire'; British socialism becomes (as it did for Mrs Thatcher) something to be totally 'destroyed'; the bourgeoisie become 'scum'.

To the extent the friend-enemy distinction collapses, we approach the remote borders of politics. Hitler's final solution, Stalin's terror, Pol Pot's return to year zero, Saddam Hussein's genocidal war against the Kurds all exhibit the foe mentality; and in turn all provoke it. But in these cases social activity has descended from the political sphere into hell on earth. The creative job of politics, both domestically and internationally, is to avoid such hell, to contain human difference and rivalry within the friend–enemy boundary. Where hell cannot be avoided, as it often cannot, we have no political script to follow; we are back in the nightmare maelstrom of Hobbes's state of nature.

So far we have argued that parliament need not be so moribund nor liberal principles so politically emasculated as Schmitt believed. We now wish to indicate how they might be reconceived within the context of a democratic liberalism that escapes some of the strictures Schmitt levelled at liberal democracy. Schmitt's analysis reveals the relationship between liberalism and democracy to be somewhat paradoxical. On the one hand, they are in many respects antagonistic, with liberalism both constraining and being under-mined by democratic processes. On the other hand, whenever in the name of enhanced democratization movements of either Left or Right have sought to abolish such standard liberal features as the rule of law, the separation of state and civil society and the conventions of parliament, they have ended up destroying democracy itself. The dilemma this paradox poses liberal democ-racy appeared intractable to Schmitt, because he doubted the political capacity of liberalism to withstand the democratic onslaught. However, we have seen more grounds for hope. First, what he took to be the liberal parliamentary goal of achieving a rational consensus between free and equal individuals can be more realistically conceived as an attempt to find a set of equitable agreements and compromises on particular matters of common concern. Suitably reformed to be more responsive to the different sections of society, central parliamentary institutions remain indispensable for achieving collective agreements between the constituent parts of a polity. Second, traditional liberal substantive constitutional constraints for the protection of openness and pluralism, such as entrenched bills of rights, can be replaced with procedural institutional checks and controls involving new forms of the division of power and representation. These might range from the establish-ment of distinct functional and cultural as well as territorial areas of legislative and administrative forms of competence on the one hand, to the development of corporatist and specialist bodies for the scrutiny and formulation of policy on the other. Within such a set-up, the norms of political participation, such as majority voting, are largely instrumental and prudential in character. They are functional components of a system designed for the peaceful resolution of social conflict.

A democratic liberalism seeks to incorporate both these features within a confederal political structure composed of a plurality of decision-making bodies designed to facilitate the influence and scrutiny of policy by all relevant groups and individuals and to disperse power throughout society. A plural system of democratic institutions, that reflects the diversity of values and interests within society and enables accommodations to be arranged between them, provides liberalism with the political tools needed to meet Schmitt's challenge. For by linking liberal values and the legitimation of norms to the distribution and division of power within society, liberalism gains a political capacity that is more in tune with the demands of a democratic age than the liberal constitutional mechanisms of the eighteenth and nineteenth centuries whose deficiencies Schmitt so acutely analysed.

Although within such a pluralist system sovereignty is shared with other organizations, a separate and superior body will be necessary to provide the funding and public services necessary for their operation and interaction, to supervise and mediate between them, and to defend the state against its internal and external enemies. As Schmitt pointed out in his criticisms of the English pluralists noted above,[73] an authoritive public power, traditionally the national parliament – although increasingly this role is shared with international institutions such as the European Parliament and the UN General Assembly – must exist both to regulate the activities of groups and to facilitate inter-group decision making. However, such institutions need not claim to represent the undifferentiated sovereign will of the people that Schmitt rightly linked to populist dictatorships and the destruction of the necessary liberal constraints on democracy. Their sphere of competence can be institutionally delimited and their recruitment be achieved through forms of representation that reflect the multiplicity of wills of contemporary societies. Moreover, as we have seen, discussion and decision need not be so sharply distinguished as Schmitt maintained.

Conclusion

A more political and democratic liberalism is one that begins by divesting itself of the rationalistic mind-set. Such a liberalism recognizes its own contingency; it understands that its 'final vocabulary' is a product of history, not necessity, but is willing to fight for the convictions this vocabulary expresses. The work of Schmitt is unconvincing as a demolition of parliamentary democracy, or liberalism more generally, though it highlights the many weaknesses of liberal democratic institutions. A democratic liberalism seeks to repair these weaknesses, by enhancing both the workings of parliament and pushing for the further democratization of society. Thus, liberalism can use Schmitt as a resource, particularly through adopting aspects of his friend–enemy distinction. By so doing, liberalism loses its gloss of universality and self-righteousness, but gains the political will to defend its values.

Notes

1. This chapter was originally written with Peter Baehr, then a colleague attached to the Sociology Department at the University of Edinburgh and now at Memorial University of Newfoundland. I enjoyed the experience of joint composition and am very grateful to him for allowing its republication here.

2. E.g. G. Poggi, *The Development of the Modern State*, London: Hutchinson, 1978; P. Piccone and G. L. Ulmen, 'Introduction', *Telos*, Special Issue on Carl Schmitt, 72 (1987): 3–14; J. Keane, *Democracy and Civil Society*, London: Verso, 1988; P. Hirst, *Representative Democracy and its Limits*, Cambridge: Polity Press, 1990; and P. Hirst, 'The State, Civil Society and the Collapse of Soviet Communism', *Economy and Society*, 20 (1991): 217–42.

3. Stephen Holmes reviewing J. W. Bendersky, *Carl Schmitt: Theorist for the Reich*, Princeton, NJ: Princeton University Press, 1983, for example, remarked that Schmitt was a 'theorist who consciously embraced evil and whose writing cannot be studied without moral revulsion and intellectual distress' (S. Holmes, 'Carl Schmitt: Theorist for the Reich', *American Political Science Review*, 77 (1983): 1067). Gianfranco Poggi, assessing *The Concept of the Political*, provides a more balanced and positive assessment of Schmitt's contribution, but feels bound to comment on its 'bloody mindedness', 'fascist irrationalism' and 'repulsive moral undertones' (Poggi, *Development of the Modern State*, pp. 9, 11). See also Martin Jay's indignant, but still reasoned, critique of Ellen Kennedy's claim that Schmitt significantly influenced the political theory of members of the Frankfurt School (M. Jay, 'Reconciling the Irreconcilable? Rejoinder to Kennedy', *Telos*, 71 (1987): 37–66.

4. C. Schmitt, *The Crisis of Parliamentary Democracy*, trans. E. Kennedy, Cambridge, Mass.: MIT Press, 1985, p. 35.

5. C. Schmitt, *The Concept of the Political*, trans. G. Schwab, New Jersey: Rutgers University Press, 1976, p. 60; and C. Schmitt, *Political Theology. Four Chapters on the Concept of Sovereignty*, trans. G. Schwab, Cambridge, Mass.: MIT Press, 1985, p. 56.

6. Schmitt, *Crisis*, p. 35.

7. Schmitt, *Crisis*, p. 42.

8. Schmitt, *Crisis*, pp. 44–5; *Political Theology*, pp. 32–3.

9. Schmitt, *Crisis*, pp. 34–5.

10. Schmitt, *Crisis*, p. 7.

11. Schmitt, *Crisis*, p. 39.

12. Schmitt, *Crisis*, pp. 39–40.

13. Schmitt, *Crisis*, p. 48.

14. Schmitt, *Crisis*, p. 10.

15. Schmitt, *Crisis*, p. 14.

16. Schmitt, *Crisis*, p. 25.

17. Schmitt, *Crisis*, p. 39.

18. Schmitt, *Crisis*, p. 15.

19. Schmitt, *Crisis*, pp. 6–7.

20. Schmitt, *Crisis*, p. 4.

21. Schmitt, *Crisis*, pp. 25–32.

22. Schmitt, *Crisis*, pp. 16–17, 34–5.

23. Schmitt, *Concept*, p. 26.

24. Schmitt, *Concept*, pp. 26–8, 37.

25. C. E. Frye, 'Carl Schmitt's Concept of the Political', *Journal of Politics*, 28 (1966): 18–30.
26. Schmitt, *Concept*, pp. 33–4.
27. Schmitt, *Concept*, p. 49.
28. Schmitt, *Concept*, pp. 34–5.
29. Schmitt, *Political Theology*, p. 63.
30. Schmitt, *Political Theology*, p. 62.
31. Schmitt, *Concept*, pp. 28, 71–2.
32. Schmitt, *Concept*, pp. 73–6.
33. L. Strauss, 'Comments on Carl Schmitt's *Der Begriff des Politischen*' (1932), in Schmitt, *Concept*, pp. 81–105.
34. Schmitt, *Concept*, p. 27.
35. Schmitt, *Concept*, pp. 35, 52.
36. Schmitt, *Concept*, p. 79.
37. Strauss, 'Comments', pp. 101–2; Schmitt, *Concept*, p. 37.
38. Schmitt, *Concept*, p. 53.
39. M. Weber, 'Politics as a Vocation', in H. H. Gerth and C. W. Mills (eds), *From Max Weber*, London: Routledge & Kegan Paul, 1948, pp. 121–8.
40. As, e.g., R. Dworkin argues in *A Matter of Principle*, Cambridge, Mass.: Harvard University Press, 1985.
41. Schmitt, *Concept*, p. 27.
42. Schmitt, *Political Theology*, pp. 12–14, 18–21; Schmitt, *Concept*, pp. 46–7.
43. Schmitt, *Political Theology*, p. 13.
44. Schmitt, *Concept*, p. 46.
45. Schmitt, *Political Theology*, p. 13.
46. Schmitt, *Concept*, pp. 6–7.
47. Schmitt, *Political Theology*, p. 5.
48. Schmitt, *Concept*, pp. 72–3.
49. Schmitt, *Concept*, p. 77.
50. A number of commentators on the New Right in Britain regarded Mrs Thatcher's espousal of the free economy and a strong state as paradoxical or incoherent, e.g. A. Gamble, *The Free Economy and the Strong State*, Basingstoke: Macmillan, 1988. Schmitt's analysis makes sense of this apparent confusion.
51. Schmitt, *Concept*, p. 22.
52. C. Schmitt, *Legalität und Legitimität*, Munich: Duncker & Humblot, 1932, pp. 28–32.
53. G. Schwab, 'Enemy or Foe: A Conflict of Modern Politics', *Telos*, 72 (1987): 194–201; Bendersky, *Carl Schmitt*.
54. Schmitt, *Legalität und Legitimität*, pp. 33–9.
55. Schmitt, *Legalität und Legitimität*, pp. 48–9, 76–87, 98. It has been argued (e.g. Bendersky, *Carl Schmitt*, pp. 283–5) that Article 21.2 of the Federal Republic of Germany's Basic Law, which prohibits as unconstitutional 'Parties which, by reason of their aims or behaviour of their adherents, seek to impair or abolish the free democratic basic order', embodies Schmitt's stricture against the 'equal chance'. However, it does so only in a formal way. For by leaving this exclusionary power in the hands of a court, it misses Schmitt's point that only a political agent, such as a popularly elected President, has the authority and decisiveness to safeguard the constitution.

56. E.g. P. Hirst, *After Thatcher*, London: Collins, 1989.
57. Schmitt, *Crisis*, p. 2.
58. Schmitt, *Crisis*, p. 9.
59. Keane, *Democracy*, p. 164.
60. Schmitt, *Crisis*, p. 5.
61. Schmitt, *Crisis*, pp. 34–7.
62. Schmitt, *Crisis*, p. 6.
63. C. Schmitt, *Political Romanticism*, trans. G. Oakes, Cambridge, Mass.: MIT Press, 1986, p. 26.
64. For an analysis of this school together with a collection of their writings, see P. Hirst, *The Pluralist Theory of the State*, London: Routledge, 1989. Hirst notes Schmitt's criticisms of the pluralists (p. 44, n. 28) but, as is argued below, is wrong to regard the two theories as incompatible.
65. C. Schmitt, 'Staatsethik und pluralistischer Staat', *Kant-Studien*, 35 (1930): 28–42; and Schmitt, *Concept*, pp. 40–5.
66. See D. Held, *Models of Democracy*, 2nd edn, Cambridge: Polity, 1996.
67. R. Rorty, *Contingency, Irony, and Solidarity*, Cambridge: Cambridge University Press, 1989, p. 73.
68. Rorty, *Contingency, Irony, and Solidarity*, p. 73.
69. Schmitt, *Concept*, p. 27.
70. Schmitt, *Concept*, p. 33.
71. E.g. C. Schmitt, 'The Legal World Revolution', *Telos*, 72 (1987): 85–9.
72. On 'foes' as distinct from 'enemies', see Schmitt, *Concept*, pp. 36, 54, 65, 67, 79.
73. Schmitt, 'Staatsethik und pluralistischer Staat'.

CHAPTER 5

Schumpeter and the Transformation of Capitalism, Liberalism and Democracy[1]

The events of 1989 produced a high degree of uncritical triumphalism amongst certain Western commentators. The collapse of the communist regimes in Eastern Europe, as a result of their failure to manage their economies and the consequent demand on the part of their citizens for more accountable government, led many to link the struggle for democracy with a desire for capitalism. Some writers went so far as to portray the demise of 'actually existing socialism' as the culmination of 'a universal human evolution in the direction of free societies' grounded in 'the empirically undeniable correlation between advancing industrialisation and liberal democracy'.[2] Re-reading Schumpeter's fifty-year-old classic *Capitalism, Socialism and Democracy*[3] in this context is a curious but, I believe, sobering experience. A liberal and a capitalist, Schumpeter nevertheless believed the future lay with socialism. Following Weber, he maintained that the increasingly cartelized and monopolistic character of capitalism had eroded the function of the entrepreneur and made its transformation into the bureaucratic type of social organization he associated with socialist states inevitable. He assumed the public acquisition of the means of production and exchange would be a mere formality. Unlike Weber, he thought the difficulties facing a centrally planned economy had been exaggerated and were remediable. Moreover, he contended that a centralized state was well adapted to the only form of democracy likely to survive in the complex mass societies of the modern world – namely, a plebiscitary contest between rival party leaders for the right to rule.

Such conclusions fly in the face of much contemporary wisdom. However, further reflection reveals them to have more substance than might at first appear. Far from being indissolubly linked, as Whiggish accounts such as Fukuyama's suggest, capitalism, liberalism and democracy frequently clash with each other. In Poland and Russia, for example, the reformers have complained that the democratic demands of the people have hampered economic recovery. There have even been calls for a benevolent dictator to manage the transition from socialism to capitalism. During the 1970s, New Right theorists made similar complaints about the 'overloading' of the economy by popular calls on the state, and in the 1980s governments influenced by their thinking sought to diminish the sphere of democratic decision-making whilst extending that of the market. In fact, historically the process of democratization has generally been promoted by those struggling against the inequality and coercion associated with the free market organization of production and distribution. Schumpeter may have underestimated both the problems associated with central planning and the resistance of the hierarchical structures of the states controlling such economic systems to any amount of democratic accountability, but he was correct in imagining that in certain crucial respects people would regard state provision and regulation as preferable to untrammelled private enterprise. Furthermore, his alternative conception of democracy captures the nature of existing democratic arrangements far better than the classical model he rejected. Indeed, on his account, rather than being the agent of the 'end of history', liberal democracy belongs to a world we have lost.

Instead of being a mere historical curiosity, therefore, Schumpeter's book remains highly relevant to contemporary debates. His thesis challenges the common contention that capitalism and liberalism offer the necessary preconditions for democracy, arguing that the internal dynamic of the first has undermined the second and seriously altered the character of the third.[4] The purpose of this chapter is to explore his analysis of the empirical constraints limiting the scope and nature of liberal democracy in contemporary capitalist societies. The first section outlines Schumpeter's criticisms of the classical conception of democracy, which he largely associates with the liberal faith in the possibility of rational agreement between free and equal autonomous individuals.[5] He maintains that the theory of agency assumed by these ideals has been progressively undermined by the evolution of modern industrial societies. He argues that the pluralism and complexity resulting from the enhanced division of labour within mass industrial economies have rendered the liberal ideal of moral autonomy inoperative. The social and human costs involved in implementing a democracy informed by such values would be too great for them ever to be a realistic option. The second section critically analyses and extends Schumpeter's alternative theory. Schumpeter proposes a conception of democracy as a mere means for choosing from amongst competing elites, which draws on his understanding of the logic of the democratic procedures of his time. Whilst this model is to a certain extent open to the standard objection that he confuses 'is' with 'ought',[6] idealizing current arrangements so that they come to embody the only valid form of democracy, at its heart lies a set of norms which may be separated from the particular institutionalized form he gives to them. Hence, the contrast between the classical theory and Schumpeter's own is not between an empirical and a normative theory of democracy, but between two normative theories of differing empirical plausibility. The third section draws on the norms within his own theory and opens up the possibility of a pluralist and largely procedural and realist account of democratic liberalism, which attempts to avoid the tendency of Schumpeter's own proposals to translate a contingent reality into a theoretical necessity.

Schumpeter's Criticism of Classical Democratic Theory

Although in the English-speaking world Schumpeter's *Capitalism, Socialism and Democracy* is generally treated as the originator of the empirical critique of classical democracy, his account drew on the work of an earlier generation of frustrated liberals such as Mosca, Pareto, Wallas, Schmitt and especially Max Weber.[7] These thinkers perceived that liberal values derived less from the inherent rights or attributes of human beings, so much as a specific cultural and social environment: namely, the Protestant ethic and the nature of early capitalism. These historical circumstances had given rise to a certain kind of individual – the entrepreneurial owner-manager, capable of and valuing autonomous, self-directed rational action. However, it appeared that the subsequent evolution of the capitalist economy was undermining the very ethos that had helped bring it into being. In a mass industrial society, dominated by large-scale corporations and other administrative organizations, on the one hand, and increased functional differentiation, on the other, they considered the type of free individual agency assumed by classical liberal theories to be increasingly untenable. The first process had gradually enveloped individuals into the rule-bound and hierarchical structures of bureaucratic agencies, replacing the entrepreneur with the administrator and professional director and deskilling a large portion of the workforce. The second had so enhanced the complexity of industrial societies that our ability rationally to encompass the resulting social diversity within a single moral and cognitive framework had been considerably reduced. The more individuals became trapped in the logic of their various and occasionally conflicting social roles and functions, and bombarded by a growing mass of often contradictory information and sources of persuasion, the more their capacity for autonomous orientation in the world became undermined.

These developments had considerable consequences for the liberal conception of democracy. This model had originated in a view of politics as the domain of a relatively coherent body of public-spirited men, deemed worthy by virtue of their education and moderate landed wealth to represent the nation in a responsible fashion and to deliberate in a rational and disinterested manner on the common good.[8] Liberal and other radicals merely sought to improve this system by making the representatives more responsive to the people's will through increasing popular participation. In the event, the social and economic changes wrought by the industrial revolution rendered this idealized and expanded version of notable politics an anachronism. The dramatic growth of urban centres, the advent of a mass electorate, the development of a popular press and the rise of large corporations and state bureaucracies, meant that individuals lacked the time, money, expertise and organization necessary either to influence and inform public opinion or rationally to deliberate on the running of the country. Far from producing a more popular government, the expansion of the electorate had been accompanied by social innovations which placed power in the hands of the professional politicians and managers in charge of party machines and the civil servants running the burgeoning state administration. The individual voter became a passive member of an organized group, recruited at elections and ignored by the politicians and bureaucrats between times. The relationship between state and society became distorted by the differential organizational capacities of particular social, economic and ideological interests and the invisible organizational and technical power of bureaucracies and experts. Rational discussion became replaced by bargaining and forms of manipulation which appealed more to the passions than to the intellect. These circumstances transformed democracy into a means whereby the political, social and economic elites in charge of the various apparatuses of state and society recruited support and gained endorsement for their control over people's lives. Appeals to the old liberal ideals of democracy, therefore, were not only unrealistic but positively pernicious. For they either aroused unsatisfiable expectations or served to give an intrinsically corrupt system a spurious legitimacy.

Schumpeter's analysis elaborates upon these themes but tries to reach less pessimistic conclusions than most of these other writers. He summarizes the classical definition of democracy as 'that institutional arrangement for arriving at political decisions which realises the common good by making the people itself decide issues through the election of individuals who are to assemble to carry out its will'.[9] This definition has been criticized for being over-synthetic.[10] As David Miller has remarked, his account of this doctrine 'is an unwieldy composite of Enlightenment rationalism, utilitarianism and Rousseauian ideas'.[11] However, in spite of these defects, it accurately captures the central normative assumption of both classical liberal democratic theory and those radical theories which seek to build on this heritage: namely, that political decisions should converge on the common good by reflecting the collective rational will of free and equal autonomous individuals.

Schumpeter's objections largely repeat the criticisms of the thinkers discussed above. He remarks that the complex and heterogeneous nature of modern industrial societies has undermined the homogeneity required for collective deliberation on the common good. The processes of functional differentiation have enhanced both cognitive and moral pluralism. People can not only rationally desire diverse and often incommensurable goods, they also frequently adopt distinct and occasionally contradictory kinds of reasoning in the different contexts within which they operate. As a result, the identities and loyalties even of single individuals can become divided between their membership of various groups – their professional, neighbourhood, family, sexual, ethnic and religious ties can all clash at times. No ethical code exists in such circumstances capable of rationally integrating the diverse dimensions – erotic, economic, familial, aesthetic, and so on – of human life into one scheme of values. Needless to say, these tensions between the various spheres of our social existence are exacerbated when seeking to produce a rational consensus between individuals and groups. For the division of labour and the fragmentation of our lives not only split up our own sense of personal identity, it seriously weakens our ability to relate to others as members of a common moral, social and political world. Under these conditions, he notes, democratic decisions lack not only rational unity but also rational sanction. The size of modern societies and the concomitant absence of face-to-face relations; the growing complexity and technicality of many social and economic tasks and the resulting reliance on experts, including a permanent professional bureaucracy; the intrusion of new technologies into all areas of life, the sphere of leisure as well as of work, and especially new information technology; and the enhanced functional differentiation and specialization which accompanied these innovations – all these forces have progressively weakened the individual's capacity for autonomous rational action and choice. The dependence on unknown, unpredictable and uncontrollable others involved in an integrated global economy; our containment within managerial hierarchies of various kinds; the proliferation of sources of information and persuasion resulting from the technological revolution within the media, etc., have rendered it increasingly hard for us to make reasoned judgements of our own about the world, since we cannot reduce its complexity to manageable levels. Our moral intuitions will often be inadequate to the world's baffling diversity and flux, so that to insist on them reflects the attitude of a narrow-minded and ignorant dogmatist rather than of a reasonable person. We may be capable of coherent moral and practical reasoning within specific local contexts of which we have direct experience, but on a range of wider issues we fall into an unavoidable deference to expertise and authority and become increasingly susceptible to psychological and non-rational forms of suasion. Within modern societies, he concludes, the only moral or political consensus likely to emerge is one that has been manufactured by the propaganda, advertising and organized manipulation of those in power.

For Schumpeter, the social homogeneity assumed by the classical model of democracy has been destroyed by the economic complexity and the resulting moral pluralism of contemporary societies. Socialism would prove no better than capitalism in this respect. Although, like Marx, he associates these developments with the internal dynamics of the capitalist system, and even shares Marx's belief that via them the inner logic of capitalism was undermining itself, he contends that they would issue in a very different form of socialism to the community of free associations of co-operative producers envisaged by many Marxists, syndicalists and other democratic socialists. Following Max Weber, he argues that the progressive increase in the scale, concentration and complexity of production had provided an additional impetus to the rationalizing and bureaucratic tendencies of modern industrial management. Only a regular administrative hierarchy, operating according to impartial, instrumental rules and staffed by trained experts, will be capable of co-ordinating a modern economy with any degree of efficiency. To the extent that socialism represented the culmination of this process, therefore, it meant that the co-ordination of production by bureaucratic authority would become increasingly centralized and pass from the private to the public sector. In these circumstances, public ownership of the means of production proves as inimical to human emancipation and the overcoming of alienation as corporate capitalism. As the former socialist countries of Eastern Europe amply demonstrated, the class divisions resulting from differential access to private property are simply replaced by inequalities stemming from differential access to the organs of power. Moreover, as Schumpeter points out, this trend proves just as damaging to liberal schemes for enhancing individual choice and autonomy by providing services through the market rather than the state, as it does to socialist plans for direct democracy. Reducing the tasks done by the state or other public bodies makes little difference if they merely get assumed by private corporations whose bureaucracies are almost, indeed sometimes more, extensive. This solution simply substitutes an even less accountable private agency for a public one. For within a market distorted by the concentration of capital, the power of organization and large differentials in wealth, the average consumer's ability to influence service provision is limited, since the system responds to effective and partially created demands rather than real need. Given this situation, Schumpeter sees no viable alternative to some form of socialism. However, unlike most of the other theorists mentioned earlier, he thinks a bureaucratic socialist system could be subjected to a degree of democratic control provided the nature and purposes of democracy were drastically rethought.

Schumpeter's 'Other' Theory of Democracy

Schumpeter's alternative theory reverses the priorities of the classical model. Instead of regarding democracy as primarily a means for the electorate to decide issues and only secondarily as a method for choosing representatives to implement the people's will, Schumpeter proposes making the direct deciding of issues secondary to the choice of politicians who are mandated to make decisions for us. The essence of democracy on this redefinition lies in providing an 'institutional arrangement for arriving at political decisions in which individuals acquire the power to decide by means of a competitive struggle for the people's vote'.[12] Schumpeter's alternative theory drastically alters the conception of representation found in the classical model. The point of elections is not to choose delegates who merely execute the policy preferences of the voters but to legitimize rulers who may make laws and formulate policies in their own right. The diversity of conflicting views and the unpredictability of complex social systems render some form of political co-ordination necessary. However, these same conditions of modern life prevent people from providing such regulation for themselves – they lack the shared norms and knowledge required for such agreement even to be a possibility. But if direct democracy is impossible for these reasons, then so is representative democracy based on an imperative mandate. The will of the people is too diffuse to generate decisions coherent enough to be represented by anybody. Schemes for proportional representation are similarly incoherent as mechanisms for securing the general will. As voting theorists have shown, within multi-dimensional societies global voting cycles will almost always arise whereby whatever option is chosen there is another which a majority of the people would rather have. This effect occurs whatever voting procedure is employed.[13] Furthermore, PR would merely replicate the particularism of society within government, rendering sensible and efficient decision-making impossible. Indeed, given the social and moral pluralism of the modern world, no form of representation, no matter how radical, can reflect adequately anyone's, let alone everyone's, aspirations. Under any electoral system, therefore, electors will always end up choosing decision-makers rather than decisions. The only alternative to either anarchy or blind obedience to completely unaccountable bureaucratic experts lies in deference to the authority of political leaders possessing some degree of popular support. For unlike ordinary people, professional politicians can both forge a consensus and have the time and opportunities for subjecting the bureaucrats to some kind of control.

Democracy on Schumpeter's reconceptualization offers a mechanism for legitimizing political authority by securing some sort of popular mandate. It achieves this end by providing a method for the manufacture rather than the execution of the general will. The crucial factor distinguishing this system from autocracy, and preserving to some degree the liberal concern with freedom of discussion, is the requirement that prospective candidates compete with each other for the allegiance of the people through free elections with a free vote. The electoral contest between different parties works in a similar manner and yields parallel benefits to the rivalry between companies in a market economy. Competition for voters keeps the party organizations efficient and ensures that good candidates emerge, in much the same way that competition for consumers and employees encourages entrepreneurship and efficiency in business. Both the electoral and economic markets respond to popular demand, but in an indirect manner. Producers and politicians only satisfy people's needs and desires as a by-product of their search for profits and power respectively. Their decisions do not reflect the 'will of the people', since they largely set the agenda with the products and policies they offer and the advertising they use to present them. Ordinary people express their views negatively, by rejecting goods and programmes that conflict with their interests, rather than through positive and well-thought-out proposals of their own – for which they lack the expertise. Just as consumer pressure operates through knowing where the shoe pinches rather than in designing shoes and deciding what skills the shoemaker must employ, so voters exert their influence by complaining when governments reduce their standard of living or curtail activities they value, rather than by advocating particular courses of action themselves. Rational criticism comes from amongst the competing sections of the political class more than from the electorate, who merely provide the occasion for it. Thus the politicians debate the relative merits of Keynesian and monetarist policies or entry into EMU, and employ rhetoric rather than argument to convince voters that their favoured strategy offers the best means for realizing their various ends.

Schumpeter argues that, far from being a corruption of true democracy, the transformation of democratic politics into a leadership contest between political parties represents a practical adaptation of the old ideals to the changed times. He believes that this system retains a balance between freedom and efficiency, preserving the liberal virtues of responsiveness and discussion in an attenuated but realistic form. The people may not be able to initiate rational debate, but they are presented with a range of reasonable options to choose from by a political class which can. The resulting artificial reduction of social complexity renders consensual decision-making possible, allowing governments to rule with popular assent even if they do not act as the implementors of an evanescent popular will.

Even Schumpeter acknowledges that this optimistic interpretation of the contemporary political system rests on a number of assumptions which are arguably just as unrealistic as those he criticized in the classical democratic model. He assumes that the politicians will be of a certain calibre, that differences between the rival parties will be bounded by a consensus about the overall direction of national policy and constitutional matters, and that on a wide range of issues these relative amateurs will defer to an independent and competent body of civil servants rather than following their own whims. The electorate too must show a high degree of self-control, tolerating differences of opinion, avoiding extremism and accepting the rules of the democratic game even when they are on the losing side. Finally, Schumpeter notes that the pluralistic nature of society must be of such a kind as to ensure sufficient cross-cutting allegiances to prevent society becoming too polarized. Only this social precondition could keep electoral competitions relatively free, by making it less likely that a particular majority or organized minority could consistently dominate all other groups, and hence provide an adequate basis for political compromises and a general acceptance of the democratic system.

If Schumpeter's analysis of modern societies is correct, however, his alternative model of democracy will be as vulnerable to their growing complexity and fragmentation as the classical theory he so ably criticizes. For these social processes endanger both of the related functions he associates with it: the selection of able leaders and the production of consensus. The calibre and responsiveness of politicians continue to depend on an element of competitiveness between parties, and a degree of rationality, independence and coherence of will amongst voters, which he has shown to be increasingly unlikely to exist. Unlike some later theorists of party competition, such as Anthony Downs, for example,[14] he appreciates that there was no reason for the political market to remain any freer than the economic market. Just as the competitiveness of the latter declines with the growth of large corporations capable of controlling supply and manipulating demand, so the restriction of politics to a relatively small group constrains political competition. As Schumpeter wryly observes, 'everyone is free to compete for political leadership by presenting himself to the electorate ... in the same sense in which everyone is free to start another textile mill'.[15] This constraint limits the choices presented to voters. Parties may collude in upholding those institutional and social arrangements which secure their own position and power – not least their monopoly over the dissemination of information. Rather than challenging the existing administrative and economic order, parties and the politicians who depend on them can seek to institutionalize their position as crucial regulatory components of the system. As a result, instead of a competition between elites, political consumers find themselves confronted by an oligopoly.

Schumpeter regards this restriction of party competitiveness as largely beneficial, for the log-rolling of disparate interests and opinions within the narrow range of the main party programmes helps produce an artificial consensus that provides the social system with a stability and coherence it would otherwise lack. However, when one adds to this the electorate's difficulties, noted above, in forming rational opinions within such a controlled and complex environment, in which many of the issues call in any case for highly specialized technical knowledge, then it is hard to see elections as anything but symbolic events. Without at least some reasonably firm and not wholly irrational or manipulated convictions about policies as well as personalities, voters will be totally at the mercy of the political class who fashion their opinions for them. In these circumstances, one can doubt the validity of calling such a system democratic for any other purpose than that of a legitimizing technical device. In this respect, the cynicism of the more right-wing elite theorists, such as Pareto and Schmitt, was both more honest and more realistic than Schumpeter's own analysis. As they observed, little distinguished democratic elitism from elitism *tout court*. No adequate safe-guards exist within Schumpeter's theory to ensure that these leaders will uphold the liberal legacy. Electoral victory merely legitimizes the suppression of all other forms of political competition and accountability, and places the whole governmental and administrative machinery at the disposal of the sovereign will of the successful leader.

As I noted, Schumpeter welcomes aspects of this development, seeing the move from people rule to the popular choice of rulers as a way of compensating for the loss of the homogeneity and common will assumed by the classical model. Modern democracy supposedly creates an artificial political unity focused around the will of the leader. However, he minimizes the dangers attendant on this change. In recent times these risks have been compounded by the fact that since Schumpeter's day the parliamentary competitive party system has declined even as an effective mechanism of social control. For like the classical model it claims to supersede, it continues to trade on an increasingly outmoded notion of the sovereignty of the nation state both within and outside its territory.[16] I remarked earlier that Schumpeter sees the move towards a centralized social and political bureaucratic authority as the only viable way to manage the growing differentiation and complexity of industrial societies. But the further unfolding of these processes renders the nation state either too large or too small to contain them. As new technology makes political, economic and social activity worldwide in scope, the effec-tiveness of action by individual states both domestically and abroad steadily diminishes. In an interconnected world, national policies to regulate pollu-tion, the flow of capital, cultural attitudes, production and employment, defence – in sum all the standard tasks of government – become to a great extent untenable.[17] Co-operation with other states is unavoidable, with the result that multinational organizations in the areas of law, trade, information, finance and armed conflict assume a new importance, further eroding state sovereignty. As a consequence, not only does the influence of the ordinary voter disappear almost to vanishing point, but that of the national politician is severely weakened as well. Within the new global politics, decisions get made through multi-bureaucratic rule by a mandarinate of officials working within the various international agencies – from ICI to the IMF – whose accountability to anything outside the norms and hierarchy of their respective organizations is very hard to achieve. (One need only think of the tirades of past Conservative governments against the EU, including their own appoint-ees amongst the commissioners, for a vivid illustration of this fact.) The perception of the state's growing ineffectiveness on the international stage produces a concomitant loosening of its grip on domestic affairs. Citizens begin to perceive where real power lies and appeal directly to these bodies for the economic aid, legal redress, military protection, and so on that national governments often cannot provide. Paradoxically, this distancing of the source of power combines with the tendency of the economic system to enhance diversification at the same time as interconnectedness to restore an element of local autonomy. Regional, socio-economic and functional differences begin to reassert themselves, giving rise to a new emphasis on the need for rules and allocations to reflect the peculiarities of particular contexts. The state becomes subdivided from below into a multiplicity of partial agencies with their own systems of representation and decision-making. Thus the social, political and economic system finds itself subject to two countervailing trends – the one stressing greater unity at the international level, the other calling for greater heterogeneity at the subnational level. Schumpeter's model of democracy appears singularly ill equipped to cope with either dimension of modern politics. Traditional parliamentary parties experience increasing difficulties in processing the diverse demands of the populace, who become either apathetic or turn to new social movements concerned with collective demands of limited scope aimed at either a sub- or supra-national level. The attempt to reassert their power in these conditions will either become increasingly impotent or despotic.

Schumpeter both underestimates and exaggerates the capacity of the elite and the political system more generally to control the complex social processes he associates with industrial economies. On the one hand, he does not explore sufficiently the functional role played by the contemporary political system as a means for containing those forces which threaten to break it apart – a function that changes the character of democracy even more than he realizes and stifles the effects of competition on the elite. On the other hand, he fails to note how the very forces which had undermined the classical conception of democracy are destroying the basis of his leadership model even as a means of stabilizing the political system. However, the weaknesses of his alternative model reinforce rather than invalidate his critique of classical democracy, for they stem from those self-same assumptions his model shares with the latter theory.

These failings reside in the details of Schumpeter's own theory, rather than the basic norms that inform it. In his programmatic remarks, Schumpeter defines democracy as essentially a method or set of procedures of instrumental rather than intrinsic value. As his critics point out, this interpretation of democracy is highly contentious and essentially favours his own model. For many theorists political participation constitutes a positive human good of considerable substantive value. However, Schumpeter's analysis of the classical model suggests that not only are the conditions for political involvement of the requisite kind unlikely to obtain, but that the perfectionist account of human nature which to a certain extent underpins it is similarly flawed. In the future, democracy must be conceived not as a form of popular rule but as a mechanism for constraining, influencing and producing government and for facilitating the compromises and rules necessary for the efficient and fair co-ordination of our lives. If his own theory fails to achieve these goals, they remain the only valid ones for democratic theorists today. The consequences of

Schumpeter's arguments for our current understanding of the relationship between liberalism and democracy forms the subject of the next section.

From Liberal Democracy to Democratic Liberalism

Twenty years ago, Schumpeter's theory might still have achieved a degree of popular and academic acceptance as a reasonable account of the democratic virtues of competitive party systems, particularly the British and American systems on which – following Weber's analysis – it was largely based. The experience of Mrs Thatcher's government has given ample evidence of both the failings outlined above. The abuse of the electoral mandate to push through unpopular policies on the one hand, and the confrontation with independent associations inside and outside the state on the other, provided the constant themes of her administration. Together they reveal how, far from coping with the complexity and plurality of contemporary societies, this system encourages a logic of exclusion of internal and external 'enemies' that threaten the putatively sovereign will of those in authority.[18] That Mrs Thatcher should have been brought down by the issues of local government and Europe was an entirely appropriate testimony to the unacceptability and increasing impracticality of this type of plebiscitary dictatorship within a pluralist and global social and economic system.

As a result of her period in office, constitutional reform returned to the political agenda. However, the main proposals being canvassed fail to address the problems for democratic theory revealed by Schumpeter. Blanket calls for more direct democracy suffer from all the defects he noted in the classical theory. Schemes for electoral reform involving some form of proportional representation (PR) leave the power of parliament and parties largely intact, and fail to tackle the fact that any single form of representation will prove 'unrepresentative' along one dimension or another. None can produce a popular will; they can only choose a variety of politicians. In which case, it remains far from obvious that coalitions held together by minority parties, a likely result of most systems of PR, would prove any more representative of popular demands than the current plurality voting procedures. Calls for a constitutional bill of rights sacrifice democracy to liberalism. They seek to constrain democratic decision-making within the strait jacket of liberal morality. In spite of their universalistic claims, all constructions of rights are relative to particular social and ethical points of view. This nullifies the assertion of their proponents that they offer a neutral way for mediating between a plurality of agents and agencies. Within a complex system, economic and social regulation to meet a variety of purposes makes talk of 'inalienable' individual rights an anachronism. Rather, rights must be matters of public debate and compromise amongst a range of competing con- stituencies.[19] Finally, New Right notions of turning citizens into consumers by divesting responsibility for service provision to the private sector will not empower them one iota. Since an imperfect market responds to effective demand rather than real need, there is no reason for supposing that corporate bureaucracies, any more than governmental ones, will prove accountable to public pressure.

For democracy to meet the pluralist challenge of modern societies, we must go beyond the liberal democratic paradigm. The achievement of a rational consensus between free and equal individuals must be replaced by the somewhat different goal of providing an equitable *modus vivendi* capable of facilitating a complex mixture of local and general agreements amongst the diverse sections of contemporary societies. This latter goal constitutes the rationale of what I call democratic liberalism.[20] A democratic liberal politics has two basic concerns. First, it aims to devolve power to a variety of social groups and organizations to allow them to formulate and to apply the norms appropriate to their particular purposes and situation. Secondly, it seeks to create a federated institutional structure, of which parties and parliamentary bodies form only a part, to enable the various elements of the social system to regulate their interaction and to resolve their disagreements. These objectives call for new forms of the division of power and representation respectively. These will range from the establishment of distinct functional and cultural as well as territorial areas of legislative and administrative competence on the one hand, to the development of corporatist and specialist bodies for the scrutiny and formulation of policy on the other.

A complete description of the institutional components of this model of democracy lies beyond the scope of this chapter. However, three general observations are in order. First, the norms regulating such a system will be of a largely formal and procedural nature. Instead of serving as a universal framework for all human interaction, a conception at odds with the heterogeneity of rules generated within pluralist societies,[21] these norms are best conceived as functional aspects of the political process. As such, they will vary according to the specific ends they are designed to advance. To the extent that traditional liberal moral concepts, such as natural rights, rest on a comprehensive morality deriving from an idealized and highly unrealistic notion of autonomous agency, they will prove largely redundant. Politics and ethics must be kept separate, for the distinctive function of the political system is to facilitate the expression of a plurality of values and to arrange accommodations between them. The institutional mechanisms of a democratic liberalism make for a truly political conception of justice,[22] replacing substantive constitutional constraints for the protection of pluralism and openness with procedural democratic checks and controls.

Secondly, new information and communication technology has rendered the securing of freedom of expression and the free diffusion of knowledge extremely difficult. The new media, computers, etc. are double-edged, offering unprecedented potential both for ideological manipulation, when controlled by a few, and creative discussion and innovation when freely open to all. Ensuring the latter will not be easy, but it is vital to an open political system allowing for a variety of competing opinions.

Finally, liberal theorists generally associate political pluralism with a capitalist economic system. Two factors motivate this linkage: the need to prevent the control of resources by a single agency and the flexibility of market allocations as opposed to planned. So long as socialism is identified with central planning by a monolithic bureaucratic state, as Schumpeter maintained, then capitalist arrangements will prove superior in these respects. However, unregulated markets based on private property rights in the means of production, distribution and exchange, result in discrepancies in wealth and hierarchical relationships which create grave inequalities of power and restrict the range of democratic control. The consequent private domination of the financial and industrial corporations may be better than that of the socialist state, but it is far from realizing the liberal ideals of freedom and equality that are often said to be synonymous with capitalism. A socialist society, composed of co-operatively owned and democratically self-managing enterprises, disperses economic power more effectively and equitably and so proves more pluralist than either capitalism or state socialism. It is compatible with both democratic decision-making in the areas of public goods and the conciliation of ideal-regarding preferences and the use of market and price mechanisms for the co-ordination of material preferences and ordinary consumption. For outside the area of essential social services, a regulated market proves far more adaptable and open than planning can ever be. Thus, although it may be unfashionable to say so, it seems not unreasonable to conclude with Schumpeter that the future of liberalism and democracy rests with socialism.[23]

Conclusion

Schumpeter's writings offer a powerful critique of the social and moral assumptions underlying liberal democracy. Contemporary theories of liberalism and democracy cannot avoid the empirical constraints posed by the pluralism and complexity of modern industrial societies. Rather than expressing the consensual general will of autonomous individuals, democracy must be reconceived as a mechanism for exercising control and influence over governmental decisions, securing the advantages of criticism and competition, and for achieving the co-ordination of a plurality of agents and the authoritative allocation of burdens and benefits amongst them. Schumpeter's alternative model fails to realize these goals. Cut off from the liberal values it seeks to supplant, competitive party parliamentary democracy deforms these aims. It becomes a mere means for the populist acclamation of a political elite. Democratic liberalism, in contrast, offers an institutional context adequate to the pluralist and complex character of the modern world, the accomplishment of mutual control and the creation of an equitable *modus vivendi*. Moreover, albeit in a manner rather different from his predictions, the union of democracy and liberalism would appear to require the transcendence of capitalism in socialism after all.

Notes

1. An earlier version of this chapter was given as a paper to a workshop devoted to Schumpeter's *Capitalism, Socialism and Democracy* at the ECPR Joint Sessions at the University of Essex, 22–28 March 1991. I am grateful to the other participants, particularly Frank Bealey, David Beetham, Christopher Berry, Joe Femia, Keith Graham, Liam O'Sullivan, Ferran Requejo, Emilio Santoro, Darrow Schecter and Danilo Zolo, from whose comments and papers on that occasion I have learnt much. Malcolm Anderson, David Held, Geraint Parry and Mario Piccinini also offered useful observations on that draft.
2. Francis Fukuyama, 'The World Against a Family', *Guardian*, 12 September 1990, p. 19.
3. J. A. Schumpeter, *Capitalism, Socialism and Democracy* (1942), 5th edn, London: Unwin, 1976.
4. Sophisticated holders of this view accept that capitalism does not provide the sufficient conditions for liberal democracy. For examples of this position from Left and Right respectively, see N. Bobbio, *The Future of Democracy*, Cambridge: Polity, 1987, pp. 25–6 and N. Bobbio, *Which Socialism?*, Cambridge: Polity, 1987, p. 44; and M. Friedman, *Capitalism and Freedom*, Chicago: Chicago University Press, 1962, pp. 10, 15, 19ff.
5. Schumpeter regarded democracy as a comparatively recent phenomenon, stemming from the recognition of the moral equality of all human beings. As a result, he does not trace democratic theory back to ancient Greece but to the eighteenth century.
6. E.g. G. Duncan and S. Lukes, 'The New Democracy', *Political Studies*, XI, 1963, pp. 156–77; G. Parry, *Political Elites*, London, 1969, p. 149; and D. Held, *Models of Democracy*, Cambridge: Polity, 1987, p. 179.
7. The books cited by Schumpeter as inspiring his work are G. Wallas, *Human Nature in Politics*, 3rd edn, London: Constable, 1920; Walter Lippmann, *Public Opinion*, New York, 1920; V. Pareto, *Trattato di sociologia generale*, 2nd edn, Milan, 1923; and Gustav Le Bon, *La Psychologie des foules*, Paris, 1895. However, he undoubtedly knew and was profoundly influenced by G. Mosca, *Elementi di scienza politica*, 2nd edn, Bari: Laterza, 1923; Carl Schmitt, *Die geistesgeschichtliche Lage des heutigen Parlamentarismus*, 2nd edn, Berlin, 1926; and above all Max Weber, 'Parlament und Regierung im neugeordneten Deutschland' (1918) and 'Politik als Beruf' (1919) in *Gesammelte Politische Schriften*, 3rd enlarged edn, Tübingen, 1971, pp. 306–443, 505–60. See Wolfgang Mommsen, *Max Weber and German Politics 1890–1920*, Chicago: Chicago University Press, 1984, pp. 406–7; David Beetham, *Max Weber and the Theory of Modern Politics*, 2nd edn, Cambridge: Polity, 1985, pp. 111–12; and Held, *Models of Democracy*, Ch. 5, for details of the Schumpeter–Weber connection. I discuss this generation of European liberal theorists in my book *Liberalism and Modern Society*, Cambridge: Polity, 1992. I

have also partially expounded my thesis in my *Modern Italian Social Theory*, Cambridge: Polity, 1987, Chs 2–3 (on Pareto and Mosca); the introduction to Richard Bellamy (ed.), *Victorian Liberalism. Nineteenth Century Political Thought and Practice*, London: Routledge, 1990; and an article 'From Ethical to Economic Liberalism: The Sociology of Pareto's Politics', *Economy and Society*, 19, 1990, pp. 431–55.

8. James Bryce provided a paradigmatic example of this model in his introduction to the English translation of M. I. Ostrogorski's classic study *Democracy and the Organisation of Political Parties*, 2 vols, London, 1902. 'In the ideal democracy,' he wrote, 'every citizen is intelligent, patriotic, disinterested. His sole wish is to discover the right side in each contested issue, and to fix upon the best man among competing candidates. His common sense, aided by a knowledge of the constitution of his country, enables him to judge wisely between the arguments submitted to him, while his own zeal is sufficient to carry him to the polling booth' (I. p. xliv). As Schumpeter observes with approval (*Capitalism*, p. 256 n. 7), Wallas's sarcasm at Bryce's and Ostrogorski's attempts to cling to this ideal against all the evidence they bring to bear against it is entirely appropriate (see *Human Nature*, pp. 142–8) .

9. Schumpeter, *Capitalism*, p. 250.

10. E.g. C. Pateman, *Participation and Democratic Theory*, Cambridge: Cambridge University Press, 1970, p. 17 and Held, *Models of Democracy*, p. 178.

11. David Miller, 'The Competitive Model of Democracy', in G. Duncan (ed.), *Democratic Theory and Practice*, Cambridge: Cambridge University Press, 1983, p. 137.

12. Schumpeter, *Capitalism*, p. 269.

13. Iain McLean, 'Forms of Representation and Systems of Voting', in D. Held (ed.), *Political Theory Today*, Cambridge: Polity, 1991, p. 181.

14. A. Downs, *An Economic Theory of Democracy*, New York, 1957. For a comparison between Downs and Schumpeter, see Miller, 'Competitive Model'.

15. Schumpeter, *Capitalism*, p. 272.

16. These reflections are inspired by D. Held, 'Democracy, the Nation State and the Global System', in Held (ed.), *Political Theory Today*, pp. 197–235.

17. The challenge of interconnectedness has been a theme of Ghita Ionescu's writings, most recently in 'Political Undercomprehension or the Overload of Political Cognition', *Government and Opposition*, 24 (1989): 413–26. Much of what I have to say in this article echoes more generally the arguments of the special issue of this journal on *Modern Knowledge and Modern Politics*, of which Ionescu's paper formed a part. However, it will be clear from section three that I am far less pessimistic about the role of democracy in the contemporary world than, with the exception of Geraint Parry, the other participants appear to be.

18. The reference is of course to Schmitt's analysis of the link between sovereignty and plebiscitary democratic leadership, which to my mind provides the best theoretical framework for understanding the political dimensions of the Thatcher phenomenon. See Chapter 4.

19. For an argument for what here I must merely assert, see my 'Liberal Rights and Socialist Goals', in W. Maihofer and G. Sprenger (eds), *Revolution and Human Rights, Archiv für Rechts- und Sozialphilosophie*, Beiheft Nr. 41, 1990, pp. 249–64.

20. As Paul Hirst has recently revealed, this approach was developed by the English Pluralists, notably Figgis, Cole and Laski, at the turn of the century. My argument owes much to his exposition and extension of their ideas in P. Q. Hirst (ed.), *The Pluralist Theory of the State*, London: Routledge, 1989 and P. Q. Hirst, *Representative*

Democracy and its Limits, Cambridge Polity, 1990. I have also found extremely useful David Beetham, 'Beyond Liberal Democracy', *Socialist Register*, 1981; J. Keane, *Democracy and Civil Society*, London: Verso, 1988; and D. Zolo, *Complessità e democrazia: per una ricostruzione della teoria democratica*, Turin: Feltrinelli, 1987.

21. See M. Walzer, *Spheres of Justice*, Oxford: Martin Robertson, 1983.

22. The contrast I have in mind, of course, is with J. Rawls's conception of political justice in his recent writings, e.g. 'Justice as Fairness: Political not Metaphysical', *Philosophy and Public Affairs*, 14, 1985, pp. 223–51. For more detailed criticism, see my *Liberalism and Modern Society*, Ch. 6.

23. For detailed arguments to this effect, see R. A. Dahl, *A Preface to Economic Democracy*, Cambridge: Polity, 1985; and D. Miller, *Market, State and Community: Theoretical Foundations of Market Socialism*, Oxford: Clarendon Press, 1989.

PART II
Rights, Pluralism and the Need for Politics

CHAPTER 6

Liberal Justice: Political and Metaphysical[1]

The God of the Old Testament is proclaimed as a just God but is assuredly no liberal. A society whose idea of justice accords with patriarchal principles of political authority is an unjust society by the test of liberal ideas about freedom, autonomy and the equality of persons. Such a dispute between conceptions of justice sounds squarely metaphysical, turning on the true character of a just society, of human nature and, perhaps, of a just God. Nor is it meta-ethically neutral: if patriarchy were to prevail, a just society would oblige citizens to lead a particular form of good and upright life, contrary to the familiar liberal tenet that questions of what is right can be settled without prejudice to questions of what is good. Yet this liberal tenet is not disputed only by patriarchs and other opponents of liberalism. There are competing conceptions of justice within the liberal camp and some of them include a specific, if carefully incomplete, account of a citizen's moral commitments.

Liberals who agree with J. S. Mill that the only freedom worthy of the name is that of pursuing our own good in our own way may seem bound to leave each of us to define our own good for ourselves.[2] This familiar conclusion does not follow simply, however. A liberal could stress 'our own way', rather than 'our own good', when designing a constitution whose primary idea of religious toleration was to allow a variety of ways to a Christian good.[3] A more agnostic liberal could tolerate wider experiments in living, provided that they embody a prescribed, if secular, notion of human flourishing.[4] A liberal with communitarian tendencies could let us choose *our* own good without letting each of us choose his or her own good.[5] This may be to approach the limits of liberalism, but there are liberal disciples of Rousseau and, in general, the line between the right and the good has never been perspicuous.

Contemporary liberals usually contend that modern democratic societies are so deeply plural that liberalism must do without any comprehensive moral framework of a distinctively liberal kind. Pluralism forces the issue. But it

111

does so neither because it is a contingent historical fact which a democratic liberal should recognize, nor because liberalism implies moral relativism or some such meta-ethical commitment. The point is, rather, that a liberal society which permits free discussion and action has to leave radically conflicting ethical viewpoints in play. To restrict this diversity by the use of state power would be oppressive.[6] Hence, it is argued, liberalism cannot defend itself by appealing to the inherent superiority of the liberal ideal without becoming illiberal. The only way to avoid this paradox is to provide principles of justice which are neutral in the 'political' sense that all involved accept them as offering fair terms of social co-operation when viewed from within their respective comprehensive doctrines. Pluralism involves a compromise between liberal and illiberal views, which, although reached in the name of justice, allows illiberal practices. (We shall test the coherence of this line later.)

Can one construct a conception of justice that eschews metaphysical claims to universal truth, for instance about the nature of persons, and instead seeks simply to provide a fair and stable basis for peaceful political co-existence? The attempt has been made most explicitly in the recent writings of John Rawls.[7] His idea of a just society as 'a fair system of co-operation between free and equal persons' is finely poised (*JF*, p. 238; *PL,* pp. 9, 26). *Fairness* is a procedural notion, falling a hair's breadth short of implying a thick conception of the good. *Co-operation* involves a notion of proper conduct Kantian enough to prevent free-riding, yet without requiring a shared moral purpose. The *freedom* envisaged leaves room for dispute between disciples of Locke (the 'moderns') and disciples of Rousseau (the 'ancients'). *Equality* constrains the distribution of power and resources without conceding to egalitarians. *Persons* are essentially participants in social life, equipped with a capacity for a sense of justice and of the good; yet this conception does not call for a metaphysical doctrine of the nature of the self. The whole idea is framed to apply not universally or eternally but to the basic structure of a modern political democracy. It 'starts from within a particular political tradition', roughly the one which emerged in Western Europe from the wars of religion and has given us an 'overlapping consensus' about the virtues required of citizens to base the construct on (*JF*, p. 225; *PL*, pp. 14–15). The revised theory of justice is thus as promised by his (1985) title, 'political, not metaphysical' (*JF*, p. 230; *PL*, p. 10).

This paper addresses two related doubts about trying to turn metaphysical water into political wine. First, there are rival non-metaphysical theories of justice on offer and, in weakening his conception of the self, freedom and equality, Rawls may have let himself be fatally squeezed between libertarian writers like F. A. Hayek and left-of-centre liberals like Ronald Dworkin. Secondly, his theory, in common with those of other philosophical liberals, is curiously *un*political. He deliberately excludes the haggling and trading of interests and the contingencies of power, characteristic of political agreements, from the rational deliberations that he believes ought to motivate the parties in a democratic society to arrive at his two principles of justice. He contrasts an articulated and normative 'overlapping consensus' on principles of justice with a mere *modus vivendi* achieved through a contingent balance of power; and he sees his two principles as removing from the political agenda certain contentious issues, such as who has the vote or what sorts of views can be expressed. This exclusion of politics threatens to render the principles of justice too abstract and far removed from people's real circumstances to yield any practical guidance to free and equal persons trying to work out what counts as fair co-operation in particular political conditions.

To focus these doubts we shall begin by asking whether a Rawlsian type of construct can be defended against libertarians without falling prey to communitarians. This enquiry will be conducted in the next two sections under the headings of 'Clubs' and 'Communities'. We shall then step back to consider whether the 'political' can be kept clear of 'metaphysics'. We explore this question in the third section under the heading of 'Commonwealths', understood as fair systems of co-operation between free and equal persons, conceived in a republican tradition updated by drawing on the earlier comments on each of the other headings. This discussion leads to the conclusion that citizenship does indeed involve a political idea of justice, where political obligations are prior to pre-political rights, but one which is, as the chapter title suggests, metaphysical for all that. The final section tests out this thesis by applying it to questions about the position of women and the distribution of welfare in an illiberal culture.

Clubs

'Clubs' refer to free associations formed for mutual advantage in pursuing limited aims. Members observe the rules for instrumental reasons. The rules embody a system of co-operation related to the purpose of the club. But not all clubs treat their members equally or even fairly. Women, for instance, may be banned from the library in a London club, expected to make the tea in a cricket club or admitted at half-price to a dating club. Rich and powerful members may fare better than others, as in clubs for landowners, yachting enthusiasts and oil barons. Since nothing in the basic idea of a club itself rules out all manner of discrimination, we need a particular sort of club to serve as a model for the liberal state.

So let us specify that the members be equal and the system of co-operation fair. Also, since they cannot easily leave, we need to construe their freedom in some broader sense, which may involve resources for pursuing their own good and not merely an absence of formal obstacles. Here liberal opinion starts to divide, with libertarians thinking in terms of a mail-order club, so to speak, and social liberals in terms of a Christmas club. In the mail-order state, all are equally free to trade, human relations are severely instrumental, everyone's penny is worth the same as everyone else's penny and it is no one's concern that all have at least a basic number of pennies. Each widow's mite is worth the same as each of the millionaire's million. In the Christmas club state, all insure themselves against some future personal calamity by contributing according to their means to some form of collective welfare and social security provision, drawing on the common fund according to need rather than contribution. On this view, which would appear to be Rawls's, mutual advantage is secured by a relationship of reciprocity.

For both versions a crucial question is whether the self-interested partici- pants will rationally accept that they have an obligation to abide by the spirit of the rules. If they do, then they will play fair even when able to avoid it. If not, then free-riding will destroy the system of co-operation, as Hobbes insisted when arguing for 'a power to keep all in awe'.[8] All participants do better if all play fair than if the system fails; but each seems to do better still by undetected cheating, not only if others cheat but also if they play fair. Where this choice is truly dominant for rational, self-interested individuals, the club is doomed. The problem is more obvious for the mail-order version, where human relations are explicitly instrumental, but also besets the Christ- mas club, which has difficulty explaining why the better off should join in the first place.

The liberal club would be safe from free-riders, if those taking part were Kantians. The problem vanishes among rational agents, if obedience to the categorical imperative is a requirement of rationality. Yet, although the Good Samaritan may have no reason to regret saving the life of a stranger who then pinches his wallet, it is hard to believe that one should rationally be as high- minded about failures of mutual trust by mail-order or even in the course of a mutual insurance scheme. Whereas moral obligations may be unconditional, obligations of prudence seem to be rendered void by reasonable suspicion of non-compliance, as Hobbes suggests.

Yet Hobbes's own remedy is not as dour as appears from remarks like 'covenants without the sword are but words, and of no strength to secure a man at all'.[9] In his reply to the 'fool' who 'questionneth whether injustice . . . may not sometimes stand with that reason, which dictateth to everyman his own good', he declares that 'it is not against reason' to honour covenants of mutual trust, unless one has reasonable suspicion that the other party will not.[10] But this conclusion is not easy to extract with as little apparatus as Hobbes provides and even his liberal admirers usually give themselves more to work with.

The snag, as diagnosed by Rawls (PL, pp. 16–17, 147–8), is that a society built on nothing but the mutual self-interest of rational agents issues at best in a mere modus vivendi. Such a society need be neither fair, depending as it does on a contingent distribution of power, nor durable, since it will collapse as soon as it suits one or more of the parties to defect. Accordingly he now advocates a solution with a moral element, injected by basing a just society on an 'overlapping consensus' among 'reasonable' agents who recognize ties of 'reciprocity'. Since reciprocity involves discharging one's obligations even when one could defect, we are being offered a version of the Christmas Club model which looks safe from free-riders.

This manoeuvre compares interestingly with the role of the 'veil of ignorance' in A Theory of Justice.[11] Behind the veil the demands of self-interest generated an extensive mutual insurance scheme by reasoning uncannily close to Kantian. It looked as if prudence pursued in ignorance was congruent with the Kantian moral point of view. Even so, that left it unclear why a rational agent, as standardly defined, would comply with the social contract, if, once the veil was lifted, defection turned out to be dominant. By making more of a distinction between rational agents and reasonable agents and relying heavily on an 'overlapping consensus', Rawls makes compliance less problematic.

Nevertheless, reciprocity is something of a mystery ingredient. Its effect is to populate the just society with reasonable agents of a neighbourly sort. Yet this would be a sleight of hand if it only worked by doctoring the passions so as to make human beings more sociable, sympathetic to one another, or prone to the pangs of a bad conscience than originally envisaged. So presumably its role is to make reasonable agents reflective and hence able to override their own preferences as expressed in their current utility rankings of outcomes: when rational choice theory bids rational agents to defect, reasonable agents sometimes refuse. But why? The obvious answer might seem to be that we are being offered a robust 'philosophical psychology or a metaphysical doctrine of the self', which includes a Kantian power of reason to override inclination, renders agents less individualistic and more sociable, and thus grounds a distinction between reciprocity and even super-enlightened self-interest.

Yet Rawls squarely refuses to elaborate any such moral ontology or metaphysics, insisting that 'no political view that depends on these deep and unresolved matters can serve as a public conception of justice in a constitutional democratic state', and remarking that 'we must apply the principle of toleration to philosophy itself' (JF, pp. 231, 223; PL, pp. 13–14, 9–10). In that case, however, the puzzle remains how to undermine free-riding, when that is a dominant choice, within a procedural theory of rationality and justice that still keeps the liberality in liberalism. Reciprocity may indeed hold the key but not as an ad hoc device.

The generic problem is that, if prudence is construed along the lines of standard rational choice theory, then it threatens to be self-defeating. The putative solution is to set the hypothetical in pursuit of the categorical by equipping rational agents with a reflectiveness which leads them to overcome this feature of prudence to their mutual advantage. Yet, while (expected) utilities remain a given element in the stock of common knowledge which rational agents have of one another and are an automatic link between preference and choice, there is simply no way for reflectiveness to make a difference. Hence we need a device for distancing rational agents from their preferences, while leaving them 'self-interested' in the pursuit of their own good.

Rawls fails to solve this difficulty. The imperative to co-operate, in Rawls's view, remains hypothetical, in that co-operation proceeds on 'terms that each participant may reasonably accept, provided that everyone else likewise accepts them' (*JF*, p. 232; *PL*, p. 16). However, there is bound to be a problem of compliance among rational maximisers, once they have a shrewd idea of their power to avoid doing their bit. This is explicit in David Gauthier's version of the club,[12] for example, where rational agents know their historical and social positions and yet choose to be 'constrained maximizers' who play fair with other constrained maximizers even when able to avoid it. That may sound promising. If it pays the weak and the strong alike to adopt a disposition to play fair, then the Hobbesian problem is solved without the trouble and expense of a fraud squad. But the burden of this solution falls very heavily on the idea that one can choose a disposition to be a Kantian among Kantians and, presumably, a rat among rats. Since the choice is prompted by self-interest and the disposition, being conditional, can be suspended when it suits, we fail to see why a rational villain will not smile and smile and still be a villain. In Rawls and Gauthier alike, the social contract needs to bring about what Rousseau called a 'remarkable change in man', putting 'justice in the place of instinct' and leading him 'to consult his reason rather than study his inclinations'.[13] Gauthier's disposition towards enlightened self-interest is not to be trusted any more than Rawlsian reciprocity, unless the self is transmuted in acquiring it.

That will disappoint those who hope that Kant can furnish the element of trust which even a mail-order market needs. But the Kantian *Rechtsstaat* is not a club, even though it seems to keep the liberality in liberalism without blending the right and the good. Despite its contractarian air, the *Rechtsstaat* firmly presupposes a theory of morality which is not contractarian and rational agents who are categorically moral in all their practical dealings with one another. In undertaking to respect one another's autonomy, these agents are not entering a contract but simply recognizing what their own autonomy implies. It may look as if autonomy is too schematic a notion to have moral content. But there is no mistaking Kant's view that someone who consults only self-interest, however reflectively, is not a fit citizen of the *Rechtsstaat*. Autonomous agents keep promises because they have made them, and regardless of their expected utilities when the time comes. *Pace* Rawls, the *Rechtsstaat* embodies a universal conception of justice, a metaphysical doctrine of the self and a refusal to apply the principle of toleration to philosophy itself.

In denying that the *Rechtsstaat* is a contract, we do not deny that it may be a construct. Such a construct would need to be the work of already autonomous agents, however, not their incentive to become autonomous. That is to build a specific principle of limited toleration into the construct and hence a refusal to compromise between liberal and illiberal views. The grounds of this refusal can only be moral and connected with a metaphysical doctrine of the self, even if the morality involved is carefully schematic rather than detailed. The Kantian self is not prior to *all* the ends which constitute it. That much is clear. But a new difficulty arises, when we ask exactly which ends are integral to a citizen of the *Rechtsstaat*. That is the cue for communitarians.

Communities

Communities differ from clubs in that, rather than individuals constituting society for distinct purposes of their own, social membership supposedly constitutes individual identity. Communitarians regard the club model of society as an impossible attempt to pull society up by its own bootstraps, since it assumes what it seeks to create: unless there is already a social setting which provides individuals with roles and standards, the notion of individual choice has no meaning. The self-interested agents of much liberal theorizing are ridiculed as compulsive shoppers in the supermarket of ends. Lacking either a sense of purpose or a shared moral framework, such disencumbered individuals as the participants in Rawls's original position or Gauthier's contractors could not establish a settled order of preferences or reach stable agreements with others.

Communitarians contend, therefore, that the Kantian *Rechtsstaat* makes sense only within the context of the Hegelian ethical state. The right cannot be separated from the good, since rules of justice reflect common understandings of ends, rather than means, which explain why certain goods are important and how they fit into a particular pattern of social relationships of which the individual is a part. Despite an established tradition of neo-Hegelian liberal communitarianism, however, many liberals have been uneasy with this way of thinking, regarding it as either conservative, with a small 'c', or downright authoritarian.

Contemporary attempts at communitarian liberalism cannot easily escape these criticisms. Communitarian liberals can be divided into relativists and rationalists, with Michael Walzer's *Spheres of Justice*[14] providing an example of the first and Joseph Raz's *Morality of Freedom*[15] an instance of the second. Walzer's argument is communitarian in so far as he argues that 'distributions are patterned in accordance with shared conceptions of what the goods are and what they are for'.[16] His theory is liberal, however, in contending that we ought to show equal concern and respect both for the different understandings of justice found in different societies and for the distributional criteria appropriate to different goods within societies.

The problem with Walzer's thesis is that the relativism need not generate

117

the liberalism. His contention that 'a given society is just if its substantive life is lived . . . in a way faithful to the shared understandings of the members'[17] can legitimize extremely coercive regimes. Public opinion may be misguided or unreliable. People are often misinformed, prejudiced or self-deluded, their views as much the product of socialization and various forms of indoctrination as of reasoned argument. Oppression is often accepted by the oppressed as a result of their acquiescence in the ideology inflicted on them. Thus a shared understanding that we are all, for instance, miserable sinners can underpin a 'substantive life' quite contrary to a liberal idea of justice.

Moreover, the relativist argument provides no basis for tolerating a plurality of views either within or between societies – something Walzer desires. Complete agnosticism about any foundations for truth or morality leads not to tolerance but to struggles between opposed ideologies in which might is right. If X seeks to impose a lifestyle on Y, on the grounds that Y's life will otherwise lack fulfilment, then Y can restrain X only by appealing to some principle transcending their respective subjective ideals. The equality of respect desired by Walzer might emerge naturally where there is an equitable balance of power. Outside this purely contingent situation, however, he needs a warrant for it in an objective claim about what makes all human lives worthy of our concern.

Rationalist communitarians seek to provide such a justification by arguing that the central human good that a liberal society should uphold is the capacity for autonomy. A communitarian liberalism must, therefore, be committed to maintaining an autonomy-supporting environment that secures those conditions necessary to make meaningful choices possible. This entails not merely protecting each individual's negative liberty from deliberate coercion by others, but also providing a range of worthwhile options. The danger with this thesis from a liberal point of view arises from the classic objection to all positive theories of liberty: namely, that they lead to the paternalistic imposition of a particular type of behaviour on individuals on the grounds that freedom requires the pursuit of certain goals necessary to realize their 'true' selves. The difficulty arises from trying to reconcile the requirements of the conditions for autonomy, which only flourishes in a certain kind of social set-up, with the capacity for autonomy, seen as our ability to create our own moral world. Once our capacity for autonomy becomes itself a conditioned product, then one can no longer appeal to it as an independent standard to prevent paternalistic interferences with individual liberty.[18] As Raz himself observes, 'for those who live in an autonomy-supporting environment there is no choice but to be autonomous'.[19]

This criticism may seem unfair. Raz does after all contend that autonomy presupposes what he calls 'competitive pluralism' and we have seen that liberalism cannot divorce itself from all metaphysical and moral considerations. However, Raz goes too far. He attempts to make the metaphysics do all the work in producing a well-ordered society. As a result, the pluralism which he allows turns out to be narrower than at first appears, consisting only in putatively 'worthwhile options'. Crucial to his thesis is a distinction he makes between 'self-interest' and 'personal well-being' analogous to Mill's famous division between the lower and the higher pleasures. The first relates primarily to our biological requirements and arouses 'pleasure' which, on Raz's definition, is both insatiable and non-diminishing. The second is orientated towards goals or pursuits of independent value and produces 'happiness', which Raz regards as a satiable and diminishing emotion. He argues that, whilst the pursuit of self-interest produces conflict, striving after personal well-being does not. Consequently, if the opportunities available within society only 'enshrine sound moral conceptions' then people will naturally 'choose for themselves goals which lead to a rough coincidence in their own lives of moral and personal concerns'. Social harmony will follow, in which 'by being teachers, production workers, drivers, public servants, loyal friends and family people, loyal to their communities, nature-loving and so on, [people] will be pursuing their own goals, enhancing their own well-being, and also serving their communities, and generally living in a morally worthy way'.[20]

This ethical liberal utopia, in which (only slightly to amend a famous phrase) the autonomy of each is the condition for the autonomy for all, is wildly optimistic. Not only does it underestimate the potential for moral conflict between different features of people's lives even within a single ethical code; it greatly overestimates the degree of moral agreement that a liberal society which encourages diversity and experimentation is likely to be able to sustain. As the following sections shall show, it is the job of politics, albeit informed by liberal morality, to conciliate and resolve such disputes.

To avoid the sort of difficulties Raz's theory raises, Rawls proposes a non-metaphysical political liberalism that avoids comprehensive meta-ethical claims. Yet, Raz is correct to the extent that such a conception cannot in itself be entirely neutral between conceptions of the good. At the very least, it requires an attachment to a specific set of political virtues which force us to exchange views rather than bullets and agree on equitable solutions and compromises. How deep such citizenly ethics need bite into our personal morality forms the subject of the next section.

Commonwealths

The members of clubs and communes lack the qualities required of a citizen of a liberal polity. The former are too detached and the latter too involved. The club model cannot show why it is instrumentally rational for atomistic individuals to adopt the impartial standpoint prescribed within the liberal framework and thus regulate their social interaction in a just manner. In any case, such an abstract and general framework is only part of what is needed. By itself, it cannot motivate a common concern for the quality of life or guide it towards a set of policies. Yet, as shall be argued below, it is the ability to formulate and motivate common concern and to translate it into policy that represents the true task of politics and hence of citizenship. Clubs are inherently apolitical.

Communities, by contrast, are unmistakably political. Communitarians are generally neo-Aristotelians and to accuse them of lacking a conception of citizenship may seem perverse. However, their civic humanist version of citizenship excludes politics in the modern sense of negotiation and bargaining in (until recently) smoke-filled rooms. For communitarians, politics simply involves participation in the public life of the community. It presupposes a pre-existing communal good, a 'tradition' which participants are to accept as a going concern. It does not start from debating a variety of different viewpoints about what that good might be so as to secure the emergence of a workable compromise. Indeed, the communitarian position denies both the pluralism of ends, at least within a community, and the public/private divide necessary to make sense of such a conception. Yet both are inescapable features of modern life with which a viable form of liberalism must come to terms. A liberalism posited upon a homogeneous moral community may have been possible in the eighteenth century, but will not be in the twenty-first.

The form of citizenship associated with 'commonwealths', by contrast, stems from the civic republican tradition. Deriving from Machiavelli rather than Aristotle, it treats political participation merely as the condition for retaining our liberty, rather than as essential to our self-realization. According to this line of thinking, since the rights and liberties available to us depend upon the laws, norms and priorities of our particular society, we shall be free only to the extent that we share in determining their character. As Rawls notes (*PL*, pp. 205–6), since this conception of citizenship involves no advance commitment to any *specific* conception of the good, civic republicanism is compatible with a pluralist democratic liberalism. Yet the schema implies an *unspecific* conception of the good, since it is underpinned by obligations. For, if these arrangements are to respect fairly the values and demands of all members of society, rather than just those of elites, then we have an obligation not only to participate personally in collective decision-making but also to ensure that others do too.

This conception of citizenship rests on the acceptance of duties whose discharge is a precondition for the political life of the commonwealth. They enjoin equal basic respect and concern for all others in this commonwealth of free and equal persons. The idea of respect looks to Kant's notion of autonomy, together with his thesis that to claim autonomy for oneself is to recognize that others have the same claim to be treated as ends in themselves. Free citizens of the kingdom of ends are separate and equal persons, in a sense which respects both their access to public life and their right to a private one. The idea of concern implies an equal minimum of resources, enough to make autonomy real. A degree of material independence is needed for public and private life alike, to give citizens the time and means to play their public part and literally to close the door on others for the sake of privacy.

These duties provide a substantive account of the preconditions for open-minded discussion among free and equal persons, including consideration of the social resources necessary for freedom of thought, expression and action. As *pre*conditions, they need to be metaphysically grounded and defended as reflecting *a priori* notions of what is due to individuals, so that no citizen is treated as less than a person. Then, within this framework of enablements and constraints, there will be room for politics of a practical kind to deliberate and settle matters of collective concern.

By putting duties before rights and making them preconditions of the life of a commonwealth, we hope to overcome two familiar problems for liberal attempts to accommodate pluralism. The first arises from the charge that liberals concede too much if they thin down their conception of justice so as to appeal to all points of view. There is a danger that a theory of justice thin enough to appeal to a plurality of groups will entail tolerating the intolerable. Moreover, it could be decidedly inegalitarian, prone to entrenching and legitimating rather than challenging the prevailing disparities of power and wealth. Pluralism combined with a thin theory of justice may mean capitulation to the existing distribution of power in society and an implicit endorsement of the belief that might is right. The second problem arises because metaphysics provides no substitute for politics. Our moral obligations prove too narrow to determine to whom our duty is owed or how it is to be discharged. Rights-based political moralities exacerbate this difficulty by upholding negative perfect obligations of non-interference so firmly that they cannot set about explaining why we *should* (as opposed to merely *could*) participate within forms of collective decision-making and co-operation. We shall return to this point in the discussion of welfare in the next section.

The first problem has surfaced forcefully in recent criticisms of liberalism by feminists who have remarked how the discourse of justice needs to be supplemented by an awareness of the sources of oppression.[21] It has also been central to criticisms of the Rawlsian project since its inception. On the one hand, Rawls's first principle of justice, which prescribes maximal equal liberties for all, has been criticized for being too formal. It fails to appreciate that judgements about maximal equal liberty, being necessarily qualitative rather than quantitative in nature, cannot yield definite resolutions of conflicts between liberties.[22] On the other hand, his second principle, which allows inequalities, provided that they benefit the worst off, has been attacked for failing to capture the importance of people's relative standing for their evaluation of their sense of worth. Moreover, the division between state and civil society, private and public, implied by giving the first principle lexical priority, underestimates the extent to which the equal liberties require a substantial social and economic empowerment.

These criticisms can be related to Rawls's attempt to draw a distinction between the right and the good so as to confine the *Rechtsstaat* to matters of procedural justice, while leaving its members autonomy to pursue their own good in their own way. This classic distinction is a liberal hallmark; but it has never come out cleanly. The snag is that there is no *purely* procedural objection to treating different people or groups differently. Any objection has to take the form of complaining that a particular difference is irrelevant and such questions of relevance are *moral* questions, even if they do not thereby cease to be questions of justice. For example, fairness between 'free and equal persons' rules out forms of the subjection of women for which some religions claim moral authority, even though the religion deals fairly between women (and fairly between men). The liberal retort is that no moral authority can infringe anyone's autonomy – a *moral* claim that women are free and equal persons. The liberal division between public and private is not one between justice and morality but one distinguishing moral commitments which the commonwealth makes from those where it stands aside.

Rawls's retreat from a metaphysical to a political theory of justice is a partial recognition of the point. 'Political' is meant to avoid metaphysics, thus letting argument about the merits of public policy proceed without having to settle questions of objectivity in ethics. But it is not meant to abolish all moral engagement. In a society marked by a 'reasonable pluralism', there are overlapping conceptions of the good with enough of a liberal consensus in the overlap to allow the emergence of reasonable policies like those implied by the Difference Principle. The consensus is morally committal, even if the warrant is only consensus itself.

Can a 'political' theory of justice rely on its own bootstraps? Rawls is ambivalent. Sometimes he presents the liberal overlap in communitarian guise as the historical product of the Western democratic tradition. We find this profoundly unsatisfactory, granted that traditions are not rigid. To continue the example: are there ways of treating women in contemporary Britain which are established practices, and so acceptable to an evolving tradition, but, by the test of a reasonable pluralism, unreasonable? For instance, sexual harassment and the exclusion of women from all-male clubs are well-established practices and Britain has lately incorporated new traditions which, it has been argued in a local government council chamber, include an established practice of female circumcision. By what test does a liberal deem these practices 'unreasonable'? Someone might perhaps reply that the crux is not what is in fact accepted but whether a liberal view can be got to prevail in a power-game where winners are always reasonable and losers always unreasonable. But that would be a desperate move. It would offer a way of making justice 'political' which recalls Thrasymachos' sardonic view that justice is what suits the strong. The test of a 'reasonable' pluralism, therefore, still needs a metaphysical backing.

Accordingly, Rawls now argues that an attempt to arrive at a political conception by striking a merely pragmatic balance between the various moral views found within society would be 'political in the wrong way' (*PL*, p. 40). Instead, he presents his theory of justice as a free-standing view derived from 'the fundamental idea of society as a fair system of cooperation', in the hope that 'this idea, with its index of primary goods arrived at from within, can be the focus of a reasonable overlapping consensus'. Yet without some transcendental reason why a liberal convergence should occur, this must surely remain a pious hope – particularly as he rejects as 'oppressive' any state action through education or legislation to uphold a political morality.

In arguing for some metaphysical foundations for liberalism we do not wish to run foul of the second familiar problem associated with liberal theory, namely that it is anti-political. Here we agree with Rawls that metaphysics must not swallow up the whole of morality. The political realm needs a metaphysical basis to define fairness for decision-making procedures, while setting only partial conditions on what may emerge from them. Thus who gets what, when and how, remains an issue where specific policies are to be settled by the pushing and shoving of different interests and points of view within the basic constraints. Whatever policy emerges from a due process of decision is to be deemed reasonable. Yet, to make it a 'due process', we require not only due formality about the procedure but also substantive conditions for political debate between free and equal persons. These conditions could be said to enable the emergence of a General Will, while also constraining its scope. From this perspective, the General Will is a matter not of discovering the objective, antecedent truth about the best policies but of constructing policies which are 'reasonable' by the test of whether they emerged by political horse-trading without breach of the conditions of communicative action.

Here lies the basis for a conception of liberal justice and citizenship that is both political and metaphysical. It is metaphysical in its connection with a form of Kantian universalism. However, unlike rights-based theories, which attach to certain putative 'natural' or 'basic' properties of the individual, our duty-based argument does not idealize any particular form of agency but is concerned solely with how one should act towards others.[23] Moreover, unlike Raz's ethical liberalism, it is directed to the preconditions of political communication rather than to the detailed conduct of social life at large. It is political in leaving the choice of specific policies for what is owed to whom to be determined by the deliberative process itself.

The Politics of the Middle Distance

To illustrate the merits of this approach, we offer two concrete examples. That such an exercise is possible in itself signals an advantage over rival conceptions of political justice, which so often fail to engage critically with the real world.

The first example, by way of comment on Rawls's Liberty principle, continues earlier remarks about what a 'reasonable pluralism' is to make of the position of women in a society marked by illiberal practices. In so far as the question is whether to tolerate the intolerant, then Milton's observation in *Areopagitica* seems apposite:

> I cannot praise a fugitive and cloistered virtue, unexercised and unbreathed, that never sallies out and sees her adversary, but slinks out of the race, where that immortal garland is to be run for, not without dust and heat.[24]

Insisting on a metaphysical grounding for a principle of equal liberties for all bypasses the subversive thought that unsexed, risk-inclined individuals behind a veil of ignorance might assign some women to drudgery and gamble on not turning out to be among them. The Liberty principle also cannot be classed as a matter where a liberal can agree to disagree with the intolerant, by deploring the subjection of women while recognizing the right of the oppressors to get on with it.

But this does not dispose of two more awkward aspects of the principle. What if there are women who are content with subservient roles and regard a liberal rescue as illegitimate paternalism? Since this can indeed be the case in a plural society, male authors cannot merely sulk, like knights expostulating that the infuriated damsel cannot possibly prefer the dragon they have slain to them. The point at issue concerns the status of preferences in a liberal theory. In market versions of the club, where the customer is always right, there is no scope for arguing that preferences may be contrary to real interests because shaped by the existing distribution of power. There is no need for a metaphysical liberalism to let itself be cloistered by this line. Nor, one might add, do liberal women feminists. Once the preconditions of reasonable discourse include considerations of social empowerment, however, preferences cease to be simply 'given'. Those formed after the dust and heat have subsided are to be respected and they can still be for a woman's role of a sort to disappoint a feminist. The liberal metaphysic insists on equal liberties for all, without supposing that no one could then reflectively choose to forgo some of them. But such a choice threatens the liberal trust in the spread of enlightenment and it may be that it has to be an option which only a few are allowed. In the last resort liberals cannot let the *Rechtsstaat* fade out unexercised and unbreathed.

Relatedly, there is an awkward question about the line between public and private for a theory which denies that justice can be purely a procedural notion. In homes, as in markets, acquiescence is not always to be read as consent. In this respect at least, the personal is the political. But that does not give the plural, yet liberal, commonwealth the right or duty to regulate pervasively. One can envisage a threefold grouping of issues into those where the Liberty principle must be upheld, those where it definitely forbids intervention and those in between, where the outcome is a matter for political debate. Examples are domestic violence, adult homosexuality and varieties of pornography respectively. But the topic is too complex for the present chapter and we leave it with the remark that a distinction between public and private remains as crucial for a liberalism whose notion of justice has a moral foundation as it is difficult to determine.

The second example is by way of comment on Rawls's Difference Principle. The issue of welfare distribution has been at the heart of recent debates about liberal justice. On the one hand, contractarians have sought to generate abstract rules of justice, ranging from Rawls's two principles to Nozick's historical theory of just transfer. On the other hand, communitarians have attempted to view welfare as a social good that should be distributed in accord either with the norms of a specific cultural context or with some view of human flourishing. Contractarian theories fail for the two reasons explored in section one. They cannot explain why the well-favoured will be moved to comply with a general welfare principle, once they know themselves to be among those who would do better by self-help. Moreover, they disagree so much about even the abstract character of an impartial theory of justice that not even an overlapping consensus on the matter is in sight. In short, they stand too far back from the problem. Yet, if contractarian theories are underdetermined, communitarian ones stand too close to prevailing practices and are overly specific. If the debate about how resources are to be distributed could be resolved by appealing to communal values, it could never have arisen in the first place.

The approach put forward here brings together metaphysical and political, individualistic and communitarian considerations. Libertarians argue that there can be no human right to welfare, on the grounds that there can be no correlative universal duties on anyone to help everyone in need. This argument stems from the individualism at the root of the club model and can be countered only if duties include imperfect obligations, which are wider than correlative individual rights and prior to them. Rawls's recent enthusiasm for reciprocity, as distinct from mutual self-interest, might do the trick. But his theory remains too grounded in an individualism of interests to generate a general social duty. Communitarians can, but in a form too specific to particular communities. Moreover, there is no intrinsic reason why the communitarian argument should relate one to other members of one's state rather than just to one's family or ethnic group, unless states have (or ought to have) a greater degree of homogeneity than they currently manifest.

From the republican perspective, by contrast, the denial of a universal obligation to help others falls foul of the central moral commitments of a political theory of justice.[25] The denial draws its plausibility from an implicit appeal to a model of idealized independent agents. These paragons of self-sufficiency apparently suffer none of the usual human frailties and requirements, such as the propensity to fall sick and the need for food, that lead ordinary men and women to call on the help and support of others at various times in their lives – particularly in childhood and old age. According to the duty-based view, however, a principle of universal indifference could never be adopted among ordinarily needy and vulnerable human beings. If we are only to adopt principles all can act on, then we must necessarily reject those that undermine or threaten the capacity for agency of others.

Nevertheless, the duty so established remains an imperfect obligation. This does not imply that we have no duty to do anything. Rather, the argument creates a requirement to create welfare arrangements and to allocate recipients of welfare to agents and agencies capable of supplying these needs. Institutional rights to welfare can be tailored to the character and conditions of particular societies. Such rights capture the more special obligations to help others which most of us feel we have or which, so far as the greater society is concerned, have been created through political commitments of a piecemeal nature. In other words, a metaphysics which makes sense of our moral obligations needs to be supplemented by more specific political obligations. I need to know, for example, why my general moral obligation to help others should be fulfilled by giving to the National Health Service rather than to Oxfam for relief in the Third World. This seems to us to be the only way to understand the growth of the welfare state.

Conclusion

Metaphysics is necessary to determine those minimum standards of just conduct which liberals insist are owed to all human beings. Politics enables us both to appreciate these basic obligations by bringing us into communication with our fellow citizens, and makes possible practical agreements that go beyond this bare minimum by providing the extensive public services necessary to the functioning of a well-ordered modern state. Liberal justice needs to be both metaphysical and political.

Notes

1. This chapter was originally written with the late Martin Hollis. A colleague at UEA and an inveterate collaborator, with whom I taught the Political Philosophy paper (amongst others), the article puts together our separate criticisms of Rawls's *Political Liberalism*. Martin believed Rawls (and indeed I) required more metaphysics than he (or I) owned up to, I that he also needed more politics. Like all who worked with and knew Martin, I owe him a tremendous amount and miss him greatly.
2. J. S. Mill, *On Liberty* (1859), ed. M. Warnock, London: Fontana, 1962.
3. E.g. J. Locke, *A Letter Concerning Toleration* (1689), ed. J. Horton and S. Mendus, London: Routledge, 1991.
4. E.g. Mill, *On Liberty*.
5. J.-J. Rousseau, *The Social Contract and Discourses* (1762), ed. G. D. H. Cole, London: Dent, 1973.

6. J. Rawls, *Political Liberalism*, New York: Columbia University Press, 1993 (hereafter referred to in the text as *PL*), p. 37.
7. Notably in J. Rawls, 'Justice as Fairness: Political not Metaphysical', *Philosophy and Public Affairs*, 14 (1985): 223–51 (hereafter referred to in the text as *JF*), revised in *PL* as Lecture 1).
8. T. Hobbes, *Leviathan* (1651), ed. Richard Tuck, Cambridge: Cambridge University Press, 1991, Ch. 13.
9. Hobbes, *Leviathan* , Ch. 17.
10. Hobbes, *Leviathan*, Ch. 15.
11. J. Rawls, *A Theory of Justice*, Oxford: Oxford University Press, 1971.
12. D. Gauthier, *Morals by Agreement*, Oxford: Oxford University Press, 1986.
13. Rousseau, *Social Contract*, Bk I., Ch. 8.
14. M. Walzer, *Spheres of Justice: A Defence of Pluralism and Equality*, Oxford: Martin Robertson, 1983.
15. J. Raz, *The Morality of Freedom*, Oxford: Oxford University Press, 1986.
16. Walzer, *Spheres of Justice*, p. 7.
17. Walzer, *Spheres of Justice*, p. 313.
18. See S. Mendus, 'Liberty and Autonomy', *Proceedings of the Aristotelian Society*, 87 (1986/7): 107–20.
19. Raz, *Morality of Freedom*, p. 391.
20. Raz, *Morality of Freedom*, p. 215.
21. E.g. I. M. Young, *Justice and the Politics of Difference*, Princeton: Princeton University Press, 1990.
22. O. O'Neill, 'The Most Extensive Liberty', *Proceedings of the Aristotelian Society*, 80 (1979/80): 45–59.
23. O. O'Neill, *Constructions of Reason: Explorations of Kant's Practical Philosophy*, Cambridge: Cambridge University Press, 1989 for this reading of Kant.
24. J. Milton, *Areopagitica* (1644), London: Nonesuch, 1952.
25. What follows is inspired by O'Neill, *Constructions of Reason*, and developed in Chapter 8 below.

CHAPTER 7

Moralizing Markets[1]

The past two decades have been characterized by a waning confidence in the capacity of the state to shape human affairs wisely.[2] This loss of faith has extended far beyond the rejection of Soviet-style centralized economic planning. Even before the collapse of the former Eastern bloc in 1989, Western democracies had progressively accepted that market forces could deliver an ever broader range of services than had hitherto been regarded as either possible or socially responsible. Particularly in Britain, but increasingly elsewhere in Europe, the public sector has been dramatically diminished in both size and scope. Not only has the state's economic role been greatly reduced by numerous privatizations of nationalized industries, it has also either relinquished or subjected to market forces a whole series of its former administrative, social policy and welfare functions as well.

Two arguments lie behind the case for supplanting state institutions by market mechanisms over a wider area of social and economic life. First, there is the claim that markets are simply more efficient and less corrupt in delivering and co-ordinating services and responding to consumer demand than state bureaucracies. Second, there is the belief that the distribution of burdens and benefits provided by the market is in some sense more just. Although distinct, the efficiency and the morality arguments are generally combined in one way or another. Two kinds of combination currently dominate. Popular defences of the market tend to appeal to a Victorian ethic of desert worthy of Samuel Smiles. This view's proponents suggest the efficiency of the market results in large part from it rewarding effort, contribution and merit, thereby encouraging individuals to cultivate the virtues of thrift, self-help, integrity and industry. Contemporary libertarian defences of the market, by contrast, drop these traditional liberal arguments for the substantive justice of *laissez-faire* capitalism. Instead, they stress the justice of the rules governing individual transactions. From this perspective,

128

the fairness of the market depends on the justice of its procedures rather its outcomes. Markets are said to embody and require individual freedom and pluralism, promoting and employing the freedom of choice of capitalist, worker and consumer alike. Whereas the first view regards the efficiency of markets as the reward for virtue, therefore, the second reduces virtue to a function of market efficiency.

The radical difference between the two points of view is particularly clear when discussing the limits of markets. The first view marks these limits in terms of their moral appropriateness; the second tends to identify moral inappropriateness with falling efficiency. The recent rolling back of the state has been largely conducted in terms of the second view. In many respects, it favours the extension of markets much more than the first. For it places the burden of proof on the statists to show why markets will not work, rather than obliging their proponents to explain why they are suitable in the first place. Even critics of the market increasingly couch their reservations in these terms. They point to market failure in the provision of public goods or the control of externalities, or raise technical problems about employing market mechanisms to deliver certain services, such as health care, rather than objecting to the substantive justice of the results of market provision.

Efficiency arguments have their drawbacks, however. The disenchantment of the market system promoted by the second view risks jeopardizing its legitimacy. As Irving Kristol has remarked: 'in the same way as men cannot for long tolerate a sense of spiritual meaninglessness in their individual lives, so they cannot for long accept a society in which power, privilege, and property are not distributed according to some morally meaningful criteria.'[3] For this reason, Hayek came close to suggesting that the popular, moralistic defence should be maintained as a 'noble lie' in order to retain support for market institutions – a position that would appear to be endorsed by nearly all New Right politicians.[4] Libertarian philosophers would be wrong to regard such considerations as simply a matter of political rhetoric, however, especially when their advocacy of the justice of certain principles is so intimately tied up with the claim that they promote efficient markets. For if it turns out that where people no longer accept their morality markets cease to be viable, then attempts to link the justice of markets simply to procedures that foster their efficient running will prove self-defeating. The moral limits of markets will mark the limits of their efficiency rather than the other way around.

This chapter explores this second view. I shall contend that, whilst it offers cogent criticisms of the first view's reliance on an outmoded, and ultimately implausible, Victorian desert ethic, it fails as a moral defence of the market. Neither individual freedom nor pluralism are as intrinsically linked to markets as these theorists contend. Indeed the very moral grounds they give for promoting the market also justify placing it within a more substantive moral framework that pays attention to outcomes.

The Efficiency and Justice of Markets: the Austrian Case

By far the most powerful arguments in favour of markets as against state planning have been offered by the Austrian school. The Austrian case is essentially epistemic.[5] The basic elements of their thesis were first developed by Ludwig von Mises in the context of the socialist calculation debate of the 1920s. He argued that rational economic planning required an efficient allocation of resources and that this in turn depended upon a knowledge of prices, which provide information on the relative scarcities of capital goods. In a market of any size and complexity, these prices are determined by the innumerable interactions between buyers and sellers and are in constant flux. He believed it would be impossible for socialist planners to solve millions of simultaneous equations in order to determine the relative value of productive resources. Such information could only be provided by a market based on private property in the means of production.

Mises's style of argument was essentially *a priori* and logical. Part of his case related to the putative computational complexities involved in simulating market pricing and the calculational impossibility of a planned economy. In fact, economists believe that in principle the relevant equations could be solved. However, his writings also contain a more profound thesis that suggests that monetary prices act as necessary 'aids to the human mind' that could only be generated within the context of a market exchange system based on private property. According to this view, the requisite knowledge needed by planners would not exist outside of a free market economy. Hayek and later Austrian theorists picked up on this aspect of Mises's work but gave it a somewhat different epistemological basis. Hayek pointed out that the difficulty confronting planners is not computational but practical. It relates to the problem of how one central agency could gather the huge amount of information necessary for accurate pricing, much of it of a concrete and contextual nature, such as the capacity of the available machines and work-force in a given locale, which is hard to represent in statistical form and which is in any case constantly changing. Moreover, as Michael Polanyi observed, much of this knowledge is tacit, embodied in practices, dispositions and intuitions that are unformulateable and often not fully conscious to the individuals concerned. Central planning not only cannot employ such knowledge, it would also probably destroy it in the attempt to articulate it in an explicit manner. The achievement of the market was its ability to collect and transmit this dispersed, local and largely transient knowledge in an intelligible and undistorted form through price signals.

G. L. S. Shackle took the Austrian approach further by developing the idea of subjective value that runs through much of their work in ways that bring out the temporal dimension of all economic transactions. According to Shackle, all possible alternatives present themselves first to individual minds. He argued that human choice involved individuals imagining not only alternative feasible uses of the means to hand, but also many alternative outcomes of each use. As Shand remarks, 'an important corollary of this view is the belief that human events are inherently unpredictable'.[6] The implications of this argument for the Austrian critique of a centrally directed economy have been brought out by James Buchanan amongst others. Central planning involves second-guessing the future. However, the economy is an open system, subject to conceptual innovation and alterations in people's subjective expectations, on the one hand, and to unpredictable changes from social, political and natural forces, on the other. As Buchanan, drawing on Shackle's work, points out, under these conditions the problem facing the economic planners is not just the co-ordination of already existing dispersed knowledge; it is much more the even greater difficulty of drawing together knowledge that does not yet exist.

What the Austrians spotted was that expectations sum to 'create' the future, so that prediction is not what markets do or planners should seek to ape (or at least, not wholly). Most recently, Israel Kirzner has built on this insight.[7] He stresses an aspect of the market first identified by Hayek: its role as a 'discovery procedure'. Whereas neoclassical economics regards the achievement of the market to consist 'in its ability to generate precisely that set of equilibrium prices that will inspire myriads of dovetailing decisions, each of them made with complete knowledge of all prices', the Austrian school stresses 'the deep fog of ignorance that surrounds each and every decision in the market'. On this second view, the merit of the market resides in the way in which

> starting at each instant of time with a background of mutual ignorance among market participants, the market process spontaneously offers the incentives and opportunities that inspire market participants continually to push back the fog of mutual ignorance. It is this fog of mutual ignorance that is to blame for the market's failure to achieve complete dovetailing of decisions; it is because the market process is continually generating insights which operate towards dispelling this fog, that markets achieve the degree of dovetailing among decisions that they do.[8]

Once again, there can be no complete body of knowledge on which central planners might draw, since this knowledge is discovered (and in part created) only through the weeding out of bad practices and products and the encouragement of good ones promoted by the competitive market.

The issue of incentives represents the point at which the Austrians' argument for the efficiency of the market meets up with their case for its justice. Given their understanding of how markets work, social justice no longer makes sense. Social justice is concerned with distributing the burdens and benefits of society according to some desirable pattern. However, the Austrians contend that market distributions neither are nor could be the product of any deliberate human agency. The unemployment and poverty which often result from market processes are not intended by either the consumers or the producers who may have inadvertently brought them about, nor could they have been. They are simply the unintended consequences of millions of acts of buying and selling. As such, they are to be regarded as misfortunes rather than injustices. Similarly, the rewards of the market are also often simply the result of luck. However, any attempt to rectify this situation would almost certainly be arbitrary and itself unjust. Not only are the concepts of need and desert essentially contestable and often in conflict with each other; in the absence of an omniscient and omnipotent central agency it would be impossible – even if the meaning of these terms were agreed – to know whose need was greatest or who had through their effort or contribution come to deserve the most. Moreover, the attempt to match resources to need or desert will break the link between reward and services rendered that is vital to market efficiency, as the disastrous results of the corrupt incentive structures of the planned economies of the former Eastern bloc amply demonstrate.

Once again Kirzner radicalizes this thesis. He insists that we cannot even know what there is to distribute prior to its distribution. In other words, the market's role is not only that of co-ordinating the dispersed actions of millions of individuals acting on their own local knowledge; the process of co-ordination is also one of creation in which the social pie is 'discovered' in the course of production and market exchange. From this perspective, there is no pre-existing pie to be sliced up and distributed. Rather, 'individual incomes are earned *simultaneously* with the process through which the size and composition of the supposed "pie" are determined'.[9] To the extent that the incentive of the profit motive encourages entrepreneurial activity, the resulting distribution can be regarded as just in a far more positive sense than Hayek and earlier Austrians maintained. It is not simply a matter of no injustice having been done in obtaining it. According to Kirzner, the uncertainty that pervades the market forces the entrepreneur to discover opportunities for enterprise and profit. Of course, a certain degree of accident and good fortune as well as flair may be involved in this discovery. Nevertheless, he argues that on the basis of a 'finders keepers' principle entrepreneurs can be regarded as entitled to the full amount of profit that results from their discoveries. Moreover, he believes that an appeal to the 'finders keepers' principle is likely to endow the market with a greater degree of popular moral legitimacy than a purely procedural theory of justice such as Hayek's or Nozick's.

The key element of the Austrian case against social justice, therefore, concerns the inseparability of the laws of distribution from the laws of production. The functional distribution of wages, for example, is linked with the marginal productivity of labour and redistribution changes that equation. Similarly, alterations in the marginal tax structure change the pattern of expectations motivating economic agents, and hence the amount of wealth produced, and not just the pattern of given outcomes. As a result, the Austrian school reject not just socialist planning but also market socialism – both the Taylor–Lange and the worker–management models. Unlike central planning, market socialism overcomes, theoretically at least, some of the epistemological objections raised by the Austrians to socialist economic systems. Although investment, and in the Taylor–Lange model the prices of production goods as well, are centrally determined, the planners use exactly the same market-generated information of surpluses and shortages deriving from consumer demand to make their decisions as individual producers employ in a free market. Even though there are doubts about how effectively they could process this information, the root difficulty does not lie here so much as in whether workers, managers and bureaucrats within such systems would have the motivation to employ it.[10] In capitalist systems, the lure of pure profit sets in motion the entrepreneurial discovery procedure in which individuals tend to learn how to arrange resources in a more effective manner to satisfy the demands of others. Moreover, private ownership makes it less likely individuals will be constrained by others from using their own knowledge. In this way, the incentive argument reinforces the epistemic case for the market and leads the Austrians to the conclusion that private property comprises an essential precondition for the learning process of competition to be enacted.

Freedom and the Market

The Austrian school provides a realistic and compelling account of how markets work, but one (as I noted) that is to a high degree morally disenchanted compared to the Victorian model outlined earlier. Even Kirzner's thesis seems rather thin in comparison, for there is a world of difference between his entrepreneur and Smiles's self-made captains of industry. The first person to spot and pick up a beautiful shell on the beach may be entitled to it, but it is hard to say whether he or she is morally responsible for it being there in the first place and hence 'deserve' or 'merit' it in some more substantive sense.

In this section and the next, I wish to argue that, contrary to the Austrian view, the fact that the market itself may work in an amoral (though procedurally just) manner does not prevent us from seeking to set it within a wider moral framework whereby we can judge its outcomes and demarcate its moral boundaries. This argument involves two elements relating to the value of freedom which, as we shall see, provides the Austrians with their principal and strongest moral defence of markets. First, a free market presupposes but does not necessarily create a free society – indeed markets may destroy it. Second, many morally valuable non-market activities may be undermined if forced to adopt the market ethos, thereby undermining freedom of choice and pluralism. I shall discuss each in turn.

The Austrian school tends to extrapolate its account of justice from its understanding of how the market works. This has the effect of making an efficient market by definition just. However, this market-centric view begs the question of the justice of what John Rawls has called the basic structure of society: the background conditions and social circumstances within which market transactions take place.[11] The Austrians' account of the market's moral attractions trades on the idea that society should reflect the free choices and fair agreements of innumerable individuals over time. But even if market processes are procedurally free and fair, critics contend their highly unequal outcomes will diminish the substantive and ultimately the procedural freedom and fairness of later exchanges. Freedom for the pike is death for the minnow, so we need to protect a minnow's liberties to prevent him being eaten. If that critique can be sustained, then a strong case will exist for periodic redistribution to maintain a level playing field amongst employers, workers and consumers.

The Austrians, in common with other libertarians, have responded to this criticism by adopting two types of moral argument: utilitarianism and natural rights theory, with a third group – represented most noticeably by Hayek – hovering uncomfortably between the two.[12] The utilitarian response, employed most clearly by Mises, states free markets promote economic growth and so maximize want satisfaction and individual choice. Minnows do less well than pikes, but the trickle-down effect means the pool can now sustain more and fatter minnows than ever before. However, this tack proves incompatible with the Austrian defence of market morality in terms of individual freedom and pluralism, and ultimately with their understanding of how markets work. For a start, the utilitarian argument suggests the free and fair agreements of the market can be overridden whenever that might increase social welfare – a position that really does suggest that the market is only moral in so far as it is efficient. Thus the freedom of individual minnows can be sacrificed for the greater good. Libertarians may have no trouble with that consequence if it is only a few workers and the odd incompetent businessman who suffer. But this approach also suggests we should see if the trickle-down effect really does operate. If unemployment levels could be stemmed through state intervention, or welfare increased through redistribution, then we should adopt such measures. Consideration of the adverse as well as the beneficial consequences of the market are now a matter of legitimate moral concern. Utilitarianism is also no friend to pluralism. As we shall see in the next section, economic growth usually erodes particular choices at the same time as expanding others. Even if one accepts that for the majority the quantity of choices is probably (if not necessarily) increased by economic development, this tells us nothing about their intrinsic worth for human beings. More importantly, utilitarianism is the planner's philosophy par excellence. The utilitarian contention that interpersonal comparisons are possible, and that all human satisfactions and goods can be regarded as commensurable, conflicts directly with the Austrians' epistemic case for the market as a mechanism that is uniquely capable of responding to the activities of diverse and widely dispersed individuals pursuing distinct and often incommensurable ends that cannot be rationally compared or co-ordinated by any one agency operating according to any single scale of values.[13]

More often, therefore, the Austrians and other libertarians, such as Nozick, claim the justice of markets rests on their contribution to and protection of individual rights. Once again, justice is concerned entirely with the market process. Justice, the Austrians maintain, is simply a matter of respecting the negative rights of individuals not to be directly and intentionally interfered with. Any more substantive account would be at variance with the nature of the market itself. As we shall see below, the absence of coercion involves more than a lack of direct, intentional physical interference, however. A wider range of human action than the Austrians acknowledge, including much market activity, can be causally related to the imposition of blocks on individual freedom.[14] Moreover, negative liberty has an additional dimension to mere non-interference – namely, the absence of domination, viewed as the capacity to exercise arbitrary power over another's life. Securing non-domination requires a degree of socio-economic independence on the part of citizens that freedom of contract alone does not secure.[15]

The Austrian account of a just market order takes the initial distribution of resources as a historical datum that can be given no more moral foundation than any other desirable patterned state of affairs. When the broader aspects of negative freedom are taken into account, though, such issues are unavoidable and the relevance of Rawls's concern with the justice of the basic structure becomes clear. It will be necessary to specify a set of resources and opportunities and a capacity to employ them which individuals need to have if they are to pursue their goals unhindered and undominated by others. In particular, it will be impossible to ignore – as libertarians try to – the ways the accumulated results of many procedurally just exchanges may erode the preconditions for free action for many groups of people. The down side of 'finders keepers' is that 'losers weepers'. Whilst the need to correct entrepreneurial failure is undoubtedly as important to the efficient working of the market as the reward of entrepreneurial success, not all of those who suffer do so as a result of their own freely chosen actions or inaction. Moreover, those who find themselves unemployed or destitute are vulnerable to exploitation and the capricious actions of unscrupulous employers and can find themselves unhealthily beholden to those who offer succour.

Libertarians raise three standard objections to such observations. First, they contend that it is impossible to provide an objective assessment of when these preconditions have been met, so that spending on welfare is infinitely elastic. But exactly the same objection can be made about ensuring the preconditions of narrowly defined liberty: what counts as coercion is similarly contestable, and the measures that might be taken to secure its absence just as prone to inflation. One can spend as much on police forces as on hospitals.[16]

Second, they maintain, as I noted above, that because the effects of market outcomes for any particular individual can be neither intended nor foreseen, the inequalities resulting from the free operation of the market cannot be regarded as unjust. However, whilst this might be true for specific individuals, it is perfectly foreseeable that some groups are prone to lose out. In addition, random individuals apart, it is also predictable that those who start with the least resources will tend to end up with least. When such likely consequences are known in advance, it is not necessary for us to have been directly or intentionally instrumental in their occurring for us to have a moral responsibility to rectify them. It is sufficient to have participated in a system that we know produces such results. Indeed, no involvement may even be necessary to generate the requisite obligations if we find ourselves able to help others. As J. S. Mill famously argued in *On Liberty*, a failure to act in such circumstances can be as much of a hindrance to individual liberty as positive action.

Finally, libertarians claim that allowing the rectification of inequalities opens the door to arbitrary and continuous interference in market processes by tyrannical social and economic engineers. This concern is where worries about non-interference meet the need to guard against domination. However, critics of economic liberalism point out that unless the state can guarantee the capacity to act independently by ensuring a certain level of educational attainment, a measure of social security, civil and political rights that give access to a system of redress and so on, then supposedly free economic agents will be similarly prone to tyrannical manipulation. No actual interference may be needed for the poor and powerless to adopt craven behaviour that seeks to pre-empt that possibility. The prevention of tyranny by private and public bodies alike requires not the absence of state controls but their regulated presence.

Hayek came to a somewhat confused appreciation of this last insight when noting that liberty depended on the rule rather than the silence of the law. Where he went wrong was in supposing that only the civil law could be framed in an appropriately non-arbitrary way. However, a system of criminal justice and a welfare system have similar benefits and risks. In each case, the goal is to secure people against harms and provide them with a stable environment in which they can plan and act free from the arbitrary interference of others. All desire these benefits. Yet, unless all enjoy them to an equally intense degree, the more privileged will be able to dominate the rest. Even libertarians accept this thesis with respect to civil rights. They acknowledge a free market depends on all parties having a formally equal status, so that contracts may be freely entered into. All that is being pointed out here, is that social rights may also be necessary to achieve this goal.

In this respect, negative liberty is both a social and a common good that can only be secured through collective action organized by a public body such as a state. Since any collective agency possesses coercive power it too needs to be checked and controlled. To avoid the dangers whilst getting the advantages of collective arrangements involves so designing the political system that laws are framed and applied in a regular manner so as to promote the common interests of citizens. As I have argued elsewhere,[17] though Hayek's formal criteria of universality and generality offer insufficient guarantees, and are sometimes inappropriate, he rightly saw the separation and balance of powers as more significant than a written constitution and judicial review in ensuring law gets made in appropriate ways.

It is worth noting that there is a growing body of evidence to suggest that markets work best when such regulative and welfare structures are in place.[18] They create the confidence needed to engage in entrepreneurial activity and create bonds of trust that discourage free-riding and other attempts to undermine the rules of market competition. Not all Austrians have been totally unconcerned with this issue. However, they have tended to argue that these supportive structures themselves spontaneously evolve in much the same way as the market itself. This thesis, however, allows the supporters of the mixed economy welfare states that emerged after the Second World War to argue that these institutions are themselves to be regarded as spontaneous social responses to various forms of market failure. Moreover, it is a singularly optimistic view that ignores the ways in which markets themselves can undermine their own moral foundations.

Markets and Pluralism

Securing individual freedom and choice also involves investigating the potentially pernicious impact of markets on non-market areas of social life. Another fundamental, yet similarly curiously unarticulated, moral argument behind the Austrian case for market, is the fact of moral pluralism. As we saw, a major part of the Austrian critique of state provision stems from the claim that there is no single criterion by which goods could be allocated. The market is praised for being an impersonal and morally neutral mechanism that allows individuals to define their own good in their own way. However, the proposition that there are a number of distinct and incommensurable kinds of good can also be used to set moral boundaries to the extension of the market on the grounds that market distributions may not always be suitable to the good in question.

This argument has been articulated most forcefully by Michael Walzer in *Spheres of Justice*. Walzer argues that goods cannot be taken as givens to be distributed according to certain universal criteria. Goods are conceived and created before they are distributed, with the result that they come into people's hands laden with value as to what they are and what they are for. Consequently, different goods in different contexts will generate different distributive criteria.[19] When bread represents the body of Christ it will need to be regarded somewhat differently to when it represents the staff of life, for example. Walzer contends the market fails to respect the plurality of goods because it treats them all as being commensurable with each other and capable of conversion into money. Rather than being a neutral medium, as supporters of the market often claim, money 'is in practice a dominant good', one 'that is monopolised by people who possess a special talent for bargaining and trading'. Walzer believes there is a danger within capitalist societies of 'market imperialism', the dominance over all other distributive spheres by the power of money. Indeed, he goes so far as to state that 'a radically laissez-faire economy would be like a totalitarian state' in this respect, transforming every social good into a commodity.[20]

Walzer's analysis is arguably a little crude, but the underlying worry of his thesis is, I believe, highly relevant to the theme of the moral boundaries of markets.[21] The crudeness lies in making the commodification of goods his main target. True, certain goods seem perverted or unobtainable in monetary terms – as the Beatles memorably put it, 'money can't buy you love', although it may purchase sex. However, human beings cannot live on love alone, and even the most collective and non-monetary organizations, such as families, will need to reflect the restrictions of limited resources in budgetary terms when identifying their priorities. The problem of market imperialism lies not so much in the extension of the sphere of money and commodities, inappropriate though this sometimes is in certain limited areas, as in the dominance of the market ethos. The two issues are often conflated by supporters and critics of the market alike, but one can clearly acknowledge the need for budgets without believing that they need or should be always set in a market manner.

The extension of the market ethos to all areas of public life in the name of financial accountability has formed a dominant theme of British politics over the last decade. The basic rationale for this policy stems from the assertion of the public choice school that civil servants, doctors, academics and other members of the professions are, like everyone else, essentially motivated by the desire for personal financial and status advancement. From this perspective, professional ethics simply serve as a cover whereby the apparatus of the welfare state has come to be organized for the benefit of those who provide and control its services rather than for the taxpayers who finance and occasionally consume them. Bureaucratic control, no matter how worthy the code of practice and norms that are said to inform it, always distorts the incentive structure by entrenching the power of the self-serving apparatchiks who manage the administration. Public services must therefore either be returned to the private sector or, where this seems either politically or economically inexpedient, turned into internal markets, as in proposals for student vouchers and the Thatcher and Major administrations' National Health Service reforms.[22]

Recent empirical studies contest the assumptions on which these extensions of the market ethos are made.[23] If, however, it is wrong to assume that *homo economicus* operates in each and every sphere of social life, then there may well be good grounds for regarding the growing domination of market norms as not only misconceived but as morally illegitimate. The reasons for this moral illegitimacy can be seen by returning to Walzer's account of the embeddedness of goods in specific social and cultural contexts or practices.[24] According to this thesis, the criteria which we use to judge individual actions and the way we conceive the goods to be distributed are intrinsic to the practice concerned. The commonest analogy is with games, where success and enjoyment in participating in the activity can only be appreciated by adopting an internal point of view. Of course, external goods and especially financial rewards may play a part in people's involvement in a given practice, especially if that is how they earn their living, but the pursuit of these rewards must not come to dominate if the practice is not to be destroyed. Rather, they must only be allocated according to criteria defined by the practice itself.

When people complain about the imperialism of the market it is almost always with reference to this kind of distortion of the incentive structure of certain practices. Those who bemoan the commercialization of sport, for example, tend to do so not because they necessarily object to tennis or football players being paid astronomical sums of money 'per se', but because they believe the pursuit of these rewards has often led to an illegitimate interference with the rules of the game, as when extra rest periods get added to make room for commercial breaks on television or rule changes are made to secure greater 'entertainment' value. Similarly, and more importantly, those who worry about the introduction of the market into the provision of certain public services such as health and education do so not because they do not wish value for money or accountability in the delivery of these goods, but because they fear that it will destroy the internal connection between standards of performance and the type of good being delivered by focusing the attention of service providers on the acquisition of the external good of money. In other words, contrary to the public choice school, they argue that the market will introduce precisely those forms of corruption it was intended to remove.

Such corruption occurs, in part, because consumer preferences may be both misinformed about the practice or at odds with it, and in part because, as a result, success in acquiring external goods need not dovetail neatly with the provision of internal goods. Of course, supporters of the market generally argue that the consequent alterations of practices and the goods they deliver should be considered highly desirable and a reflection of consumer choice. However, there are two prime objections to this move, both of which relate back to our earlier discussion of freedom. First, freedom of choice assumes the existence of a range of worthwhile options from which individuals can choose, embodying different aspects of human flourishing. A commitment to the fostering of this freedom, therefore, will necessarily involve the protection of a wide range of cultural and other goods and practices irrespective of how many individuals at any given time express a preference for participating in them. Second, freedom of choice implies a capacity to discriminate. One does not come into the world possessing this capacity, nor do people autonomously develop it. It is in large part acquired through education, culture and other forms of socialization. Once again, the practices that define and cultivate this capacity may well need to be protected from market choices which fail to differentiate between reflective and conditioned preferences.

For both these reasons, the protection of moral pluralism can be regarded as part of the basic or background structure within which the market works. Indeed, there are grounds for regarding a number of putatively market institutions as part of this basic structure. Such would appear to be the rationale of the neo-corporatist policies of such capitalist economies as Austria, Germany and Japan, where the internal relations of companies are protected from the market ethos advocated by Anglo-American free market-eers and greater attention is paid to securing investment in long-term research and development rather than short-term profits for share holders. Finally, the recognition that certain institutions and goods can generate different incentive structures to the market that are just as valuable suggests that the motivational problem associated with socialism may not be as intractable as is sometimes claimed. A public service ethos may not be a viable alternative to the market ethos, but advocates of both the mixed economy and market socialism may be correct to suggest that it forms a necessary and workable complement to it.

Conclusion

Economic libertarians give accounts of morality and justice that are internal to their understanding of the nature of markets. The argument presented here has been that such internal perspectives overlook the wider moral framework within which markets operate and which provides the conditions for the freedom of the producer, entrepreneur and the well-informed consumer. In addition, there may well be forms of activity antithetical to the market ethos that are nevertheless worth maintaining for their own sake. There are also moral grounds for taking responsibility for the victims of market failure. In all these cases the moral legitimacy of markets turns on recognizing their limits.

Notes

1. I am grateful to Jeffrey Friedman, the editor of *Critical Review*, where this piece first appeared, two anonymous referees and my colleagues Martin Hollis and Shaun Hargreaves-Heap for useful comments on an earlier draft.
2. As Alexander Shand observes in the introduction to *Free Market Morality: The Political Economy of the Austrian School*, New York: Routledge, 1990, p. 1: 'during the last

decade many confident and widely agreed beliefs as to the ability of the state or its agencies to shape human affairs wisely have been severely shaken.'

3. Irving Kristol, ' "When Virtue Loses All Her Loveliness": Some Reflections on Capitalism and "The Free Society" ', *The Public Interest*, 21 (1970): 8.

4. F. A. Hayek, *Law, Legislation and Liberty: The Mirage of Social Justice*, London: Routledge, 1976, pp. 73–4.

5. See Shand, *Free Market Morality*, Part I and John Gray, *The Moral Foundations of Market Institutions*, London: IEA Health and Welfare Unit, Choice in Welfare No. 10, 1992, Chs 1 and 2, whose arguments I here summarize.

6. Shand, *Free Market Morality*, p. 26.

7. I. Kirzner, *Discovery, Capitalism and Distributive Justice*, Oxford: Blackwell, 1989.

8. Kirzner, *Discovery, Capitalism and Distributive Justice*, p. 11.

9. Kirzner, *Discovery, Capitalism and Distributive Justice*, p. 8.

10. See Allen Buchanan, *Ethics, Efficiency and the Market*, Totowa: Rowman and Littlefield, 1988, pp. 111–14.

11. See John Rawls, *Political Liberalism*, New York: Columbia University Press, 1993, Lecture VII.

12. This tension within Hayek's work forms the main theme of Chandran Kukathas's *Hayek and Modern Liberalism*, Oxford: Clarendon Press, 1989. As H. L. A. Hart noted, the same tension runs through most recent political philosophy. See his 'Between Utility and Rights', in A. Ryan (ed.), *The Idea of Freedom*, Oxford: Oxford University Press, 1979.

13. It is sometimes argued that indirect utilitarianism avoids these difficulties. For a detailed argument that it does not, see John Gray (who attributes this thesis to Hayek) 'Hayek on Liberty, Rights and Justice', in *Liberalisms: Essays in Political Philosophy*, New York: Routledge, 1989, Ch. 6.

14. See Onora O'Neill, 'Between Consenting Adults', *Philosophy and Public Affairs*, 14 (1985): 252–77 and D. Miller, 'Constraints on Freedom', *Ethics*, 94 (1983–4): 66–86.

15. For the republican concept of 'non-domination' as a negative view of liberty, and its consequences for how we ensure a free market, see P. Pettit, *Republicanism: A Theory of Freedom and Government*, Oxford: Clarendon Press, 1997, Ch. 2 and pp. 140–3, 158–65.

16. I develop this argument in Chapter 9, section 1.

17. See R. Bellamy, ' "Dethroning Politics": Constitutionalism, Liberalism and Democracy in the Political Thought of F. A. Hayek', *British Journal of Political Science*, 24 (1994): 419–41 and *Liberalism and Pluralism: Towards a Politics of Compromise*, London: Routledge, 1999, Ch. 1.

18. See Michel Albert, *Capitalisme contre capitalisme*, Paris: Editions du Seuil, 1991. Gray, *Moral Foundations*, Ch. 7 defends the German notion of the social market economy on these grounds.

19. Michael Walzer, *Spheres of Justice: A Defence of Pluralism and Equality*, Oxford: Martin Robertson, 1983, Ch. 1.

20. Walzer, *Spheres of Justice*, pp. 21–2, 119–20.

21. I owe the refinement of Walzer's thesis and much of the argument that follows to Russell Keat, 'The Moral Boundaries of the Market', in Colin Crouch and David Marquand (eds), *Ethics and Markets*, Oxford: Blackwell, 1993, pp. 6–20. See also my 'Justice in the Community: Walzer on Pluralism, Equality and Democracy', in D.

Boucher and P. Kelly (eds), *Social Justice: From Hume to Walzer*, London: Routledge, 1998, Ch. 9 and *Liberalism and Pluralism*, Ch. 3.

22. For an argument along these lines, see Shand, *Free Market Morality*, Part IV.

23. See Leif Lewin, *Self-Interest and Public Interest in Western Politics*, Oxford: Oxford University Press, 1991, for a detailed empirical assessment of the public choice account of democratic politics, that reveals citizens, politicians and bureaucrats to be motivated by far broader considerations of the long-term common good than the theory allows.

24. See Keat, 'The Moral Boundaries', pp. 16–20.

CHAPTER 8

Liberal Rights, Socialist Goals and the Duties of Citizenship[1]

The question of the compatibility of socialism and rights is usually seen as part of the broader issue of the desirability or possibility of combining socialist goals with liberal means.[2] On the whole, these two traditions have been regarded by their respective adherents as intellectually and politically antagonistic. Liberals have argued that only a capitalist economy can guarantee the preservation of individual rights and political liberties,[3] and this view has been mirrored in many socialist condemnations of such principles as intrinsically 'bourgeois' and only necessary within an economic system based on private property and exploitative contractual relations between owners of capital and sellers of labour.[4] However, a number of distinguished thinkers have attempted to combine the liberal respect for individual liberty with the socialist concern with social justice. John Stuart Mill, to mention the most prominent exponent of this school of thought, regarded this proposition as 'the social problem of the future'.[5] More recently, socialists sympathetic to the activities of dissidents within the Communist block on the one hand, and disturbed by the erosion of civil liberties and welfare services by New Right governments in the West on the other, have returned to the Millian project with renewed interest. These writers maintain that the liberal commitment to giving citizens an equal right to freedom can only be met within a socialist economy which grants individuals social rights to the resources required for the full exercise of those civil and political rights traditionally associated with liberalism. Socialism, on this view, is presented as the natural extension of liberal values, and the political shortcomings of both existing socialist countries and Western democracies are attributed to a failure to appreciate the close relationship between the two systems of thought.[6]

This chapter explores the rights-based road to socialism. Such an approach has manifest practical attractions for socialists seeking to tackle increasingly aggressive liberal governments on their own terms, and seems to offer the possibility of achieving the new society through gradual reform of the old. My primary concern will be with the theoretical coherence of these arguments, although I believe my conclusions have some (negative) consequences for assessing their pragmatic usefulness. The first section discusses the nature of liberal rights. I examine whether they are relative to a specific set of social arrangements or of universal application, providing criteria for establishing the legitimacy of any modern society. I argue that in important respects liberal rights only make sense within a particular sort of community, and that this fact renders the use of the language of rights to achieve the transition to socialism a dubious undertaking. Once all rights, liberal or otherwise, are seen to be relative to particular social and personal values rather than 'natural', one can no longer talk of expanding rights in the way those thinkers who see socialism as an extension of liberalism claim. The second section explores the question of whether socialists might nevertheless require a framework of rights analogous to the liberal's. Whilst I maintain they do, in section three I challenge the view that rights have to be isolated from the normal political process within a rigid constitution if individual liberty is to be preserved. I contend that freedom in both liberal and socialist systems is realized only through political institutions giving citizens control over the shape of their public culture, an arrangement which is inhibited rather than promoted by a constitutionally entrenched Bill of Rights. I argue instead for a procedural view of rights as the outcome of a democratic process.

The Nature of Liberal Rights

Most liberals see rights as following from the priority they accord to individual liberty. Since restraints on liberty are to be reduced to a minimum, our rights reflect the maximal set of compossible equal liberties capable of being consistently exercised by all individuals. Although liberals disagree about how liberty is to be interpreted, such theories all presuppose the existence of a coherent conception of liberty.[7] Only then is it possible to talk of maximizing freedom. Socialists seeking to extend liberal freedom trade on a similar thesis. The problem with this approach, as Onora O'Neill has forcefully argued, becomes clear once we consider the difficulty of making 'on-balance' judgements about freedom in the event of a clash of liberties.[8] How do we decide, for example, whether freedom of information is greater than freedom of privacy, or in what ways might freedom of association be considered more or less extensive than the freedom not to be discriminated against? Many different sets of equal liberties could consistently be assigned to all. In the absence of a metric for adjudicating between them, prioritizing liberty in this way will be indeterminate. This dilemma undermines the aim of deontological liberals to make rights basic in a manner which is neutral between conceptions of the good and of the person.

Natural rights theorists claim to circumvent these kinds of conflict by conceiving rights as part of a system in which no right need violate another. It is my intention to show that no such set of absolute basic compossible rights exists. Even the natural law originators of this tradition, such as Locke and Smith, were forced to admit that moral life regrettably fails to evidence the regularity this thesis demands. The coherence of such systems derives from their promoting a particular conception of the person and conceiving society in a particular kind of way. Far from being fundamental aspects of human well-being, liberal rights function to uphold those collective goods necessary for a characteristically liberal communal way of life. It is only in reference to this ulterior purpose that conflicts between rights can be resolved. Once this is admitted, then the project to ground liberalism in universally valid principles must be conceded to have failed. Liberalism will be forced to compete with alternative forms of social organization offering divergent modes of human flourishing of equal legitimacy and validity, socialism amongst them.[9]

My argument can be illustrated by looking at traditional packages of liberal rights. Libertarian defences of the minimal state and the market system arguably offer the strongest defence of a set of basic liberal rights. Proponents of this thesis maintain that because the market system only requires negative passive rights to function, then rights violations can be avoided simply by all individuals exercising self-restraint. The rights to non-interference from others require no redistribution of scarce resources to be upheld and allow individuals to trade with each other and exercise their talents and opportunities in whatever way they please. Superficially, the market system offers the most plausible realization of the vision of liberal politics as consisting in the maximization of the greatest possible area for individual action compatible with the minimal demands of social life.

Closer reflection reveals that it is quite implausible to characterize the market as the spontaneous outcome of exchanges between right-bearing individuals. Far from this system being constituted by individual rights, these rights depend upon certain social institutions and values which give them point and facilitate their exercise. In spite of the apparent liberal reliance on the invisible hand to derive public benefits from the selfish pursuits of egoistic individuals, the successful operation of this mechanism assumes all recognize the collective good of the market itself. As the originators of this theory, notably Adam Smith, well knew, the market consists of a complex network of conventions concerning such notions as fair dealing, promise keeping and the avoidance of restrictive practices like the formation of price cartels or monopolies which would destroy its competitiveness. The market only benefits the public, as opposed to certain private individuals, so long as these regulatory structures remain in place. For someone to insist on their right to the point of destroying these social arrangements, thereby preventing others from enjoying the same rights in the future, would be nonsensical. At the extremes, radically individualist theorists of rights, such as Nozick, recognize this paradox – for example, when they admit the owner of the only water hole in a desert infringes the rights of others by charging extravagantly for them to use it.[10] This concession amounts to an acceptance that rights cannot exist in a social and moral vacuum. They can only be enjoyed in a certain milieu, defined by the presence of certain collective goods and shared understandings. Thus, the benefits arising from the various rights protecting economic freedom presuppose the market and its values. To subvert them is ultimately to destroy those rights. The upshot of this recognition of the market as a public good is to compromise the stringency of the natural rights thesis. For the vital conditions necessary for the form of life allowed by the market may require in certain circumstances that some rights be violated in order to protect the whole system of rights. Moreover, not even the most basic and minimal of the negative rights can in practice be treated as simply requiring the passive non-interference of individuals in order to be operative. To be sure of one's physical integrity and privacy, for example, a police force and judiciary paid out of public funds will be necessary. This requirement makes the possibility of clashes between rights over the employment of scarce resources for divergent purposes highly likely, leading to 'on balance' judgements about liberty with all their attendant pitfalls.

Similar difficulties arise with the usual liberal civil and political rights to vote, to freedom of speech and association, and to participate in some form in the making of collectively binding decisions. As with the economic rights examined above, such citizen rights assume the existence of a complex of collective structures and practices – in this case political institutions which provide a place for popular involvement at one level or another, and which enable people to express and give effect to their opinions. None of these rights make sense for individuals isolated from the rest of their fellow citizens in some putative state of nature: after all, I would hardly want freedom of speech merely to talk to myself. Rather, they take their place within a communal form of life which provides them with their justification, and hence limits their application. For example, all societies draw boundaries around the right to freedom of expression. In the United Kingdom, these limitations range from laws against slandering another person, to censorship of obscene or violent material, and restrictions on the reproduction of classified information. Similarly, American lawyers interpreting the First Amendment normally treat certain ways of expressing yourself, such as maliciously shouting 'fire' in a crowded room or incitement to racial hatred, as falling outside the constitutional right to free speech. Many of these limitations are notoriously contentious; however, they point to the fact that we value freedom of expression primarily for communication and the benefits deriving from the unrestricted exchange of information, feelings and ideas. We uphold the right of the political dissident to speak not because it is in his or her interest that we do so, but because it is in the interests of all individuals living in a political

146

society which depends for its openness on the free discussion and criticism of the policies and opinions of those in power.[11] When the dissident's views appear to threaten the character of that society, then his or her right to express them becomes called in doubt. To deny this would be analogous to saying that democrats must allow the demos to choose an undemocratic form of government. Clearly they do not, which is why many modern democracies refuse the right of parties committed to their overthrow to participate in elections without contradiction.

The argument so far has aimed to show how the specification of rights within a liberal, or indeed any society, derives from their worth in fostering a particular set of practices which favour the development of a certain quality of human flourishing and interpersonal relations. They defend the interests not of an isolated individual, but of individuals engaging in a variety of forms of interaction within a given kind of community. If each person exercises his or her right for themselves, so that some may choose not to vote, speak in public, or deal on the stock market, and so on, every member of society benefits from the fact that the majority do take advantage of them. This communitarian aspect of rights becomes especially clear when rights clash, as we have seen they inevitably do. For conflicts of rights can only be resolved, as the examples above illustrate, with reference to the common good or forms of life valued by the community.

This thesis stands opposed to the argument that the only acceptable political and moral theories are those in which rights alone are basic and all duties and goals occupy a derivative and secondary place.[12] As Joseph Raz has persuasively argued, a moral theory consisting entirely of rights would be immensely impoverished.[13] A world in which people's actions were entirely co-ordinated and motivated by the obligation to respect one another's rights would be a dreadful place, in which the spontaneous bonds of affection had dried up and been replaced by mechanical chains of duty enslaving us to each other. Raz notes how an exclusively rights-based society would be devoid of those 'oughts' which are other than duties, such as acts of supererogation, virtue and the disinterested pursuit of excellence. These often provide weightier reasons for action than those deriving from duty alone. Thus, if I have promised to meet someone at a certain time but witness an accident on the way, we are inclined to believe that I ought to see what I can do to help the injured rather than hurrying along regardless to keep my appointment as duty requires. A rights-based society would hardly be a social world at all. When, for example, intimate relations, such as those between lovers or parents and their children, have to be cashed out in terms of the separate entitlements of those involved, we conclude that the relationship has broken down. Much the same can be said of social relationships generally. We only have the rights we have, and know how to exercise them in a responsible manner which does not insist on their absolute nature but allows for other considerations to be taken into account as well, because we have learnt to relate our own desires and goals to those of others through social interchange. To assert our rights against the social environment that gives them their worth would be absurd, yet this is the argument that those who affirm the primacy of rights would have us accept.[14]

The collective goods on which we have seen rights depend, such as the market or an open and democratic society, cannot be reduced to a set of individual claims of rights. In a widely cited article, Neil MacCormick has insisted that rights 'concern the enjoyment of goods by individuals separately, not simply as members of a collectivity enjoying a diffuse common benefit in which all participate in indistinguishable and unassignable shares'.[15] According to the view of rights propounded here, this is true only in a qualified sense. As I remarked earlier, specific entitlements to welfare, a fair trial, freedom of association and religious belief, and so on are claimed on an individual by individual basis. Some people may not take them up. To this extent MacCormick is correct to say that rights defend the interests of specific individuals. But even those who do not choose to exercise them continue to benefit in a diffuse way from the fact that most of their fellow citizens do. Moreover, these rights exist as part of a public culture and both help to secure and derive from various collective goods within the community, such as tolerance, education, democratic institutions, etc. They would not have the importance we accord them if this was not the case. Nevertheless, whilst no one can be excluded from the advantages such goods bring to the society, different individuals benefit from them to different degrees according to their aptitude, tastes and effort. The derivative package of individual rights following from a collective good, the rights to vote or to stand for elected office within a representative democracy for example, reflects the fact that to an extent enjoyment of these goods is individualizable.

This said, I agree with MacCormick (and Raz, who adopts a parallel argument) that the collective goods themselves could not be secured by rights. For rights presuppose, they do not create, a way of life. We have our rights as members of a society which seeks to provide a range of options enabling various patterns of human development and social interaction, not as the inhabitants of some putative state of nature. To assert a right to live in a particular kind of society would be a very odd demand. It is one thing to say that individuals within a given polity have certain rights, quite another to suggest that they have the right to impose on their fellow citizens a whole new set of duties and patterns of existence. Imagine a single individual claiming a right to establish communal property relations within a capitalist society where everyone is contented with their lot. To achieve this would involve both the curtailment of a valued form of life and the more or less active participation of his or her fellow citizens in sustaining a new kind of community they do not care for. There may well be sound moral grounds for instituting such a change. The interest of an individual in living in a certain way is certainly a reason for taking his or her proposal seriously and weighing it against the interests of those other people who will have to bear the burdens of imple-menting it. However, this is a long way from regarding such a person as having an absolute right.

This communitarian and relativist explanation of the nature of rights goes against the doctrine of universal human rights. Supporters of the latter, however, might counter that properly understood the two views are perfectly compatible.[16] A theory of rights need not claim to be a complete moral system. Human rights provide a baseline protecting the capacity of individuals to enter into communitarian relationships by both securing them against the harmful interference of others and guaranteeing them the minimum necessary to engage in an uncoerced manner in any acceptable social set-up. According to this line of argument, since human agency and the free making of social agreements presuppose freedom from hunger or physical restraints, and the ability to reason and communicate with others, we can build up a picture of basic rights which should be met in some form in any legitimate society. Recent formulations of such lists typically include not just the classic rights to defend ourselves, acquire the necessities of life and not be wantonly interfered with by others, but also rights to freedom of speech and association, minimal education and welfare.[17] They argue that none of these rights needs to be identified with specifically liberal democratic societies, since a variety of types of community can embody different conceptions of the same basic concepts of human rights within their divergent social practices. Rights are not intended to provide detailed guidelines as to how people ought to live their lives. They merely indicate vital aspects of human well-being essential to individual freedom of choice, which, because of their universality, set limits on what individuals or governments can do in pursuing their private goals. They are preconditions for our communal engagements, no more, and so can be met in a number of ways. Moreover, if insisting on one's rights may be out of place in many kinds of relationship, they become necessary in the event of their collapse. Thus, even the most happily of married couples might at some stage need to stand on their rights in the event of a divorce. Indeed, a relationship in which one of the partners regularly rode roughshod over the interests of the other would in itself constitute grounds for such a reassertion of the aggrieved person's rights.

I have a certain sympathy with this line of argument, which has an undeniably prominent place in the liberal contractarian tradition.[18] However, I feel that nothing is lost by saying that the rights such theories establish belong very much to the liberal and related political traditions, and have no claims to universality. Indeed, I believe these theorists have no choice but to make just this concession. For the very form of moral agency they presuppose, namely that of the autonomous and purposive agent, forms an integral part of liberalism, and is not necessarily found in other cultures. Their starting point takes for granted precisely that which the moral sceptic or relativist seeks to question. To concede this does not in any way diminish one's ability to insist that we all ought to live in communities which do recognize such rights. There is no need to translate 'A ought to have a right to X', in order to realize him or herself in a certain kind of way, into 'A has a right to have a right to X'. In fact, because different packages of rights derive their value from the moral ideals and communal goals they serve, we must resist this temptation. As I noted above, asserting a right to live in a specific kind of social environment seems a very strange demand. Yet, if my argument is correct, an assertion of the existence of universal human rights will amount to just such a claim. The minimalist aspirations of such theorists cannot be sustained, because one cannot separate the narrow morality of rights from the broader ideal they seek to promote as this thesis assumes. We can only identify people's rights and duties with reference to the values and goals that make for a meaningful social life, knowledge of which can only be gained through the experience of living in society itself. From this perspective, liberalism offers just one amongst a plurality of possible and often incommensurable types of human flourishing, each one of which generates its own distinctive system of rights. Rights are therefore secondary rather than primary principles of social organization.

Similar points are made by John Rawls when he rejects Dworkin's proposal 'that the original position with the veil of ignorance be seen as modeling the force of the natural right that individuals have to equal concern and respect'.[19] This right, Dworkin argues, is presupposed by the activity of moral argument itself, which lies at the heart of Rawls's contractarian derivation of the principles of justice. As a result, the *Theory of Justice* offers a paradigm case of a modern rights-based moral and political philosophy. Rawls explains his refusal to follow Dworkin's 'ingenious suggestion' as follows:

> Dworkin's classification scheme of right-based, duty-based and goal-based views is too narrow . . . I think of justice as fairness as working up into idealised conceptions certain fundamental intuitive ideas such as those of the person as free and equal, of a well-ordered society and of the public role of a conception of political justice, and as connecting these fundamental intuitive ideas with the even more fundamental and comprehensive intuitive idea of society as a fair system of cooperation over time from one generation to the next. Rights, duties, and goals are but elements of such idealised conceptions. Thus, justice as fairness is . . . an ideal-based view, since these fundamental intuitive ideas reflect ideals implicit or latent in the public culture of a democratic society. In this context the original position is a device of representation that models the force, not of the natural right of equal concern and respect, but of the essential elements of these fundamental intuitive ideas as identified by the persons for principles of justice that we accept on due reflection. As such a device, it serves first to combine and then to focus the resultant force of all these reasons in selecting the most appropriate principles of justice for a democratic society.[20]

In other words, Rawls now accepts the contention of many critics of his *Theory of Justice* that it is impossible to provide an 'Archimedian point for judging the basic structure of society' by abstracting the individual choosers of the original position from any specific historical or social context. Rawls only reaches the conclusions he does because the contracting parties have all the characteristics typical of idealized liberal citizens. As a result, the principles of justice and the reasoning that leads to them only have validity relative to the 'social and historical conditions' which have produced what he terms 'an overlapping consensus' about the basic values of a liberal democratic society.[21] Liberal theorists of rights unwilling to adopt some contentious form of ethical naturalism should accept a similar starting point. Liberalism has to be understood as a historically contingent set of practices which cannot be grounded in universally valid principles. Liberals have to acknowledge the existence of different political systems offering just as valuable forms of well-being.

The above picture of liberal rights suggests that socialists will not simply employ different conceptions of the same basic human rights. Ultimately they are looking for another sort of community, involving different qualities of personal development and social interaction to those available within a liberal economic and political system. To a large extent, therefore, liberal rights will always appear inextricably bourgeois to them. This fact does not mean that socialists have no interest in insisting on these rights. Capitalist states frequently break with the principles of generality, impartiality and equivalence underpinning the liberal ideology of 'equal rights' in order to sustain profitable capital accumulation. Rights play a valuable defensive role by forcing liberal societies to live up to their ideals. However, this protective function is a far cry from the aspiration of some socialists to achieve a transition to socialism via the progressive extension of liberal rights. For securing individuals their recognized entitlements as liberal citizens is quite different to holding the rest of society duty bound to provide them with the preconditions for a totally different form of existence. In practice, the current popularity of rights talk among socialists reflects the more limited purpose. Thus, recent attempts to include a right to welfare amongst the social conditions of citizenship typically involve little more than an obligation on governments to relieve poverty through general taxation.[22] This goal amounts to considerably less than the more comprehensive services currently provided by modern welfare states and comes nowhere near the far-reaching schemes for redistribution desired by socialists. It is indicative of the political weakness of the Left that in order to counter the assaults of the New Right they have to reaffirm the values of the Social Democratic consensus of the 1950s, 1960s and early 1970s. No doubt, they are justified in insisting that most members of developed Western societies still assume these standards.[23] However, it is for this reason alone that their rights as citizens seem infringed when access to education, medical treatment, unemployment benefit, and so on are deliberately reduced or placed on a new footing by conservative governments. No basic, universal rights have been infringed. Of course it would be wrong to diminish the importance of this more relativist argument. People's expectations are important, and governments usually flout them at their peril. As a result, politicians are usually reluctant to admit that they are doing anything so drastic as altering the basis of citizenship. But socialists concerned with changing the world can hardly insist that no expectations can ever be legitimately overturned, and no positive rights ever infringed. On the contrary, they believe all sorts of time-hallowed privileges are unjust and ought to be abolished. Many are committed to a thorough-going alteration in people's motivations and rights, particularly those relating to material incentives and private property. They desire major changes in the ideals and public culture of contemporary societies. Indeed, if this had not happened in the past, the welfare state would never have arisen.

Many socialists have treated the process of political advocacy and conflict whereby rights come to be created or curtailed as part of the progress of humanity to the full enjoyment of their true rights. This argument involves adopting a teleological view of history which is hard to justify.[24] On what basis, for example, can socialists claim against their New Right opponents that the extension of welfare rights rather than rights to private property advances the true course of social evolution? Such Whiggish accounts generally serve those in power rather better than their opponents. As I shall argue in section three, the existence of rights cannot be removed from the contingencies of politics – indeed political discussion may only be possible by excising the discourse of basic human rights from it altogether.

The Nature of Socialist Rights

The above criticisms of rights as instruments of political struggle does not mean that they would have no place within a socialist system. Socialist criticisms of rights have generally turned on the way they separate the individual from the community. In a society based on communal relations of production, in which there is widespread altruism and an abundance of resources, rights no longer serve a purpose. The circumstances of justice result from an economic system based on the competition between self-interested individuals for scarce resources. Within a socialist society, however, individuals realize themselves in co-operation with others through collective projects. Marx and Engels gave this ideal its classic expression in the *German Ideology*:

> only within the community has each individual the means of cultivating his gifts in all directions: hence personal freedom becomes possible only within the community . . . In the real community the individuals obtain their freedom in and through their association.[25]

Rights are necessary when the interests of an individual or group clash with the common interests of all individuals, something which only occurs within a class-divided society in which the dominant class uses the legal machinery of the state to secure its own power within a given set of relations of production. Once 'the old bourgeois society, with its classes and class antagonisms' was abolished, then 'we shall have an association, in which the free development of each is the condition for the free development for all'.[26] Without economically derived conflict between individuals, not only rights but the whole mechanism of law and the state as well become redundant.

How plausible is this view?[27] In making an assessment, it is desirable to distinguish between assumptions which seem reasonable and those which, as far as one can tell, appear highly unrealistic. Thus, whereas one can expect that under socialism people will be better disposed towards each other, and their social relations more solidaristic and fraternal, it is unreasonable to suppose that the ordinary human weaknesses resulting from imperfect knowledge, carelessness and our essential fallibility will have been transcended by a new race of superbeings. Similarly, whilst it can be assumed that wealth will be more equitably distributed and that people will be less materialist in their desires, to believe that there will be such superabundance that no constraints of resources exist stretches the bounds of credibility too far. The implausibility of this totally harmonious picture of the socialist future derives from its reliance upon both the flawed presuppositions criticised above for its coherence.

If we remove the assumptions that human beings will have been transformed into omniscient creatures possessing a saintly rectitude, and that the world could be made so bountiful as to satisfy each of our wildest desires, then the likelihood that law, rights and politics will have their place within a socialist world becomes more certain. A more charitable reading of Marx, which does not rest on utopian beliefs about the future, argues that it will be the essential agreement on socialist values which allows the making of decisions to lose their 'present political character' and become a 'business matter that gives no one domination'.[28] Once there exists a broad consensus on the ends to be fulfilled, then debate will be restricted to finding the most appropriate means to achieve them. However, even supposing that such a distinction could be made, social processes within a society of any size and sophistication will be so complex that people are liable to err due to either insufficient information about their fellow citizens' needs, or a lack of expertise about how best to meet them. The road to hell is paved with good intentions, and even the most altruistic of individuals may be simply wrong about what his fellow citizens need or want. For all but the smallest groups, some formal framework establishing the norms of conduct and conditions for entering into agreements is unavoidable. In these circumstances, a set of rules embodying the moral values governing social interaction within a socialist community becomes necessary. These would guide behaviour into mutually advantageous and beneficial channels, reconciling claims on common resources, for example, and settling disputes over matters of interpretation or fact. Since some of these rules, like the moral principles from which they derive, will be directed towards the satisfaction of the interests or welfare of individuals, they will confer rights. Where the social norm lays down an obligation on all citizens not to physically harm others, for instance, then that will result in each of them having a correlative right against everyone else not to be harmed. Similarly, if the social norm lays down a welfare principle whereby we all have an obligation to bring into being or secure the conditions necessary for individuals to act as autonomous agents, then equally everyone has an entitlement to concern and respect as a purposive being. These norms give us rights ensuring that we can formulate our own projects by being able to choose from a number of worthwhile options free from the coercion of others or the constraints imposed by a wretched standard of living.[29]

Since the moral values underlying socialism differ in key respects from those of liberalism, socialist rights will be correspondingly different. As Campbell remarks, they will be

> more positive, less dependent on the right-holder, more directed towards the protection and furtherance of those concerns which express the needs of active and creatively productive social beings than is the case with capitalist rights. Socialist rights are more organizational than political in that they inform the co-operative social effort rather than represent demands to be disputed and traded-off against each other. They are devices to secure the benefits which can be derived from harmonious living, not protections for the individual against the predations of others.[30]

Although this conception of rights 'retains the individualism inseparable from the idea of obligations being owed to others', 'interest' has been detached from 'selfishness' and 'obligation' from 'burden'.[31] Such rights 'are more typically directives and enablements than claims', and involve no departure from a socialist vision based on communal relations.[32] However, they exist in recognition of the 'inevitable limitations in human knowledge, the requirements of educating the young into the way of life of socialist societies and the need to establish normative standards of what counts as harm and benefit'.[33] Moreover, not all human purposes are realizable in combination with others. Whereas certain activities, like playing in an orchestra or a football team, involve individual self-realization through joint production with others, the historical trend of industrial manufacture in particular suggests that self-realization and integrated work processes conflict rather than complement each other. Nor can one suppose that all the different sorts of relationship and activities through which individuals express their social selves will always be in perfect harmony with each other. The relations between friends, workmates, lovers, neighbours, other citizens, parents and children, strangers, and so on, all of which would presumably persist under socialism, are not all of the same quality and with the best will in the world cannot always be harmonized. Some set of priorities will be necessary to resolve potential conflicts, producing rules which will give rise to rights in a number of instances. However, these rights will reflect the distinctive values of socialism. There is no need for socialists to adopt liberal rights.

Rights, Freedom and Democratic Citizenship

The discussion so far has been designed to show that the rights, and hence the liberties, available within liberal and socialist societies derive from the public culture of these two systems. As such, my argument rejects the traditional liberal picture of rights, which regards them as having a privileged status in securing the protection of individual liberty and as providing criteria for the legitimacy of any political system.[34] Rather, the importance of rights stems from the role they play in upholding the collective goods on which the quality of life and freedoms of individuals within a particular sort of community depend. The traditional liberal view treats rights as moral constraints upon the political process, which preserve certain essential 'natural' properties of individuals against the coercive or paternalistic interferences of tyrannical majorities or powerful minorities. Recently some socialists have been persuaded of the necessity of incorporating these liberal constitutionalist arrangements into any form of socialism which seeks to preserve individual civil liberties.[35] The interpretation of rights offered above implicitly challenges the characterization of the human subject on which this thesis rests, regarding the capacities and statuses of individuals, like the rights which protect them, as depending upon the social forms which give them effect and purpose. Individuals are only free by virtue of the culture which nurtures them, giving them the ability to use and value not unqualified freedom, an impossible and meaningless notion, but a certain quality and range of liberties. Advocates of the primacy of rights must posit the existence of some natural law or espouse a form of ethical naturalism for the coherence of their position – as, indeed, the classical exponents of this doctrine, such as Locke, did. For they must assume that individuals have certain inherent characteristics and duties towards each other which are presupposed by all social systems. Such claims are very difficult to ground. They tend to be either too abstract and generalized to provide any sort of guide to political action, or too specific to be true, for the individual attributes they treat as 'natural' or 'inherent' can only be acquired through the experience of living within a particular kind of society. Assertions of universal human rights inevitably degenerate into irreconcilable conflicts between rival ontological claims. The debate over abortion illustrates this feature of rights discourse particularly well. This debate has shown both the difficulty of agreeing on a common conception of what counts as life and the impossibility of rationally adjudicating between a conflict of supposedly basic rights such as the right of the foetus and the right of the mother in whose body it resides. Even the most essential of civil and political rights come into conflict with each other at times. For example, it is correctly believed to be essential in a liberal democracy that everyone has a right to the fair procedures which guarantee an unprejudiced trial. However, suppose it is discovered that some of these rights lead to guilty individuals getting off and committing crimes which infringe the equally important rights of innocent citizens. Such a situation is not at all implausible. The British government's decision to modify the right to silence reflects just such a perceived conflict of rights. In such instances we are faced with tragic choices in which doing right involves committing wrong. No ethical theory can adequately resolve such questions. If policy decisions and social reforms are to be possible, then argument about the merits of different proposals has to be pitched at a less absolute level.[36]

Given that our freedom depends upon the society and culture in which we live, we will be freer if we have a say in determining the character of our community. This activity requires the existence of democratic institutions through which we can deliberate on our collective interests. Traditional rights theorists have argued that a set of constitutionally entrenched rights must provide the framework for this deliberative process. But this is to place the cart before the horse. When rights lose their absolute and inalienable status, and come to be seen in their true light as merely protecting important aspects of a given public culture on which the interests and possibilities of a particular society's members depend, then this argument loses its point. The constitutional entrenchment of a given set of rights attempts to make a given conception of social life unalterable. Yet discussion of what sort of world we would like to live in and the kinds of collective goods the state ought to provide form a vital part of the subject matter of politics, and so cannot be legitimately excluded from the political agenda. To do so has the effect of raising the temperature of political debate so that every challenge to the existing system gets turned into a revolutionary proposal. It places political disputes on a level where the opposing positions of the contesting parties cannot be discursively redeemed.

Citizenship itself does not assume the recognition of rights to participate, express opinions, and so on. After all, the Greeks had a conception of citizenship without being able to distinguish the term 'right' from notions of something being 'just' or 'correct'.[37] Skinner's writings on Machiavelli and Rousseau reveal a tradition of political thought in which the practice of civic virtue is a condition of retaining our liberties.[38] Within the civic republican tradition we only have our rights as a result of performing our *duties* as citizens. Those rights we do have emerge from a political struggle regulated by certain democratic procedures. There is no guarantee of course that such rights will be either liberal or socialist — it will depend on the will of the community concerned. The safeguards for individual freedom emerge from the distribution of power such mechanisms afford. In my view, these controls offer a better guarantee against coercion than a Bill of Rights based on a contestable view of human nature. If socialists desire to achieve a peaceful transition to an open socialist society these are the sort of arrangements they must seek to establish. Rather than constructing socialist theories of citizenship which attempt to offer an expanded version of liberal rights, they must undertake the task of designing constitutional arrangements which will enable political debate and the arbitration of conflicting goods to take place. Only within such a framework can they hope to achieve their goals in a democratic manner which preserves the freedom of an eventual socialist polity. Needless to say, the same goes for liberals concerned to defend their own values in a way which recognizes the pluralism which now characterizes modern societies. The only alternative is a moral and political totalitarianism.

The above argument is as much practical as it is theoretical. In practice, formal statements of rights establish very little. After all, even under Stalin the USSR boasted a written constitution guaranteeing the rights of its citizens. Individual freedom is not protected by written statements, however worthy, but by the existence of agencies which enable agents to act in certain ways and offer them a means of defence against being hindered by others. Rights signify the capacity of individuals to do or not do certain things, and are best secured by a democratic institutional structure which distributes power within the community. The protection of minority groups, which forms a major part in the desire of rights theorists to limit the scope of democratic decisions, can best be served by having a variety of different loci of power and decision making which restrict the possibilities for any one agency or group to dominate all others. Without a differentiation of political functions which recognizes the plurality of society by preserving the autonomy of different spheres and levels of social life, separating, for example, judicial and executive functions and local from central government, constitutional rights will be worthless. Once disproportionate power falls into the hands of a restricted group or a single agency, individual freedom will soon be curtailed.

Two further benefits derive from such an institutional framework which avoids reference to inalienable constitutional rights. First, not only does it promote the instrumental exercise of freedom by citizens, it also educates them through participation and discussion into a perception of the dependency of their social relations and individual autonomy upon collective rules and arrangements – discouraging free-riding and other self-defeating forms of self-interest. Moreover, by providing a forum for public discussion it enables preferences to be transformed and not just aggregated, allowing opposed interests to find agreement on common values which can offer new forms of individual expression to all.[39] Second, the legal rights which emerge from the deliberations of such bodies involve none of the drawbacks I have associated with notions of natural human rights. Instead of representing inherent ontological attributes, they reflect socially determined purposes which are capable of reformulation to meet changing circumstances and attitudes. Legislation can be used to mediate between competing claims, granting rights which reflect the divergent requirements of different areas of social life rather than conforming to some idealized image of the human subject which imposes a particular pattern of human agency upon a society.

Finally, liberal theorists generally associate political pluralism with a capitalist economic system. Two factors motivate this linkage: the need to prevent the control of resources by a single agency, and the flexibility of market allocations compared to planned. So long as socialism is identified with central planning by a monolithic bureaucratic state, then capitalist arrangements will prove superior in these respects. However, unregulated markets based on private property rights in the means of production, distribution and exchange result in discrepancies of wealth and hierarchical relationships which create grave inequalities of power and restrict the range of consumer choice and democratic control. The consequent private domination of the financial and industrial corporations may be better than that of the socialist state, but it is far from realizing the liberal ideals of freedom and equality that are often said to be synonymous with capitalism. A socialist society composed of co-operatively owned and democratically self-managing enterprises arguably disperses economic power more effectively and equitably, and so proves more pluralist than either capitalism or state socialism. It is compatible with both democratic decision making in the areas of public goods and the conciliation of ideal-regarding preferences, and the use of market and price mechanisms for the co-ordination of material preferences and ordinary consumption. For outside the area of essential services, a regulated market proves far more adaptable and open than planning can ever be. Thus, although it may be unfashionable to say so, it seems not unreasonable to conclude that a democratic socialism may prove far more amenable to the freedom of citizens to exercise their rights than liberal capitalism.[40]

Conclusion

Since rights owe their origin to the preservation and co-ordination of a given way of life, it is important for individuals to participate in sustaining and developing the political culture of their society. Individual freedom can only be realized and developed through democratic institutions that allow us to control the fashioning of the common good on which our ability to pursue our personal projects depends. Civil liberties in both liberal and socialist systems rely for their continuance on an institutional framework which gives people power over their collective destiny, not a contestable but inviolable Bill of Rights. Only thus can they reform their society without promoting irresolvable conflicts between opposed positions and defend themselves against the illegitimate incursions of powerful groups or agencies. This conclusion is far from novel – it is to repeat the lesson of one of the shrewdest analysts of the political significance of the French Revolution, Benjamin Constant. Namely, that if we wish to enjoy the liberties of the moderns celebrated in the French Declaration of Rights, we will have to continue to practise the liberty of the ancients and take part in the political process and be prepared to control and support the public sphere ourselves.[41] Prior to insisting on our rights, therefore, we have an obligation to participate in sustaining and completing the community which makes their exercise possible.

Notes

1. I am grateful to Malcolm Anderson, Richard Gunn, Peter Jones, David Miller, Paul Smart, Andrew Williams and Richard Vernon for their comments on earlier versions of this chapter.
2. E.g. T. Campbell, *The Left and Rights: A Conceptual Analysis of the Idea of Socialist Rights*, London: Routledge, 1983, Ch. 1.
3. E.g. M. Friedman, *Capitalism and Freedom*, Chicago: Chicago University Press, 1962, pp. 19 ff.; F. A. Hayek, *The Road to Serfdom*, London: Routledge, 1944.
4. E.g. K. Marx, *On the Jewish Question: Early Writings*, Harmondsworth: Penguin, 1975; V. I. Lenin, *State and Revolution, Collected Works*, 25, London: People's Press, 1969; E. P. Pashukanis, *Law and Marxism*, London: Lawrence and Wishart, 1978. Campbell *Left and Rights* comments on this agreement between right-wing liberals and revolutionary socialists at a number of points.
5. J. S. Mill, *Autobiography*, ed. J. Stillinger, Oxford: Oxford University Press, 1969, p. 138.
6. E.g. B. Crick, *Socialism*, Milton Keynes: Open University Press, 1987; D. Held, *Models of Democracy*, Cambridge: Polity, 1987; J. Keane, *Democracy and Civil Society*, London: Verso, 1988.
7. E.g. both J. Rawls, *A Theory of Justice*, Oxford: Clarendon Press, 1971 and F. A. Hayek, *The Constitution of Liberty*, London: Routledge, 1960 adopt this starting point. R. Dworkin, 'Liberalism', in S. Hampshire (ed.), *Public and Private Morality*, Cambridge: Cambridge University Press, 1978, pp. 113–43 is unusual in founding liberalism in equality. However, as I have argued at length elsewhere, his value of equal concern and respect proves just as indeterminate as the ideal of liberty he seeks to supplant. See my 'Defining Liberalism: Neutralist, Ethical or Political?', in R. Bellamy (ed.), *Liberalism and Recent Legal and Social Philosophy, Archiv für Rechts- und Sozialphilosophie*, Beiheft Nr. 36 (1989), pp. 23–43.
8. O. O'Neill, 'The Most Extensive Liberty', *Proceedings of the Aristotelian Society*, 80, (1979/80): 45–59 and O. O'Neill, *Faces of Hunger: An Essay on Poverty, Justice and Development*, London: Allen and Unwin, 1986, Ch. 6.
9. The following argument is indebted to J. Finnis, *Natural Law and Natural Rights*, Oxford: Clarendon Press, 1980, Ch. 8 and J. Raz, *The Morality of Freedom*, Oxford: Clarendon Press, 1986, Chs 7, 8 and 10.

10. E.g. Hayek, *The Constitution of Liberty*, pp. 135–7 and R. Nozick, *Anarchy, State and Utopia*, Oxford: Blackwell, 1974, pp. 178–82.
11. This argument gets its classic expression in J. S. Mill's *On Liberty* (1859).
12. E.g. R. Dworkin, *Taking Rights Seriously*, 2nd edn, London: Duckworth, 1978, pp. 171–2, J. L. Mackie, 'Can There be a Right-based Moral Theory?', in J. Waldron (ed.), *Theories of Rights*, Oxford: Oxford University Press, 1984, Ch. 8, esp. p. 176.
13. J. Raz, 'Right-based Moralities', in Waldron (ed.), *Theories of Rights*, Ch. 9, reproduced in slightly modified form in his *Morality of Freedom*, Ch. 8.
14. For a development of this criticism see C. Taylor, 'Atomism', in *Philosophical Papers 2*, Cambridge: Cambridge University Press, 1985, Ch. 7.
15. N. MacCormick, 'Rights in Legislation', in P. M. S. Hacker and J. Raz (eds), *Law, Morality and Society: Essays in Honour of H. L. A. Hart*, Oxford: Clarendon Press, 1977, p. 205.
16. The arguments set out and criticized below come from Jeremy Waldron, *Nonsense on Stilts: Bentham, Burke and Marx on the Rights of Man*, London: Routledge, 1987, Ch. 6.
17. E.g. G. Vlastos, 'Justice and Equality', in Waldron (ed.), *Theories of Rights*, pp. 41–76 and A. Gewirth, *Human Rights: Essays on Justification and Applications*, Chicago: Chicago University Press, 1982.
18. See J. Waldron, 'Theoretical Foundations of Liberalism', *Philosophical Quarterly*, 37 (1987): 127–50.
19. Dworkin, *Taking Rights Seriously*, Ch. 6. Waldron, *Nonsense upon Stilts*, pp. 202–9, and in his introduction to *Theories of Rights*, p. 20, makes similar claims for the contractarian foundation of rights doctrines based on Rawls, *A Theory of Justice*.
20. J. Rawls, 'Justice as Fairness: Political not Metaphysical', *Philosophy and Public Affairs*, 14 (1985): 236, n.19.
21. J. Rawls, 'The Idea of an Overlapping Consensus', *Oxford Journal of Legal Studies*, 7 (1987): 4.
22. E.g. D. King and J. Waldron, 'Citizenship, Social Citizenship and the Defence of Welfare Provision', *British Journal of Political Science*, 18 (1988): 415–43 and Raymond Plant, *Citizenship, Rights and Socialism*, Fabian Society Tract 531. The concern of the British Left with the erosion of civil and political rights came to head with the Charter 88 call for a Bill of Rights, a defensive move if ever there was one. For a critique of the Human Rights Bill that develops these arguments, see my *Liberalism and Pluralism: Towards a Politics of Compromise*, London: Routledge, 1999, Ch. 7.
23. See King and Waldron, 'Citizenship', pp. 431–6, for evidence to this effect.
24. T. H. Marshall, 'Citizenship and Social Class' (1949), reprinted in his *Citizenship, Social Class and Other Essays*, Cambridge: Cambridge University Press, 1950 is a classic instance of this sort of argument. It has been particularly prominent within the British socialist tradition, e.g. E. P. Thompson, *Whigs and Hunters*, Harmondsworth: Penguin, 1977. In these hard-pressed times Thompson's almost Whiggish optimism, e.g. *Writing by Candlelight*, London: Merlin, 1980, p. 153, seems particularly contentious.
25. K. Marx and F. Engels, *The German Ideology* (1845–6), *Collected Works*, Vol. 4, London: Lawrence and Wishart, 1975, p. 78.
26. K. Marx and F. Engels, *The Communist Manifesto*, *Selected Works*, Vol. 1, Moscow: Progress Publishers, 1969, p. 127.
27. The following discussion draws on the excellent analysis of Campbell, *Left and Rights*, esp. Ch. 2.

28. K. Marx, 'Conspectus of Bakunin's "Statism and Anarchy" ', *The First International and After*, ed. D. Fernbach, Harmondsworth: Penguin, 1975, p. 336.
29. For an argument to this effect, see A. Weale, *Political Theory and Social Policy*, London: Macmillan, 1983, p. 42 and Campbell, *Left and Rights*, Ch. 10. Alone amongst theorists of welfare rights, Weale and Campbell make plain that socialists are interested in more than mere poverty relief. Contrast their view with King and Waldron, 'Citizenship, Social Citizenship', for example.
30. Campbell, *Left and Rights*, p. 213.
31. Campbell, *Left and Rights*, p. 95.
32. Campbell, *Left and Rights*, pp. 148, 55.
33. Campbell, *Left and Rights*, p. 46.
34. The classic argument stems from J. Locke, *Two Treatises of Government*. See Nozick, *Anarchy, State and Utopia* and Dworkin, *Taking Rights Seriously*, Ch. 9 for contemporary versions of this thesis.
35. E.g. Held, *Models of Democracy*, Ch. 9.
36. This point is well made by P. Hirst, 'Law, Socialism and Rights, in P. Carlen and M. Collinson (eds), *Radical Issues in Criminology*, Oxford: Blackwell, 1980. Hirst's paper has inspired much of the argument of this section, although I diverge from him on a number of crucial points.
37. H. L. A. Hart, 'Are there any Natural Rights?', in Waldron (ed.), *Theories of Rights*, pp. 77–90.
38. Q. Skinner, 'The Idea of Negative Liberty: Philosophical and Historical Perspectives', in R. Rorty, J. B. Schneewind and Q. Skinner (eds), *Philosophy in History: Essays in the Historiography of Philosophy*, Cambridge: Cambridge University Press, 1984, pp. 193–221 and Q. Skinner, 'The Paradoxes of Political Liberty', in S. McMurrin *et al.* (eds), *The Tanner Lectures on Human Values*, VII, Cambridge: Cambridge University Press, 1986, pp. 225–50.
39. See J. Elster, *Sour Grapes*, Cambridge: Cambridge University Press, 1983, on the educative virtues of public dialogue.
40. For a detailed argument to this effect, see D. Miller, *Market, State and Community: Theoretical Foundations of Market Socialism*, Oxford: Clarendon Press, 1989.
41. B. Constant, 'The Liberty of the Ancients Compared with that of the Moderns', in *Political Writings*, ed. and trans. by B. Fontana, Cambridge: Cambridge University Press, 1988, esp. pp. 326–8.

CHAPTER 9

Three Models of Rights and Citizenship

Political debate is currently suffused by the language of rights. All the main
political parties, most pressure groups and individuals of almost every
ideological persuasion make their demands and define our identity as citizens
in terms of rights. Thus, groups campaigning against discrimination, such as
women or ethnic minorities, regularly turn to rights to articulate and
institutionalize their demands. Similarly, rights are also increasingly used in
international relations by those, such as the poor in the Third World, seeking
to emphasize the obligations of countries other than their own towards them.
Over the whole range of political issues, therefore, rights have become the
preferred method for pressing one's case and judging a state's, a government's,
or a social and economic system's legitimacy.

Perhaps because our political thinking and practice have become so
suffused with talk of rights, we rarely question its attractiveness or coherence.
The appeal of rights, like the rights themselves, is frequently regarded as
being self-evident. In this chapter, I want to challenge that assumption by
pointing out some theoretical difficulties with the concept of rights which
weaken its practical effectiveness. I shall start off by examining the two main
ways of characterizing the links between rights and citizenship found in the
most recent literature on the subject. In the first section, I shall discuss some
of the abstract philosophical arguments for what I call a 'rights-based
conception of citizenship'. In the second section, I turn to the more sociological form of analysis that underpins a 'communitarian conception of
citizenship and rights'. I shall claim this second conception articulates many
of the unexamined and, in my opinion, dubious social assumptions of the first
view. Finally, in the third section I shall outline an alternative 'republican
conception of citizenship', which places duties before rights.

In laying out my argument in this fashion, I also wish to achieve a
secondary purpose, that of illustrating a particular approach to political

theory. I hope to show that, whilst clear and logical thinking is indispensable, abstract theorizing of the kind discussed in section one is insufficient in itself to mount a convincing argument. Rather, it needs to be supplemented with the sorts of sociological and distinctively political or institutional considerations raised in sections two and three respectively.

Rights-based Citizenship

Rights-based conceptions of citizenship draw on doctrines of human rights. An initial distinction needs to be made at this point between human rights and institutional rights. Human rights claim to be fundamental and universal. As such, they must be capable of being extended equally to all persons regardless of social status, country of origin, colour, creed or sexual inclination. They ought to be upheld by all legitimate states, whatever their particular cultural, ideological or religious traditions and practical commitments. In certain important respects, therefore, human rights make us citizens of the world – an aspect that those campaigning on behalf of relief for the hungry or oppressed have often sought to exploit in order to generate international co-operation to tackle these issues. However, the universality of rights does not negate our membership of different states or cultures, nor does it mean that all states must adopt precisely the same laws and institutional structures. Human rights only aim to define the essential moral conditions that ought to be guaranteed citizens in any social and political order. They are necessary but not sufficient elements of morality or politics, which purport to be compatible with a wide variety of different sets of moral beliefs and political and economic systems. As a result, human rights are usually framed in sufficiently abstract and general terms to be met in a number of highly diverse ways.

Institutional rights consist of the rights recognized and incorporated into the laws and regulations of particular countries or other associations. Clearly, for any human right to be operative, it will need to be institutionalized and formulated in detail. Thus, the right to a fair trial will in practice require further specification in numerous institutional rights detailing what sort of evidence the police can or cannot bring against you, the composition and procedures of the court, access to legal support, the framing of the laws used against you, and so on. Similarly, a right to welfare will need spelling out in terms of a system of social security benefits, health care, housing provision, etc. These institutional rights give members of a particular society an entitlement to a whole range of benefits subject to meeting certain well-defined criteria. However, a country's institutional rights may be deemed to conflict with or fail to provide for certain human rights. In these instances, human rights activists believe that the laws, and in some cases even the entire political system, have to be reformed, possibly radically.

This distinction between human and institutional rights lies behind attempts to get international agreement on various charters of rights, such as the United Nations Universal Declaration of Human Rights of 1948 or the European Convention for the Protection of Human Rights of 1953. None of the signatory nations to these charters have precisely the same legal, social, economic or political arrangements, and there are often huge cultural differences not only between countries but within them too. Yet all claim in their different ways to meet certain standards safeguarding basic civil rights, such as the right to a fair trial; political rights, such as a right to vote; and usually certain social rights as well, such as rights to a certain level of education, health care and housing. However, when either the policies or the institutional rights enshrined within the law or conventions of a particular signatory state are deemed to have conflicted with human rights, then, according to the proponents of human rights, it is the offending law or policy that ought to change, even if that law reflects the democratic will of the population at the time. For example, Britain has been taken to the European Court of Human Rights on numerous occasions over matters such as its interrogation methods and policy of internment in Northern Ireland, corporal punishment in schools and employment legislation which endorses or gives inadequate protection against discrimination against women. In each of these cases, individuals who had no rights according to the institutional laws of Britain, and hence no case in British courts, were able to force the British government to introduce new legislation institutionalizing new practises in line with the European Convention.

The thinking behind the human rights project should now be clear. Human rights aim to offer a meta-political moral framework for politics and social interaction, which is capable of providing criteria by which we can judge a given system or set of arrangements as just or not. The declared purpose of human rights is to ensure the just treatment of individuals, and on some theories groups as well, either by protecting them from the incursions of others, as with rights against torture or unfair imprisonment, or, at least on certain interpretations, by enabling them in some vital respect, as with rights to food or shelter.

Human rights have an obvious political appeal for activists of all kinds. By getting their claims accepted as rights, they can seek to alter established conventions, policies and legal and institutional frameworks by questioning their moral validity. They can insist that the legally accepted authorities – governments and the courts of the land – do not have the final say. There are universal principles by which their decisions may be evaluated and called to account. A demand that human rights be respected can have a liberating effect, therefore. For those that invoke rights may challenge not just the practices but the very values of the established order. In this guise, rights can serve to promote radical changes, as in the cases cited in the opening paragraph. However, they may equally operate to block reforms or preserve the status quo if the proposed innovations are held to infringe individual rights. Some of the ambivalence that both the Left and Right have expressed about rights arises from the fact that, whilst Conservatives have generally deplored the first aspect of rights discourse and welcomed the second, socialists have usually liked the first and condemned the second. The current Labour government, for example, saw the Social Chapter of the Maastricht Treaty as offering a means for securing workers' rights. Their Conservative predecessors, by contrast, regarded it as involving undue interference with the property rights of employers and the individual's freedom of contract.

These sorts of disputes reveal a paradox generated by the very appeal of rights: to be at all useful, human rights must speak not only to those seeking change but also to those capable of instituting it. To achieve this goal, human rights must be able to lay claim to a degree of universality and objectivity that places them above political debate. As a result, they must meet two fairly stringent conditions. First, to achieve widespread support, human rights must be capable of appealing to a plurality of different people and types of institution motivated by often diverse principles and goals. In particular, they must be able to sustain in a plausible manner their claim to be fundamental and universal conditions of a just social order, that are capable of applying equally to all individuals. To meet this condition, a distinction needs to be drawn between the 'right' and the 'good', between the framework of basic rights and the conceptions of the good people may pursue within that framework. Human rights cannot themselves be based on any particular ethos or conception of the good, therefore. Second, whilst being sufficiently general and abstract to meet the first condition, rights must also be precise enough for us to be able to apply them to concrete circumstances, and the criteria defining what counts as a right stringent enough to prevent each and every goal or preference we have becoming the subject of a human right. Those who doubt the usefulness of rights language have usually been particularly critical of the tendency for the class of human rights to expand seemingly indefinitely to include each and every person's favoured cause.

Most philosophers now believe that the two traditional foundations for human rights, a divinely ordered natural law and an appeal to human nature, are inadequate because they fail to meet these two conditions. Given that the world contains not only wide differences of religious belief but also a large proportion of atheists as well, God is too contentious a starting point for a theory of rights aiming at near universal acceptability and applicability. The secularism of modern science has rendered human nature a similarly problematic basis for rights. Those theorists who begin from here argue that our rights should protect and possibly promote the conditions necessary for human beings to flourish. We establish these rights by identifying the distinctive characteristics of the human species and the circumstances necessary for them to develop. However, numerous difficulties arise with this procedure.[1] In the first place, one immediately comes up against the 'is'/'ought' problem. That something happens to be a fact about human beings tells us nothing in itself about its moral significance. After all, there are many human traits that mark us out from other animals, such as cruelty and killing for reasons other than food, which most people would find morally repugnant. Moreover, even those traits that appear to be rather more attractive, such as rationality or creativity, may be put to morally ambiguous or positively immoral uses, such as devising sophisticated and subtle forms of torture. Indeed, the empirical evidence tends to suggest quite a variety of often conflicting forms of human flourishing even within the range that most people would find acceptable. Thus, the selection of the distinguishing marks inevitably presupposes certain moral judgements about the nature of the good life, so that it is our views about morality rather than any empirical facts about human beings *per se* that actually does the work in our selection of human rights. As a result, the appeal to human nature will not get us very far. It will generate as many conceptions of rights as there are moral views and hence fail to pass our two conditions.

Most contemporary philosophers faced with this dilemma have followed Kant and opted for a 'transcendental' argument for human rights. In other words, they have tried to associate rights with the preconditions necessary for us all to make moral judgements and choose to flourish in any recognizable form at all. This basis for rights is generally held to issue in an equal right to liberty. On this view, claims to particular rights will be settled on the basis of whether they can be construed as a universal right to liberty that can be held equally by all. If there are many consistent such sets of compossible rights,[2] then the maximum set guaranteeing the greatest degree of individual liberty compatible with a like freedom for everyone else is to be preferred. John Rawls's 'first principle of justice' offers a neat summary of this formulation, according to which 'each person is to have an equal right to the most extensive total system of liberties compatible with a similar system of liberty for all'.[3]

Even if the form of moral agency assumed by this argument is clearly the Western liberal one of the autonomous chooser, and hence not so uncontentious as its proponents often assert, the reasoning behind it appears perfectly cogent. Namely, to provide the optimal framework for a plurality of individuals living together in society to carry out their various projects in a peaceful and just fashion. Since freedom seems necessary to undertake any project at all, by making liberty the basis of rights they claim to have satisfied the two conditions for a coherent theory of rights set out above. Unfortunately, matters are not so simple. To be plausible, this thesis requires near universal agreement on a common conception of liberty. Most of the recent debates about rights arise because, rhetoric apart, no such consensus exists.

Although there are a number of intermediary positions, the debate over rights to liberty is essentially between those who take a 'negative' view of liberty and those who hold a 'positive' view. For the former, mainly New Right libertarians,[4] freedom consists of an absence of intentional interference by others. The most important rights are, therefore, the traditional civil and political rights guaranteeing a right to life, security of property, freedom of speech and belief, and rights to engage in economic activity free from the intervention of the state or others. For the latter, who range from social liberals to democratic socialists,[5] freedom also includes the capacity to undertake certain actions, and hence must include a number of social or welfare rights to basic human needs, such as to food, health care, shelter and education.

If a conception of rights based on liberty is to work, this debate has to be settled. For these are not just two different views of liberty rights but two incompatible views. As New Right theorists eagerly point out, if I have an unrestricted right to property and to trade in the market, I cannot have unrestricted rights to welfare (and, of course, *vice versa*). To avoid this dilemma, these thinkers have insisted that only a negative conception of liberty can make sense of the rights project. They argue that basing rights on positive liberty inevitably leads to conflicts between rights and so brings into play unresolvable moral questions about the quality as opposed to the quantity of our liberty, and so renders the concept of liberty rights inherently unstable. In the rest of this section I shall very briefly examine their case against positive liberty rights and show that it is equally telling against their own arguments for negative liberty rights. I will conclude that these criticisms seriously weaken the whole rights-based conception of citizenship.

Negative libertarians standardly argue that rights based on 'negative freedom' merely require restraint on the part of others.[6] As a result, they are capable of being universally applied to all and generate perfect duties on everyone that do not infringe any other negative liberty rights. For example, in sitting quietly at my wordprocessor, as I was when writing this sentence, I can respect each and every person's right not to be attacked and everybody else can show an equal respect for my right just as easily. Positive liberty rights, in contrast, require action on my part which is often costly, frequently conflicts with some of my other rights, and is in some instances impossible to extend equally and universally to all.

These three criticisms of positive rights are related. Because they are costly, they lead to conflicts and so cannot be universal equal rights. If I tried personally to meet the welfare rights of my fellow human beings, for example, I would quickly exhaust my financial and physical resources, thereby restricting the exercise of my own liberty rights to do other things, and make only the smallest of contributions to the relief of suffering. Many of these difficulties remain even if I attempt to get around some of the problems, as most advocates of positive rights propose, by holding that respecting other people's welfare rights merely entails an obligation to support agencies, such as social workers and a national health service, that can provide a more universal system of benefits than any single individual could. For the negative libertarian, there would still be a conflict between the taxation needed to run these services and my right to do what I will with my own rightfully acquired property. Robert Nozick goes so far as to argue that such taxation is the moral equivalent of granting property rights in another person and 'is on a par with forced labour'.[7]

Even if we do not accept this extreme view of property rights, proponents of welfare rights admit that the scarcity of resources means that competing claims will result in conflicts between rights that will have to be sorted out somehow.[8] If two people require a particularly expensive form of treatment, for example, and there only exists resources for one of them, then inevitably one person's right to health care will have to be weighed against the entitlement of another person. Equally, governments are likely to be faced with competing claims between different sorts of rights, between education and housing for instance, which may prove even trickier to resolve. In each of these sorts of cases, it will be hard for anyone to say which policy maximizes freedom. What metric could we use to say whether housing, health care or education produces more freedom, or to decide whether one person's liberty would be increased more than another's?

Resolving conflicts between rights in this way places the whole concept in jeopardy. To engage in these sorts of interpersonal comparisons in order to maximize the utility of the whole goes against what is traditionally regarded as one of the chief virtues of rights – namely, that rights attach themselves to individuals and prevent or 'trump', in Dworkin's phrase,[9] any attempt to sacrifice a person or minority for the good of a majority or collectivity.[10] To countenance calculations of interpersonal utility, therefore, constitutes a slippery slope that undercuts the very logic of rights theories. Moreover, negative libertarians believe it reveals what they regard as the central incoherence at the heart of positive liberty rights: the confusion of freedom with ability. For once liberty gets linked to my capacity to do something, then the only way clashes between different liberty rights could be avoided is by everyone becoming omnipotent.[11]

Proponents of positive liberty rights usually grant a watered-down version of these criticisms, but respond by pointing out that negative liberty rights give rise to the self-same problems.[12] After all, my negative rights to security of my person and possessions, a fair trial and the like require a police force, prisons, courts of law, and so on if they are to be upheld, all of which are just as costly to keep up and lead to similar utilitarian comparisons between rights and persons. Indeed, the cost of total security is probably as beyond our resources as meeting everyone's welfare needs, and could only be achieved at a similarly unacceptable moral price. For as most attempts to increase security lead to clashes and trade-offs with other rights, such as the right to privacy or free speech, a totally secure society would not only bust the exchequer but have to be an extremely coercive police state as well.

Developing this argument, advocates of positive liberty counter the charge of having absurdly identified freedom with omnipotence by arguing that any view of freedom will be bounded by qualitative moral judgements, at least some of which will entail notions of ability.[13] Negative libertarians have attempted to avoid this dilemma by adopting physicalist accounts of liberty that define coercion in the narrowest terms as a direct, intentional, absolute, and practical hindrance to our performing a given action, such as imprisoning someone. However, outside the realm of metaphor, the view of the individual sheltering behind a barricade of rights within an 'inviolable moral space' proves very hard to sustain.[14] To be remotely plausible, this conception has to rely on a number of debatable empirical assertions, such as the view that people's choices are not constrained by prevailing social prejudices or fears, for example, or that the effects of market transactions can neither be intended nor foreseen. But even if we grant these usually unargued assumptions, evaluative difficulties will still crop up about defining when the individual's physical space has or has not been infringed. Thus, is the loud music emanating from the flat below mine a hindrance to my freedom or not? If so, to what degree, and at what point does it cease to be so? It seems hard to answer these questions without getting embroiled in knotty questions concerning the various degrees to which different physical acts impose on people. Such questions involve making some sort of appeal to basic human interests and our differential capacity for protecting them. These considerations in turn will lead to the problem of how to make on balance judgements between conflicting liberty rights. After all, stopping my noisy neighbours surely will entail some interference with their property rights?

If no objective view of freedom exists, then the project to make universal equal rights to liberty foundational runs into grave problems. Faced with differing and often conflicting views of freedom, it may not be possible even to agree when collisions between liberties occur, let alone to rationally resolve such disputes. Moreover, we have seen that this dilemma arises even within attempts to deduce rights from a single conception of liberty. These theoretical weaknesses give rise to even more debilitating practical difficulties. Once the 'right' can no longer be separated from the 'good', then in a pluralist society one will be faced with an ever expanding number of rival and incommensurable assertions of rights between which no mediation is possible. Think, for example, of the way the debate over abortion and related issues, such as population policies in the Third World, degenerates once it is conducted in terms of rights. Between the 'right-to-lifers' and the defenders of the mother's right to control her own body, little or no compromise has been possible without what has usually been felt to be an unacceptable compromising of one or other side's principles.

As we saw in Chapter 8, the only way to circumvent these obstacles to a coherent theory of human rights is to smuggle certain communitarian assumptions into the foundationalist position. The tacit reliance on communitarian reasoning is apparent, for example in the way classical rights theorists typically appealed to a pre-political 'natural' society in order to ground their argument, Locke's *Second Treatise of Government* being the paradigmatic example of this approach.[15] Whereas foundationalists seek to separate the right from the good and come up with a set of human rights valid for all societies, communitarians situate rights within the context of a certain kind of community that promotes a particular conception of the individual and his or her relations with others. From this communitarian perspective, rights emerge in their true character as secondary rather than primary principles. Instead of being prior to the good, rights operate to co-ordinate a given way of life motivated by a certain common conception of the good. Different conceptions of human community and flourishing will generate different conceptions of rights. It is to the coherence of these various communitarian justifications of rights that we must now turn.

Communitarian Conceptions of Rights and Citizenship

If foundationalists maintain that rights inhere in individuals and are both logically and morally prior to any society or state, communitarians associate our rights with membership of a particular kind of society or state.[16] However, we have seen that the foundationalist position ultimately collapses into the communitarian one, since any coherent theory of rights necessarily proposes an ideal form of membership and hence a certain type of community. A number of rights theorists have deliberately grasped this nettle. They argue that the foundationalist enterprise can be given a communitarian basis in the nature of modern industrial societies. They contend that the evolution of contemporary capitalism has promoted the very form of agency presupposed by foundationalist theories of human rights – namely, the view of the individual as an autonomous chooser of ends, capable of freely contracting into different social relationships.

As we saw in Chapters 7 and 8, New Right proponents of negative liberty rights believe this mode of action is best satisfied within a somewhat idealized model of the capitalist market. By contrast, proponents of positive rights have argued that, although capitalism provided the initial impetus for the development of notions of rights, the subsequent elaboration of this doctrine by a variety of groups struggling to gain a degree of control over their lives has radically transformed both the capitalist system and the character of rights themselves.[17] Consequently, rights can no longer be assessed solely in terms of their ideological significance for class relations within capitalist society. Rather, new claims of rights have created new forms of citizenship and community. In what follows, I shall offer a different interpretation of this process. I shall argue that the changes within modern societies that both these sets of theorists have correctly associated with the growth of rights have served to undermine the communitarian assumptions on which any coherent conception of human rights must rely.

To focus my argument, I shall centre it around an analysis of probably the most influential sociological explanation of the development of human rights,

T. H. Marshall's famous essay 'Citizenship and Social Class'.[18] Marshall linked modern rights-based citizenship to the growth of capitalist relations based on the division of labour within the context of the modern nation state. The creation of a national economic infrastructure and the resulting need for a mobile workforce, possessing a generic training and able to communicate in a standard idiom, produced a transformation of the relationship between the individual, society and the state. State and society become gradually separated, with the state's role shifting from one of direct control to the regulation, albeit of an increasingly extensive nature, of the social relations of free and equal rights bearing individuals. Nationalism played an important part in this new economic and administrative structure. It provided the common cultural identity required by a form of citizenship that was defined by adherence to a shared set of legal, socio-economic and political norms and institutions. Within this set-up, rights co-ordinated our relations both with each other and with the state and other agencies. However, like the proponents of positive liberty rights, Marshall believed that rights not only served to stabilize the industrial capitalist order, but to reform it. He saw the establishment of welfare rights as a prime instance of this reformist potential, regarding them as one of the principal means whereby the working class acquired full membership as equal citizens of the modern state.

Marshall provided a brilliant synthesis of the historical evolution of the modern conception of citizenship and rights in Britain. He divided this process into three phases. The first phase took place roughly speaking in the eighteenth century and saw the consolidation of civil rights, such as 'liberty of the person, freedom of speech, thought and faith, the right to own property and to conclude valid contracts, and the right to justice'. The second phase, occurring generally during the nineteenth century, witnessed the consolidation of political rights 'to participate in the exercise of political power, as a member of a body invested with political authority or as an elector of the members of such a body'. Finally, the third phase, which was largely a twentieth-century phenomenon, involved the creation of social rights extending 'from the right to a modicum of economic welfare and security to the right to share to the full in the social heritage and to live the life of a civilised being according to the standards prevailing in society'.[19]

Marshall did not regard these three categories of rights as distinct or exclusive but as complementary. Our exercise of our political rights, for example, entails not only the civil rights guaranteeing our freedom to speak without fear of harassment or arbitrary arrest, but also (on his view) a sufficient level of education and welfare to be able to make informed and independent decisions. The three phases of their establishment formed part of a dialectical process whereby rights had been changed from the privileges of a few, within the hierarchical social order of the feudal system, into the universal entitlements of all members of modern egalitarian societies.[20] The three only appeared to be in conflict during the intermediate stages of their transformation, as when the establishment of the civil right to freedom of contract clashed with the semi-feudal social rights based on ascribed status protecting the privileges of certain classes and categories of worker to pursue particular trades or professions. However, when all three came to reconstituted as aspects of our equal status as citizens of the community, he believed they would be harmonized once again. Summing up his argument, he observed how

> Citizenship is a status bestowed on all who are full members of a community. All who possess the status are equal with respect to the rights and duties with which the status is endowed. There is no universal principle that determines what those rights and duties shall be, but societies in which citizenship is a developing institution create an image of ideal citizenship against which achievement can be measured and towards which aspiration can be directed. The urge forward along the path thus plotted is an urge towards a fuller measure of equality, an enrichment of the stuff of which status is made and an increase in the number of those on whom the status is bestowed ... Citizenship requires a ... direct sense of community membership based on loyalty to a civilisation which is a common possession. It is a loyalty of free men endowed with rights and protected by a common law. Its growth is stimulated both by the struggle to win those rights and by their enjoyment when won.[21]

Marshall's linking of modern citizenship rights to the shift from status to contract, as the organizing principle of modern societies, essentially offers a historicist and communitarian explanation of the foundationalist view that we possess our human rights as persons entitled to equal rights to freedom to pursue our own lives in our own way. Indeed, given the pivotal role of social rights in his argument, foundationalist advocates of welfare rights have happily welcomed his interpretation of rights as providing an empirical grounding of their own case for positive rights.[22] They thereby acknowledge the commmunitarian background informing their own justification of rights.

However, Marshall's communitarian thesis has a number of advantages over the foundationalist position. First, although the general justificatory principle informing his discussion is the same, namely our entitlement to equal concern and respect, Marshall's more relativist perspective can accommodate different understandings of this principle far more consistently than the foundationalist position. Second, because Marshall's argument makes better historical and sociological sense of the meaning of rights, in many ways it makes better philosophical sense too. Rather than viewing rights as universal dictates of pure reason, an approach we saw to be largely vacuous, Marshall's account unites the theory and practice of rights and plays the two

Appeals to human rights in such circumstances have only resulted in a hardening of their respective positions.

The argument of this section has been that modern societies fail to provide a secular communitarian substitute for the natural societies of classical natural rights theorists. Rather than converging on the sort of common moral framework needed for either an extended or minimal conception of human rights, modern societies appear increasingly differentiated and pluralistic. The contention that human rights can offer a framework for the pluralism of modern societies is confuted by the fact that theories of rights presuppose a high degree of social and ethical homogeneity for their coherence. Within a pluralistic society, particular assertions of rights can only be successful at the cost of squashing or driving out all rival assertions by others. If this dilemma is to be avoided, then we need an account of the political mechanisms whereby the struggle for rights may be institutionalized without degenerating into a raging war between polarized camps. In the next section I shall argue that such an enterprise rests on a very different conception of citizenship to those examined so far, one which places duties before rights.

Republican Citizenship: From Duties to Rights

Rights-based theories of citizenship see human rights as defining and delimiting the sphere of the political. The existence of certain basic rights, such as freedom of speech and the right to vote in regularly held elections, not only ensures equal access by all citizens to the political process. These fundamental rights also are held to prevent governments from illegitimately interfering with or failing to promote certain vital liberties of individual citizens. Such thinking lies behind schemes for a written constitution and a Bill of Rights. From the perspective of a republican view of citizenship, however, this approach inverts the true relationship between politics and rights. Republicans regard rights as the products of the political process, rather than its presuppositions. They believe the moral framework of politics to be defined by a duty to participate in collective decision-making and to take the views of one's fellow citizens seriously, rather than a right to participation that one may or may not exercise. I shall argue that this offers the most plausible conception of rights and citizenship within modern pluralist societies.

Two important clarifications need to be made about the republican conceptions of rights and citizenship respectively. First, the rights that emerge from political deliberations are institutional rather than human rights. In other words, they are rights they derive from the particular laws and accords arrived at between citizens participating within the political process, rather than supposedly transcendent normative verities. Institutional rights of this kind have a number of advantages over doctrines of human rights. Unlike the latter, they do not invoke an idealized form of human agency and community of a putatively universal kind. Instead of representing inherent ontological attributes, they reflect socially determined purposes which are capable of reformulation to meet changing circumstances and attitudes. Legislation can be used to mediate between competing claims, granting rights which reflect the divergent requirements of different areas of social life, as in the case of reproductive rights for women, rather than conforming to a uniform standard. Furthermore, when rights are institutionalized then the counterpart duties can be allocated with precision so as to settle conflicts. These characteristics of institutional rights make them far more suited to the heterogeneity of modern societies than human rights.

Second, the term republican is used advisedly and in contrast to the civic humanist conception of citizenship, with which it is often confused. As Quentin Skinner has pointed out,[39] classical republicanism differs from civic humanism in seeing politics as a means rather than an end in itself. A form of Aristotelianism, the civic humanist tradition regards human beings as essentially political animals for whom political participation forms a necessary aspect of the good life. Civic humanism is a variety of communitarianism, therefore, which sees citizenship in terms of involvement in a common enterprise orientated towards a shared conception of the good. This view has been rightly ridiculed by rights theorists as advocating an unrealistic return to the solidary communities of the past. Moreover, it trades on a similar sort of ethical naturalist thesis to that employed by those who seek to derive a doctrine of natural rights from a view of human nature, a position we have already criticized for its circularity. Neither the ethics nor the practices of ancient Greece can be plausibly revived in the modern world.

Classical republicanism, by contrast, originates with Machiavelli and treats civic involvement as merely the condition for retaining our personal liberty. According to this line of reasoning, since the rights and liberties available to us depend upon the priorities, norms and laws of the society in which we live, we shall only be free to the extent that we share in determining the character of that society. In addition, if these arrangements are to respect fairly the values and demands of all members of society, rather than just those of particularly well-placed and powerful persons and groups, then we have an obligation not only to participate personally in collective decision-making but to ensure others do so too.

At the heart of the republican conception of citizenship lies a set of prudentially motivated political duties. These duties provide the preconditions for political discussion and decision-making between a plurality of roughly equal agents and agencies. They reflect a situation in which no agreed transcendent principles of reason and truth exist, so that the only ground for a claim that a particular policy or decision is just or the object of a right is that it has been consented to by a public that allows the free expression of all relevant points of view. The sorts of duties to emerge from this kind of reasoning would be those that entail only adopting those forms of conduct that are compatible with free communication between all members of the polity. Thus, deceit would be ruled out since it undermines the basis of discussion and could not be adopted as a universal obligation without self-contradiction: there is no point in lying when everyone else is. Similarly, to be systematically indifferent to human vulnerability is to ignore the degree to which our acts affect others and our independence is mutually dependent and socially engendered. Such considerations operate in most welfare legislation which aims to secure the conditions of agency for all, for example.

It has been objected that the notion of free consent which lies at the heart of this argument inevitably involves making the very sorts of idealization about human agency I criticize in theories of rights.[40] The universal duties which I claim define citizenship are said to be too abstract to enable one to know whether particular agents are coerced or not. Since the actual consent of agents may be the product of coercion or indoctrination, the deliberative process itself cannot provide a foundation for the specification of our rights. This thesis must inevitably fall back on some notion of hypothetical consent between ideal rational agents, therefore, if it is to provide a legitimate foundation for principles of justice. This approach gives rise in turn to a theory of those rights necessary to take part in the process of moral and political deliberation.[41]

Against these critics, I believe that it is not only possible but necessary to steer a path between the idealized citizens of rights-based theories and the relativist view of the communitarians. If the problem with relativized accounts of citizenship is that they risk legitimizing the forces constraining individuals' choices within particular circumstances, the difficulty with idealized accounts is that they often completely ignore such issues altogether. As feminists have observed of liberal social contract theories, for example, such approaches all too frequently assume that agents enter the world white, middle class, adult and male.[42] To avoid the Scylla of idealization and the Charybdis of relativism, we must rely neither on the hypothetical consent of idealized agents nor the actual consent of possibly oppressed agents to ground moral principles. Rather, to quote Onora O'Neill, whose thesis I am here developing, the appeal should be to the *'possible consent* of *actual agents'*.[43] In other words, the specific interpretations of these duties must reflect the views of those actually involved. However, to avoid the problems of false consciousness or coercion inherent to this thesis, consent must be capable of refusal or renegotiation. This emphasis on the opportunity for refusal follows from the general approach of defining duties through the rejection of those principles that could not be coherently universalized amongst a plurality of potentially interacting agents and agencies. On this view, it is the possibility of dissent rather than actual or hypothetical consent that guarantees the legitimacy of policies and that should guide the framing of those democratic institutions that, in a pluralistic world, provide the only adequate basis for constructing the norms regulating social life.

O'Neill has shown how making duties fundamental in this way avoids many of the difficulties we encountered with rights-based arguments.[44] First, whereas the coherence of constructions of basic human rights require that we identify the whole set of consistent, compossible rights, duties can be identified successively via the rejection of those principles of action that are incompatible with a heterogeneous public sphere within which all participate on roughly equal terms. Second, universal duties can be formulated in ways that are both general and abstract without entailing the idealization of a particular form of human agency, a requirement that mars the aspiration to universality of any conception of human rights. This non-idealizing feature of duties makes them far better candidates as the fundamental principles for a pluralistic society than rights. Third, a moral theory consisting exclusively of rights is immensely impoverished. For it allows only for the perfect duties entailed by respecting the reciprocal rights of others. Acts of supererogation, virtue and the disinterested pursuit of excellence often provide far weightier reasons for action than those generated by a respect for rights alone, but tend to become debased within rights-based discourse. Note the way the demands of rights-based justice have relegated charity to the level of an optional extra, for instance. Fourth, rights by themselves give no indication as to how they might be exercised. Far from always requiring decent behaviour, within their sphere they give a title to do wrong if the right-holder so wishes.[45] Indeed, the logic of rights can lead us to ignore the social environment that makes their exercise possible and valuable. Making duties primary, in contrast, forces us to consider the collective arrangements entailed by a system of rights and their effects on the lives of others. Finally, the emphasis on duties provides a far more effective framework for action than rights because they speak directly to what ought to be done. There is a tendency for rights to be promulgated or asserted with little regard for what might be entailed for other people to meet them. This rhetoric speaks more to the powerless seeking a slogan around which to organize, than to those who are being called upon to act, for whom the assertion of a right is liable to appear too indeterminate. What really defines a right is the complex of obligations within which it is situated. When we seek to work out what is involved in a right to life, for example, we are asking essentially what kinds of things we ought or ought not to be doing if certain risks are to be avoided and needs met. To make a discussion of rights primary, therefore, is to approach such problems of applied ethics from the wrong end.

These advantages of making duties rather than rights fundamental are well illustrated by the issue of welfare.[46] As I noted in section one, libertarians are able to object to the idea of a human right to welfare on the grounds that there can be no universal correlative obligations on the part of an individual to help all those in need. The most any single person can offer is selective help. This argument reflects many of the distortions of the rights-based view. A universal refusal to give aid draws its plausibility from an implicit appeal to a model of idealized independent agents. These paragons of self-sufficiency apparently suffer none of the usual human frailties and requirements, such as the propensity to fall sick and the need for food, that lead ordinary men and women to call on the help and support of others at various times in their lives – particularly in childhood and old age. For according to the duty-based view, amongst ordinarily needy and vulnerable human beings a principle of universal indifference could never be adopted. If we are only to adopt principles all can act on, then we must necessarily reject principles that undermine or threaten the capacity for agency of others. True, the duty so established remains an imperfect obligation, but it does not follow that we have no duty to do anything. Rather, the argument creates a requirement to institutionalize and allocate recipients of welfare to agents and agencies capable of supplying these needs. Institutional rights to welfare will thereby be created which can be tailored to the character and conditions of particular societies. These rights, however, clearly depend on the prior establishment of both a fundamental general duty and more special obligations to help others.

Duty-based thinking places greater rather than less attention on the preconditions for action than rights, since it emphasizes the need to pay attention to those real circumstances of actual persons that may inhibit their option of refusal. This approach also has profound consequences for how we think about politics. A duty-based politics yields a very different style of citizenship to a politics derived from rights. Rights-based forms of citizenship are ultimately passive and anti-political. The universalizing and homogenizing character of rights displaces politics from smaller forms of association and relocates it at a more comprehensive level – in the past the nation state, in more recent formulations some kind of global organization.[47] At the same time, however, power gets shifted from democratic institutions, such as the legislature, to bodies, such as the judiciary and bureaucracy, that claim to be untainted by popular pressures, and hence better able to decide issues of principle in an objective manner and uphold the individual's basic rights against the tyranny of the majority. Although rights are often presented as protecting the individual against the state, in reality they strengthen it and reinforce the concentration and centralization of power. For every demand for rights necessarily entails a greater regulation and institutionalization of social life so as to conform to a uniform pattern, and a concomitant withdrawal of more and more issues from the realm of democratic decision-making. As a result, individuals find themselves enmeshed in a growing array of obligations not of their own making. However, their self-image as free-choosing rights-bearers cannot sustain this degree of engagement in the affairs of others. By an almost dialectical process, continual insistence on the priority of right ultimately alienates individuals from public responsibility. Political discussion gives way to irreconcilable conflicts between rival rights claims. A framework of duties, in contrast, provides the basis for a participatory form of citizenship in which we collectively decide on our legal rights through the exercise of our civic obligations.

This republican conception of citizenship may seem as elegiac as the civic humanist's. Within complex and large-scale social systems, individuals simply lack the time, knowledge, or ability to participate directly in the political process. Even if new technology could help them to do so, consensual decision-making seems hardly plausible amongst such a massive number of people, and involving such a wide range of opinions and interests. The advantage of a rights-based political system, its proponents claim, is that the entrenchment of rights within a constitution frees individuals from politics and enables them to get on with their lives in peace and security. Similarly, international conventions of rights can regularize the relations between states and introduce a measure of justice and order into an otherwise anarchic world.[48] However, as we have seen, such stability can be acquired only at the price of a high degree of imposed conformity. Since moves in this direction go against the trend towards greater plurality and differentiation within modern societies, appeals to rights are far more likely to prove as destabilizing as they are ineffectual.[49]

To meet the challenge of the complexity and pluralism of modern societies, we need to move away from the model of the sovereign, centralized state and conceive of politics as operating within a complex plurality of interrelated political units. This approach fits with the duty-based, participatory model of citizenship far better than it does with the rights-based view. It also draws on the classic republican view of avoiding domination by so dispersing power as to achieve a balance of the social interests and ideals involved when making collective decisions.[50] It requires the distribution of decision-making power throughout society and the designation of distinct areas of competence so as to limit the scope of central authority. Such a system increases the areas of public life where a more active participation by citizens is possible. Putting pressure at the lower levels of the political system also serves to improve the accountability and responsiveness of our representatives to the views and aspirations of people at large.[51]

A framework of duties also offers a better starting point for international co-operation and the mediation between the different spheres of our lives than rights. As I noted above, duties provide more effective action-guiding principles than rights. Above all, they encourage the creation of the political mechanisms through which it is possible to establish the policies and priorities which institutionalize rights and so give them a meaningful existence. The various charters of rights have only had an impact on international politics to the extent that they have been authenticated by a political process capable of mobilizing the interests of a significant number of states behind them. As a result, human rights have been appealed to in a highly selective and frequently hypocritical manner. However, this situation will not be ameliorated by promulgating ever-more sophisticated and detailed conventions of human rights. Because of the unstable foundations of rights, discussed in section one, such proclamations will only increase the number and contestability of rights claims, increasing in the process the ability of states to recognize only those rights, and only in those circumstances, that suit them. As in the domestic arena, rights-based theories approach the problem of justice in international relations from the wrong end. Here too, the legitimation of value cannot be distinguished from the distribution of power. The rethinking of the international political system in ways that foster co-operative decision-making and supply the means for interest aggregation between states is a precondition for, rather than a product of, a coherent policy of world rights.[52]

Conclusion

This chapter has made the following three points. First, I showed that a coherent theory of fundamental human rights assumes a fairly homogeneous human community oriented around a common human good, a thesis traditionally provided by a doctrine of natural law. Second, I contended that modern societies are too fragmented to provide a secular communitarian foundation for a doctrine of human rights. Indeed, the complexity and pluralism of modern societies lead to unresolvable and infinitely expanding claims of rights. Third, I argued that resolving these disputes between contesting rights claims is a distinctively political matter, calling for a duty-based conception of participatory citizenship. This approach involves a shift from assertions of human rights to the formulation of institutional rights built around particular policy initiatives.

Notes

1. B. Williams, *Morality: An Introduction to Ethics*, Cambridge: Cambridge University Press, 1972.
2. The notion of compossibility derives from the metaphysics of Leibniz and was introduced into moral and political philosophy by Bertrand Russell, a distinguished Leibniz scholar. Here the term denotes non-conflictability and harmony. With regard to theories of rights, the idea is that rights should dovetail in such a way that the upholding of one right need not involve contravening another. See J. Gray, *Liberalisms: Essays in Political Philosophy*, London: Routledge, 1989, p. 147.
3. J. Rawls, *A Theory of Justice*, Oxford: Clarendon Press, 1971, p. 302. David Held offers a similar view, whereby 'persons should enjoy equal rights (and, accordingly, equal obligations) in the framework which limits the opportunities available to them; that is, they should be free and equal in the determination of the conditions of their own lives, so long as they do not deploy this framework to negate the rights of others' (D. Held, 'Democracy, the Nation-State and the Global System', in D. Held (ed.), *Political Theory Today*, Cambridge: Polity, 1991, p. 228).
4. E.g. R. Nozick, *Anarchy, State and Utopia*, Oxford: Blackwell, 1974 and N. Barry, 'Markets, Citizenship and the Welfare State: Some Critical Reflections', in R. Plant

and N. Barry, *Citizenship and Rights in Thatcher's Britain: Two Views*, London: Institute of Economic Affairs, 1990, pp. 34–77.

5. E.g. R. Plant, 'Citizenship and Rights', in Plant and Barry, *Citizenship and Rights in Thatcher's Britain*, pp. 1–32 and A. Gewirth, *Human Rights: Essays in Justification and Applications*, Chicago: University of Chicago Press, 1982.

6. E.g. M. Cranston, *What Are Human Rights?*, London: Bodley Head, 1973.

7. Nozick, *Anarchy, State and Utopia*, p. 169.

8. J. Waldron, 'Rights in Conflict', *Ethics*, 99 (1989): 503–19.

9. R. Dworkin, *Taking Rights Seriously*, London: Duckworth, 1977.

10. E.g. Rawls, *Theory of Justice*, pp. 3–4, for an explicit statement to this effect.

11. F. A. Hayek, *The Constitution of Liberty*, London: Routledge, 1960, p. 19.

12. E.g. Plant, 'Citizenship and Rights' and R. Plant, *Modern Political Thought*, Oxford: Blackwell, 1991, Ch. 7.

13. Lack of space dictates that my treatment of this issue can be only very brief. My account draws on the following, who provide the detailed arguments I can only hint at: O. O'Neill, 'The Most Extensive Liberty', *Proceedings of the Aristotelian Society*, 80 (1979/80): 45–59; D. Miller, 'Constraints on Freedom', *Ethics*, 92 (1984): 66–86; Plant, *Modern Political Thought*, Ch. 6; and, for (at that point of his career) a libertarian's acknowledgement of the same difficulties, Gray, *Liberalisms*, Ch. 9.

14. The metaphor is Nozick's in *Anarchy, State and Utopia*, pp. 10, 56, 57.

15. The communitarian nature of Locke's account of rights is one of the implications of the analysis of J. Tully, *A Discourse on Property: John Locke and his Adversaries*, Cambridge: Cambridge University Press, 1980. For an important study of the links between classical rights doctrines and their modern counterparts, see I. Shapiro, *The Evolution of Rights in Liberal Theory*, Cambridge: Cambridge University Press, 1986. Shapiro's realist account of liberal theories of rights inspires much of the argument of the next section.

16. Communitarian arguments are as ideologically and epistemologically diverse as foundationalist views of rights. There are different versions of communitarianism: conservative (E. Burke, *Reflections on the Revolution in France*, Harmondsworth: Penguin, 1969; M. Oakeshott, *On Human Conduct*, Oxford: Oxford University Press, 1975) and socialist (K. Marx, 'On the Jewish Question', in D. McLellan (ed.), *Karl Marx: Early Texts*, Oxford: Oxford University Press, 1972; D. Miller, *Market, State and Community: Theoretical Foundations of Market Socialism*, Oxford: Clarendon Press, 1989); rationalist (J. Finnis, *Natural Law and Natural Rights*, Oxford: Clarendon Press, 1980) and relativist (M. Walzer, *Spheres of Justice: A Defence of Equality and Pluralism*, Oxford: Martin Robertson, 1983). Since the rationalist versions tend to rely on the sort of contentious view of human nature that I have already criticized as a basis of rights, I shall not consider them here. My concern will be with the widely held tacit communitarian assumptions about modern societies that I believe ground most contemporary rights-based theories of citizenship.

17. E.g. T. H. Marshall, *Citizenship and Social Class and Other Essays*, Cambridge: Cambridge University Press, 1950; A. Giddens, *The Nation State and Violence: A Contemporary Critique of Historical Materialism Vol. II*, Cambridge: Polity, 1985; and D. Held, *Political Theory and the Modern State*, Cambridge: Polity, 1989, Ch. 7.

18. In Marshall, *Citizenship and Social Class*.

19. Marshall, *Citizenship and Social Class*, pp. 10–11.

20. Marshall, *Citizenship and Social Class*, pp. 11–14.

21. Marshall, *Citizenship and Social Class*, pp. 28–9, 40–1.
22. E.g. R. Plant, *Citizenship, Rights and Socialism*, London: Fabian Society, 1988, Fabian Society Tract 531 and D. S. King, and J. Waldron, 'Citizenship, Social Citizenship and the Defence of Welfare Provision', *British Journal of Political Science*, 18 (1988): 415–43.
23. Marshall, *Citizenship and Social Class*, 59, 70.
24. E.g. Giddens, *The Nation State and Violence*, pp. 226–9; M. Mann, 'Ruling Strategies and Citizenship', *Sociology*, 21 (1987): 339–54.
25. Held, *Political Theory and the Modern State*, Ch. 7 and B. S. Turner, *Citizenship and Capitalism: The Debate over Reformism*, London: Allen & Unwin, 1986.
26. See Turner, *Citizenship and Capitalism*.
27. G. Esping-Anderson, *The Three Worlds of Welfare Capitalism*, Cambridge: Polity, 1990.
28. Marshall, *Citizenship and Social Class*, pp. 47, 77.
29. See M. Freeden, *The New Liberalism: An Ideology of Social Reform*, Oxford: Oxford University Press, 1978; A. Vincent, and R. Plant, *Philosophy, Politics and Citizenship: The Life and Thought of the British Idealists*, Oxford: Blackwell 1984. See too R. Bellamy, *Liberalism and Modern Society: An Historical Argument*, Cambridge: Polity, 1992, Ch. 1 for a much more critical examination of this movement, that places it in a comparative perspective with similar changes in other European countries. The parallel with E. Durkheim, *Division of Labour in Society*, trans. W. D. Halls, London: Macmillan, 1984, examined in Ch. 3, is particularly strong.
30. E.g. T. H. Green, *Lectures on the Principles of Political Obligation*, ed. P. Harris and J. Morrow, Cambridge: Cambridge University Press, 1886, paras 5–7 and E. Durkheim, *Sociology and Philosophy*, trans. D. F. Pocock, London: Routledge & Kegan Paul, p. 52.
31. See M. Freeden, 'Human Rights and Welfare: A Communitarian View', *Ethics*, 100 (1990): 489–502 and M. Freeden, *Rights*, Milton Keynes: Open University Press, 1991 for an explicit defence of rights along these lines.
32. D. Bell, 'The World and the United States in 2013', *Daedalus*, 116 (1987): 14.
33. Turner, *Citizenship and Capitalism*, pp. 85, 92; Held, *Political Theory and the Modern State*, pp. 199–203.
34. Held, 'Democracy, the Nation-State and the Global System' and D. Held, 'Democracy: From City-states to a Cosmopolitan Order?', in D. Held (ed.), *Prospects for Democracy, Political Studies*, Special Issue, XL (1992): 10–39.
35. E.g. I. M. Young, 'Polity and Group Difference: A Critique of the Ideal of Universal Citizenship', *Ethics* (1989) 99: 250–74.
36. E.g. M. Sandel (ed.), *Liberalism and its Critics*, Oxford: Blackwell, 1984, 'Introduction'.
37. The view that the contrast between communitarian and rights-based theories has been overstated has become increasingly common. See W. Kymlicka, 'Liberalism and Communitarianism', *Canadian Journal of Philosophy*, 18 (1988): 181–203.
38. Rawls, *Theory of Justice*, p. 563.
39. Q. Skinner, 'The Paradoxes of Political Liberty', in S. McMurrin (ed.), *The Tanner Lectures on Human Values*, VII, Cambridge: Cambridge University Press, 1986.
40. By David Held and Leo McCarthy in their helpful and detailed comments on an earlier version of this chapter.
41. See Gewirth, *Human Rights*, for an example of this sort of argument.

42. C. Pateman, 'Women and Consent', *Political Theory*, 8 (1980): 149–68.
43. O. O'Neill, *Constructions of Reason: Explorations of Kant's Practical Philosophy*, Cambridge: Cambridge University Press, 1989, pp. 216–18.
44. O'Neill, *Constructions of Reason* and O. O'Neill, *Faces of Hunger: An Essay on Poverty, Justice and Development*, London: Allen & Unwin, 1986.
45. Waldron, 'A Right to do Wrong', *Ethics* 92 (1981): 21–39.
46. O'Neill, *Constructions of Reason*, Ch. 12.
47. E.g. Held, 'Democracy: From City-states to a Cosmopolitan Order?'.
48. A. Cassese, *Human Rights in a Changing World*, Cambridge: Polity, 1990; R. J. Vincent, *Human Rights and International Relations*, Cambridge: Cambridge University Press, 1986.
49. H. Bull, *The Anarchical Society: A Study of Order in World Politics*, London: Macmillan, 1977, Ch. 4.
50. For the republican lineage of this scheme, see R. Bellamy, 'The Political Form of the Constitution: The Separation of Powers, Rights and Representative Democracy', *Political Studies*, 44 (1996): 436–56.
51. I have given a full picture of the republican design of a pluralist polity in *Liberalism and Pluralism: Towards a Politics of Compromise*, London: Routledge, 1999, Ch. 5.
52. I provide an account of how this model might be extended to the European Union in R. Bellamy and D. Castiglione, ' "A Republic if You Can Keep it": the Democratic Deficit and the Constitution of Europe', in A. Gagnon and J. Tully (eds), *Justice and Stability in Multinational Societies*, Cambridge: Cambridge University Press, 2000.

CHAPTER 10

Liberalism and the Challenge of Pluralism

Pluralism permeates modern societies. Their growing differentiation and complexity both highlights and partially generates the plurality of morals, underlining the latent tensions between the various ethical codes and commitments associated with the different spheres of people's lives. Obligations to work, family, friends and strangers frequently pull in opposed directions, as do the claims of ethnicity, religion, ideology and locality. We experience such clashes both within ourselves and in our everyday dealings with other people and institutions whose outlook and attachments differ from our own.

This social and moral pluralism has important consequences for politics. Modern states are less homogeneous than they once were. The enhanced variety amongst the religious, ethnic, occupational and other loyalties of citizens leads them to hold increasingly divergent and often conflicting interests and ideals of social and personal morality and of what gives value to life. The central problem confronting contemporary polities, therefore, is whether it is possible to co-ordinate the various activities of their citizens and generate collectively binding agreements amongst them in ways that respect the diversity of their beliefs and concerns, and so can command their uncoerced allegiance.

Liberalism has traditionally offered itself as the best solution to this issue. A special affinity is often presumed to exist between liberalism and pluralism, with both being seen as distinctive products of modernity. Further analysis, however, shows this relationship to be more ambiguous, both historically and substantively. Of course, it is true that liberalism is associated with various concepts that can be related to a certain kind of appreciation of the plurality of values – such as toleration, autonomy, rights and equality. Moreover, earlier liberals held a historicist faith that the progress of society had inscribed their understanding of these concepts within the economic, social and political transformations that brought the modern world into being – a view still shared implicitly and sometimes even explicitly by many liberals today.[1] But the traditional liberal justification of these principles was essentially monistic. Liberalism was a militant ideology that offered a distinctive and comprehensive moral vision tied to a particular view of the good society. Diversity was only valued for its contribution to that vision.[2]

To the extent pluralism is embedded within modern societies such arguments are no longer plausible.[3] As the first section of this chapter will show, in such circumstances no single ethical code can integrate without remainder the diverse dimensions of human life. Consequently, liberal social and political arrangements require an alternative basis to the ethical liberalism of old. Many contemporary liberal philosophers have come to accept this conclusion and have sought to rethink liberalism in appropriate ways. The second section evaluates their responses. Market-based libertarianism, communitarian liberalism, and the putative neutral constitutionalism of liberal democrats are examined in turn and all found wanting. The first and second options trivialize pluralism by associating it with subjectivism and relativism respectively, whilst the third vainly strives to evade it by seeking agreement on principles of right that are supposedly independent of all notions of the good. The third section puts forward a fourth approach – democratic liberalism – whereby competing ideals and interests are reconciled through compromises negotiated via the political process. The concluding section considers whether this argument falls foul of certain standard liberal fears about the dangers posed by democracy to minority rights.

The Challenge of Pluralism and the Need for Compromise

Pluralists contend that human beings have very different life experiences, hold a wide range of world-views, pursue a variety of goods, goals and interests, and are pulled in diverse directions by various sorts of moral claim.[4] These forms of human flourishing and types of ethical argument are said to be equally reasonable and incommensurable. Consequently, there can be no rationally best life or way of living for human beings to lead. Incommensurability involves both the rational incomparability of values and a failure of transitivity between them. This fact poses grave problems when, for either logical or practical reasons, interests, ideals, moralities or conceptions of the good prove incompatible. For incommensurability suggests that no common currency, such as happiness, exists in terms of which goods and values might be expressed or weighed. It also implies that there is no greatest good towards which all human projects should contribute or tend, or against which they might be evaluated. Nor can any other mechanism be found, such as a lexical priority rule, that can provide an order of precedence amongst all norms, virtues, concerns or preferences, and yet respects each of their distinctive qualities.

Pluralists differ from relativists in contending that different values and goods all have objective worth, rather than simply being relative to particular individuals and societies. They maintain merely there is no hierarchical ordering of, and the ever-present possibility of conflict between, the plurality of goods and values. The basic, universal values which most human societies have recognized, underdetermine the possible forms of human flourishing. Indeed, there may be clashes even between the various elements of the basic universal minimum that are resolved in diverse and incompatible ways within different communities or moral codes.

It is the objectivity of value-pluralism that creates the experience of moral conflict. It also forces us, as individuals or members of a given society, to make choices between moral and other values or interests, and amongst both different sorts of moral claim and the various spheres of human activity within which we either are or could be engaged. Whilst these choices may be reasonable and coherent, they cannot always be said to be the most or the only reasonable or coherent option open to us. Almost every choice involves a sense of lost opportunities or the sacrifice of equally worthwhile goals. As Joseph Raz has noted, incommensurability between plural values entails that 'even in success there is a loss, and quite commonly there is no meaning to the judgement that one gains more than one loses'.[5]

This circumstance poses grave difficulties in the sphere of politics. It is here that the range of values, goods and interests in contention is likely to be greatest, and the need to make collectively binding decisions that reconcile these conflicts between incommensurables hardest to avoid. Moreover, any attempt to resolve the dilemmas thrown up by pluralism will be partial – for both individuals and groups. Certain theorists insist that only radical, and occasionally tragic, choices are possible in such cases.[6] Indeed, for Machiavelli and Weber it was the capacity to make such choices and carry the people with them that marked out political leaders.[7] Similar reasoning has led certain theorists to reject the 'classical' model of liberal democracy and its aim of achieving a rational consensus on the common good. At best, it becomes a mechanism for throwing up appropriately charismatic politicians.[8]

A less drastic view of the consequences of pluralism for democratic politics is possible, however. For an alternative to the radical choice of one option over all others can be a compromise between them. If such compromises are to be distinguished from the simple capitulation of certain of the parties involved, then they must entail all those concerned modifying their positions in some mutually acceptable way. To achieve that latter result requires political negotiation and a willingness to face up to the full moral and epistemological complexity that characterizes most modern societies.

I shall defend the art of compromise as the chief virtue of a democratic liberalism in section three. As we shall see, it stands in marked contrast to the approaches of contemporary liberal theorists, the subject of the next section. For instead of confronting the political choices and conflicts associated with pluralism, they seek to avoid them by pursuing an elusive apolitical consensus grounded in the invisible hand of the market, community traditions or a neutral constitution. These respective strategies of libertarians, communitarians and liberal democrats all prove inadequate.

Contemporary Liberalism

Although liberal doctrine grew out of the religious and class conflicts of modern Europe, it attempted to accommodate and contain them within the context of relatively homogeneous nation states. Liberals conceived individuals as enjoying an equal status as members of largely well-defined and culturally cohesive societies. A shared constitutional framework, democratic institutions and the economic market all served as supposedly impartial mechanisms that enabled individuals and groups to pursue their own ends with a minimum of mutual interference. This view of society and politics depended in its turn on certain ethical naturalist assumptions concerning human agency and flourishing that suggested that individual goals could be harmonized within a social and political system guaranteeing the most extensive equal liberty to all.[9]

Recent liberal philosophers have attempted to hold on to this conception of the liberal social and political system, whilst placing it on less contentious metaphysical foundations to those of the ethical liberal tradition of Locke, Kant and Mill. Whilst they accept that pluralism undermines the attempt to found liberalism on a comprehensive conception of the good, they believe that liberal practices have distinctive virtues of their own that prove compatible with a wide range of values and beliefs.

Libertarians commonly assert that the market fosters pluralism because it promotes individual choice. Its distributions reflect the multifarious subjective preferences of consumers rather than the value scheme of any single central planning agency.[10] The pluralist credentials of this argument are highly dubious, however. Unlike pluralism, subjectivist and emotivist moral theories do not see moral conflicts as a clash between objective goals, values and types of reasoning which are independent of the will or inclination and can all claim an equally rational basis. Similarly, the normative individualism of market theories is no respecter of collective goods, as early conservative and socialist critics of capitalism who bemoaned its destructive impact on tradition and social solidarity pointed out. Such criticisms have come to seem ever-more relevant in recent years, and have been added to by certain religious and ethnic groups wanting to stress the worth of forms of life where individual choice plays little or no part. More important, the market reduces all goods and values to a common medium of exchange, namely money, and hence treats all goods as commensurable. This process of commodification goes hand in hand with the diffusion of a market ethos that imputes a certain form of self-interested, utility-maximizing agency to individuals in all spheres of activity.[11] Finally, justifications for the market tend to be on the basis of either utilitarian considerations that stress its economic productiveness, or rights-based arguments usually related to the individual's right to private property. But what Charles Larmore has called the heterogeneity of morality is such that neither of these types of moral claim tells the whole story.[12] Consequentialist and deontological reasoning often pulls us in different directions, and are themselves in conflict with partialist considerations.

Criticism of the individualist bias of markets and of the imperialist extension of the market ethos into all spheres of social life has formed a constant refrain of communitarian theories. Some communitarians have argued that pluralism can be more easily accommodated within an Aristo-telian version of liberalism.[13] The pluralist credentials of this kind of argument derive from Aristotle's criticism of the Platonic doctrine that all goods are ultimately one. However, recognition that human flourishing draws on a diversity of goods is different from an acceptance of pluralism. Aristotle not only remained convinced that both individuals and society at large could bring all values and interests into a coherent vision of the good life, he also ranked the contemplative life above all others. As Stuart Hampshire has remarked, he retained Plato's picture of the soul 'as corresponding to the due gradations of social order', with 'reason as the governing class and desires as the restless proletariat'.[14] Pluralism, in contrast, both denies that either a conception of the best life or a single just ordering for society can be rationally derived from human nature, and contests the hierarchical model of society to which this thesis tacitly appeals.

Other communitarians accept that different but equally valuable forms of human flourishing have been adopted by societies at various times and places.[15] Unfortunately, their argument rests on a relativist picture of morals and social relations that proves just as dubiously supportive of pluralism as the Aristotelians' view. Bernard Williams has pointed out that relativism does not so much account for pluralism as explain it away, regarding different moral claims and values as appropriate within their respective contexts.[16] Moral conflicts become a matter of boundary disputes rather than genuine dilemmas, many of which arise within all but the most narrowly defined of culturally determined moral spheres.

Neutrality forms the third main contemporary liberal response to plural-ism. In a major restatement of his theory, Rawls has related pluralism to 'the burdens of judgement' and the presence of reasonable disagreement between people holding different moral convictions.[17] Rawls contends that the diffi-culty of identifying conclusive evidence in ethical debates and interpreting its relevance, together with differences in individual experience, produce insur-mountable problems for the weighing and ranking of values and interests. Consequently, pluralism is a 'fact' that liberal societies which allow freedom of thought and expression must inevitably confront.[18] Whilst he remains agnostic on the objective existence of a plurality of values, he believes that these limits to reason mean that many value conflicts cannot be rationally resolved. Liberalism should steer clear of all controversial metaphysical and epistemological views, therefore – including any appeal to pluralism *per se*.[19] It must rest on only those principles that reasonable people could agree to as necessary for the regulation of their common life despite (or, perhaps, because of) the various convictions that divide them.[20]

To be generally acceptable, he maintains, such principles must be neutral with regard to the good life. This neutrality is obtained by the removal of thorny topics from the political arena. When deliberating within the public sphere, citizens agree not to refer to their background beliefs and to make their case solely in terms of a circumscribed set of core political values that reflect an 'overlapping consensus' between a plurality of different ideological and ethical perspectives. These core values consist of the basic liberties enshrined within the constitutions of liberal democratic regimes. Liberalism becomes in this way the framework for democracy.[21]

Rawls's difficulty lies in explaining why people should feel obliged to practise such self-abnegation. At times, his argument appears to be merely pragmatic – we all have a reason to avoid contentious issues for the sake of peace and stability. However, as he recognizes, this solution will only prove attractive so long as there is no chance of my being able to enforce my view or I have no desire to become a martyr (or at least to risk martyrdom), as some terrorist groups seem prepared to do. In addition, he fails to appreciate the danger that one's opinions will not count for as much as they should if one cannot voice the genuine interests and principles that lie behind one's taking a certain standpoint. One's interlocutors will be ignorant of the strength of one's feelings, for example raising the problem of 'intense' minorities.[22]

At other times, however, Rawls suggests that our adherence to the political core reflects a moral conviction deriving from a certain ideal of citizenship. Yet, Rawls proves unable to ground this ideal without either appealing to contentious metaphysical views of the self, such as he wishes to avoid, or falling into relativism. On the one hand, his neo-Kantian view of the citizen as possessing both 'a sense of justice' and 'a capacity to revise and pursue a conception of the good' derives from a recognizably liberal understanding of autonomous agency.[23] It will not attract those who regard certain of their moral commitments as constitutive of their personality and not to be revised or bracketed at will. On the other hand, Rawls claims that far from drawing this picture of citizenship from certain contestable metaphysical foundations, he is just reporting the perspective of a certain political tradition.[24] At this point, worries about relativism return, which we have seen is no more compatible with pluralism than a comprehensive liberalism of a Kantian kind.

Rawls's search for an allusive 'overlapping consensus' between plural points of view seems doomed. The very notion of separating the right from the good simply makes no sense for holders of numerous reasonable ethical positions – from consequentialist utilitarians to the various Church officials who recently condemned British political parties for not seeing that taxation was a 'moral' issue. Different views of the true and the good generate divergent understandings of the right. The 'burdens of judgement' can even give rise to reasonable disagreement over how agreed principles of justice might be applied in given circumstances – as when Constitutional Courts divide over whether a given right has been infringed or not. Rawls's failure nonetheless neatly sets the agenda for a pluralist liberalism. Namely, is it possible to steer a middle course between the Scylla of metaphysical rationalism and the Charybdis of moral relativism? In what follows, I wish to suggest that we can by turning to what I call a democratic liberalism.

Democratic Liberalism

Though apparently intractable from a theoretical point of view, practically the conflicts posed by pluralism have to be resolved – either by opting for one good or package of values at the expense of another, or by arriving at some sort of compromise. The task is to recognize the diversity represented by pluralism, whilst meeting liberal criteria of admissibility. I shall maintain that the solution lies in collective decisions that avoid coercion, are regarded as legitimate and possess authority, even if not everyone fully agrees with them. In other words, where no *a priori* right answer exists we must construct an agreement which a plurality of agents and agencies will find acceptable.

Democratic politics has formed the traditional mechanism for achieving such agreements. Following Jon Elster, one can characterize the democratic process as involving both 'bargaining' and 'arguing'.[25] We standardly employ the former to resolve what Albert Hirschman has called 'more-or-less' conflicts, where it is possible to 'split the difference'.[26] Wage bargaining typically takes this form. The latter, in contrast, is more appropriate to Hirschman's category of 'either–or' conflicts, involving competing moral principles. Ethnic, religious and linguistic quarrels often have this character. For argument enables views to be transformed as opposed to simply combined in some mechanical fashion. Needless to say, most political discussions involve elements of both types of debating and a complex interaction of interests and values. Decisions over environmental issues typically have this form, with economic concerns over employment or development interacting with the need to protect places of beauty and scientific interest, on the one hand, and rights to property, health and security, on the other.

When democracy is seen as the process of constructing justice rather than being framed by it, as in Rawls's theory, pluralism can be accommodated more fully. This end is achieved through a politics that allows the making of compromises that avoid discrimination, attain legitimacy by demonstrating mutual accommodation and respect, and are recognized as authoritive. First, the application of norms of justice from the outside, with no account of the interests or values of those to whom they are to be applied, often leads to a blindness to people's limited capacities or opportunities. Feminists, for example, have pointed out how equal opportunities legislation has often embodied a 'male comparator' test that is insensitive to gender differences and the structural difficulties women face.[27] By allowing preferences, interests and values to be voiced, rather than excluding them from debate as Rawls proposes, democratic politics enables the attitudes of hegemonic groups to be challenged, forces minority or hitherto marginalized positions to be addressed, and so is sensitive to difference and avoids domination.

Second, a democratic liberalism involves a different conception of legitimacy to the standard liberal democratic view – namely, that a legitimate decision reflects general deliberation rather than a pre-existing general will.[28] Theorists of deliberative democracy standardly see rational consensus as the goal of this style of politics.[29] I noted in section one, however, that pluralism makes consensual agreement in the sense of a convergence on common values and interests highly unlikely. Fortunately, democratic debate need not assume that all interests can be ranked along some single dimension, or that people share some common good. Deliberative decisions may reflect a compromise resulting from mutual accommodation rather than a consensus on shared norms or the general welfare.[30] How much accommodation and of what nature will largely depend on the issue, the audience one is addressing, and the radicalness of one's views and their impact on others. Debate, and the need to justify oneself in terms that people holding a variety of positions can recognize and relate to, prevent individuals from adopting a purely self-regarding point of view and encourage them to state their case in the most general and publically accessible terms possible. But what form and degree such generality and publicity must take cannot be decided *a priori*.[31]

Different types of conflict will generate different styles of politics and compromise. Compromise is most familiar to us in 'more-or-less' contexts where we can 'split the difference' so as to coverge on an agreed decision through incremental mutual concessions. Haggling over the price of a commodity such as a house, or wage bargaining are typical examples. Such conflicts, however, are usually along a single dimension and involve a common denominator. As such, this procedure is unsuited to the conflicts associated with pluralism. Compromises in 'either–or' situations involving plural and competing values and interests prove more exacting but not impossible. They have to take the form of constructing a distinctive position through argument that seeks to accommodate at some level or another the various claims, values and interests at stake.

How such compromises are to be achieved will vary according to the nature of the case.[32] Thus, a compromise might take the form of a composite agreement in which each party gets some but not all of what it wants. This strategy usually proves easier when more than one policy is involved. Because groups often have rather different priorities with regard to a range of policies, it frequently proves possible for them to concede on issues they do not feel strongly about but others do in order to obtain similar concessions from them or other allies on the matters they regard as most important. Such processes are crucial to the log-rolling and coalition-building practised by political parties. This practice does not entail that all views are reducible to interests, as is sometimes assumed. In fact, these sorts of deals are more like bartering than normal bargaining. Indeed, they generally occur precisely because people hold a plurality of moral positions that lead them to evaluate goods and even what constitutes a matter of morality differently — much as beads can be exchanged for gold when one group's worthless shiny substance is another's valuable commodity. The exchange entails incommensurability, since it might well not have taken place had it been conceived in standard 'more-or-less' terms, with all goods translated into a single common currency. It also proves more responsive to intensity of feeling than a simple bargaining model. However, it will only work if those involved can avoid judging particular issues on their merits.

When a compromise has to be reached on a single issue, such trade-offs cannot be achieved. Moreover, a mutual adaptation of views may be highly unsatisfactory, producing a result that nobody wants rather than something for everyone — precisely the situation critics who accuse compromise of incoherence most abhor. One way out of this dilemma, recently proposed by Robert Goodin, is an agreement on a second best.[33] A notion adapted from economics, the basic idea is that modifications to one's preferred option may be less desirable than obtaining one's next best or an even lower ranked choice. A cheap sports car that pretends to be an expensive one may have less appeal than an unpretentious family estate, for example. Indeed, individuals or groups with conflicting first preferences may have shared second preferences. A compromise on an agreed second best may prove a more coherent and acceptable decision, therefore, than an attempt to combine first preferences in ways that transform them out of all recognition or involve inconsistencies of various kinds.

When a group makes a claim that involves special treatment or imposing burdens on others, they may have to compromise more unilaterally by appealing either to some norm of equity that the others also share, or to ideals or interests that their interlocutors can identify with through appeals to precedent, use of analogy or *a fortiori* arguments.[34] Thus, a religious group seeking public recognition for its beliefs, say in state support for its schools, will be unlikely to get very far if it desires to set up a theocratic state. But they may be able to invoke a norm of equal treatment by pointing to the existence of other publically funded religious schools. Or, where state education has hitherto been secular, the claim might involve drawing a parallel with state support for some humanist analogue to religious belief, such as the arts, in which the cultural aspect of religion is emphasized.

Nonetheless, sometimes no compromise on substance proves possible. This dilemma often arises for purely practical reasons to do with the nature of the decision rather than because of any lack of good will amongst those making it – such as a choice between two somewhat different but equally good candidates for a post, for each of whom a sound case might be made. Only one can be chosen, and a compromise candidate does not always make sense. In such circumstances the compromise might have to be on accepting the outcome of a fair procedure, such as tossing a coin. Within purely procedural versions of democracy, the majoritarian principle can be seen as a compromise of this sort.[35]

This brings us to the third element. For the majority principle also acts as a means for resolving conflict in an authoritative manner when a compromise on substance cannot be achieved. Authority here rests on neither claims to superior reason nor coercion but the simple acceptance of the procedure as authoritative (in the sense of being 'in' authority) for the disputing parties. This point is important because there may not be any 'correct' or 'most just' way of resolving a clash between incommensurable values, only acceptable ways of ending the dispute.[36]

Democratic procedures allow the negotiation and settlement of principled differences by linking justification with the overcoming of dominance, the attainment of legitimacy and the acceptance of authority. All three of these elements involve the different interests and ideals in play being weighed in a public manner that obliges both those making a particular claim and those responding to it to take account of the views of others. Justified agreement amongst diverse groups and individuals emerges in this way from politics and its capacity to generate mutually acceptable solutions based on compromise.

Liberal Doubts

Many liberals will feel uneasy about placing liberalism within democracy rather than the other way around, and find the emphasis on compromise merely reinforces their disquiet at this approach. For compromise suggests a lack of integrity that neatly captures the moral ambivalence felt by liberals about politics at large: to adopt a 'compromising position' is the mark of politicians motivated by pure self-interest and ready to do any deal for the sake of furthering their careers or holding on to power. As such, a 'democratic liberalism' may fuel traditional liberal worries about populism and the tyranny of the majority, and the democratic tendency to pander to those with the loudest voices rather than the best case.[37]

Majoritarianism in the sense rightly feared by liberals consists in the imposition of purely self-serving preferences on others. Clearly there is a danger that if a society is not pluralist enough to contain cross-cutting cleavages, then a group could mobilize itself so as to get its way all the time without ever taking account of others. Resolving this problem is a basic task of any well-designed political constitution. In recent times, a Bill of Rights and judicial review have been assumed to be the main means of achieving this goal. The standard rationale has been that of Rawls's political liberalism: namely, the securing of those basic liberties that are intrinsic to the political sphere. However, constitutional design can also be viewed in more institutional terms as the design of political rather than legal mechanisms, that serve to promote rather than constrain politics, and ensure that minority opinions get heard and deliberation takes place. Different kinds of representation, the separation of powers, federalism and consociationalism are the classic devices employed for this purpose. All aim at producing inclusive forms of decision-making capable of delivering bargained or argued compromises. In other words, they oblige majorities to confront and engage with minority opinion and search for novel solutions that meet their concerns. Unlike judicial forms of minority rights protection, this political approach proves more sensitive to the role of unequal power in creating discrimination and the need to give hitherto oppressed groups a voice if laws are to incorporate their interests and ideals and so obtain their allegiance.

Though the net effect of these political devices is to weaken the capacity of majorities unilaterally to impose their will, there are certain instances where democratic liberalism is more favourable to majority decisions than other liberalisms. A common liberal argument insists that certain rights ought never to be sacrificed and need constitutional protection lest a democratic majority seek to abridge them.[38] By contrast, democratic liberalism regards such rights as being grounded in democracy. Even if Bills of Rights have often been formulated by elite groups, they have usually required popular endorsement. Moreover, their ongoing effectiveness and endurance depend on their commanding wide support. It would be implausible, however, to expect that they would ever achieve unanimous assent. To this extent, rights cannot be treated as totally at odds with majoritarianism, since this would render their original enactment and continued respect somewhat mysterious.

Rights are also more problematic than is sometimes supposed. For a start, they can conflict, as we saw, with other forms of moral reasoning. Both sides in discussions over capital punishment, for example, normally combine rights-based retributive and consequentialist inspired deterrent arguments. It is doubtful that a totally watertight case could be given for prioritizing one form of moral reasoning over the other, since this would be to deny the complexity of the issue. Similarly, the different moral viewpoints and related empirical evidence cannot be said all to come down either for or against the death penalty. Rather, it is a matter of balance, with different people validly placing more or less weight on different sides of the issue. Even amongst rights, conflicts can occur. Thus, one aspect of the capital punishment debate concerns weighing up the claims of potential innocent victims of crime against the danger of condemning an innocent person to death. Indeed, divergent views of human flourishing can lead people not only to prioritize different rights but also to give incompatible and incommensurable interpretations of the same right. This is clear from disputes between libertarians and egalitarians over the meaning of liberty.

A democratic liberalism regards the majority as having the legitimate authority to resolve these sorts of disputes. In part, this is because when democracy is conceived as involving deliberation then individual voters are not simply expressing personal preferences but striving to promote a general view that balances the various rights, interests and other moral considerations in play. In such cases, the usual objections to majoritarianism do not hold.[39] There has been no overriding of rights here, merely an attempt to evaluate different opinions about them. However, when a deadlock is reached, then a fair procedure is required to resolve the dispute. Here the procedural authority of democracy comes into play. Objections to majoritarianism on the basis of rights are inappropriate at this stage for the different reason that the whole point of invoking majority rule is to settle a disagreement about rights.[40]

Of course, it might be that a democratic majority would consider the best way to ensure that rights got due consideration was to accord them special constitutional protection. Even so, some forum would be required to deal with problems of conflict and interpretation. If that turned out to be a constitutional court, then in many 'hard' cases judges would be forced to deliberate and act on majority decisions in the same manner as the demos. In such cases, judges can no longer claim to act as authoritative experts on justice. Instead, their decisions have merely the procedural authority conferred by the democratic process. Consequently, a democratic liberal would want there to be mechanisms for the democratic review and amendment of such constitutional provisions. This proviso leaves open the door for arguments to be restated or new cases to be made about the relative standing of certain liberties, rather than permanently excluding them from political debate as certain liberals desire. Such a provision not only shows greater respect towards dissenting opinions but arguably proves more effective in sustaining the support of opponents and proponents alike in the resulting settlement.[41]

Democratic liberalism differs from judicial rights-based liberalism in holding that a just and liberal settlement amongst diverse groups is the product of politics, not its precondition.[42] Justice from this perspective rests on the adversarial principle of hearing the other side.[43] It can only be done if it is seen to be done, and opportunities exist for mutual adaption and a fair compromise between equally reasonable yet opposed points of view. That involves dropping the legalistic constitutional paradigm of the ethical liberal tradition from Locke to Kant, and recently revived by Rawls, and adopting the more political approach put forward here – albeit one with an equally impeccable liberal lineage in the work of Montesquieu, Madison and Weber.[44]

Conclusion

A democratic liberalism focused on the achievement of agreements through the deliberative process enables the claims of different values and goods to be taken seriously. Unlike the market championed by libertarians, political deliberation does not treat individual or group interests and beliefs as mere subjective preferences but as objective forms of flourishing. Consequently, it takes their intrinsic as well as their instrumental worth into account. Nor are people's allegiances regarded as mysterious social facts that are beyond reasonable defence and should be immune to criticism, as communitarian relativists end up arguing. Finally, instead of treating pluralism as a threat to consensus and seeking to exclude it, as Rawlsian neutralists propose, democratic liberalism regards competing viewpoints as providing an incentive for individuals to take a broader perspective. People are accorded the capacity to engage in principled dialogue with others as to the arrangements that are to frame their lives, and to meet those with whom they disagree halfway.

Notes

1. I offer a full exposition and defence of these contentions in R. Bellamy, *Liberalism and Modern Society: An Historical Argument*, Cambridge: Polity Press, 1992.
2. See R. Vernon, 'Moral Pluralism and the Liberal Mind', in J. M. Porter and R. Vernon (eds), *Unity, Plurality and Politics: Essays in Honour of F. M. Barnard*, London and Sydney: Croom Helm, 1986 and G. Crowder, 'Pluralism and Liberalism', *Political Studies*, 42 (1994): 293–305, who show that the liberal belief in autonomy, toleration and diversity does not follow from a commitment to pluralism.
3. Bellamy, *Liberalism and Modern Society*, Ch. 5.
4. The following account of pluralism draws on J. Kekes, *The Morality of Pluralism*, Princeton, NJ: Princeton University Press, 1993. See too I. Berlin, *The Crooked Timber of Humanity*, London: Fontana Press, 1991; J. Gray, *Post-Liberalism: Studies in Political Thought*, London: Routledge, 1993, pp. 287–306; S. Hampshire, *Morality and Conflict*, Oxford: Blackwell, 1983; S. Hampshire, *Innocence and Experience*, Harmondsworth: Penguin, 1989; C. Larmore, *Patterns of Moral Complexity*, Cambridge: Cambridge University Press, 1987, Ch. 6; C. Larmore, 'Pluralism and Reasonable Disagreement', *Social Philosophy and Policy*, 11 (1994): 61–79; T. Nagel, *Mortal Questions*, Cambridge: Cambridge University Press, 1979, Ch. 9; B. Williams, *Moral Luck*, Cambridge: Cambridge University Press, 1981, Ch. 5; J. Raz, *The Morality of Freedom*, Oxford: Clarendon Press, 1986, Ch. 13; and S. Lukes, *Moral Conflict and Politics*, Oxford: Clarendon Press, 1991, Ch. 1. I give a full account of the pluralist challenge to liberalism in *Liberalism and Pluralism: Towards a Politics of Compromise*, London: Routledge, 1999, 'Introduction'.

5. J. Raz, 'Multiculturalism: A Liberal View', in *Ethics in the Public Domain*, Oxford: Clarendon Press, 1994, p. 179.
6. E.g. J. Gray, *Enlightenment's Wake: Politics and Culture at the Close of the Modern Age*, London: Routledge, 1995, pp. 70–1.
7. M. Weber, 'Science as a Vocation', trans. in H. H. Gerth and C. W. Mills (eds), *From Max Weber*, London: Routledge, 1948, p. 148; N. Machiavelli, *The Prince and Other Writings*, ed. J. Plamenatz, London: Fontana, 1972, Ch. 15.
8. This has been the view of the Machiavellian-minded classic elite theorists. For an analysis and critique of this position as exemplified by Pareto and Weber, see Bellamy, *Liberalism and Modern Society*, Chs 3 and 4.
9. For further details, see Bellamy, *Liberalism and Modern Society*, esp. Chs 2 and 3.
10. This is the central claim of F. A. Hayek, *Law, Legislation and Liberty*, 3 vols, London: Routledge, 1973–9, esp. Vol. 2.
11. For further criticism along these lines see R. Keat, 'The Moral Boundaries of the Market', in C. Crouch and D. Marquand (eds), *Ethics and Markets*, Oxford: Blackwell, 1993,
    pp. 6–20 and R. Bellamy, 'Moralizing Markets', *Critical Review*, 8 (1994): 341–57.
12. Larmore, *Patterns of Moral Complexity*, Ch. 6.
13. E.g. Raz, *Morality of Freedom*.
14. Hampshire, *Innocence and Experience*, p. 34.
15. E.g. M. Walzer, *Spheres of Justice*, Oxford: Martin Robertson, 1983.
16. Williams, *Moral Luck*, p. 75; see too Lukes, *Moral Conflict*, p. 4.
17. J. Rawls, *Political Liberalism*, New York: Columbia University press, 1993, pp. 54–8.
18. Rawls, *Political Liberalism*, p. 36.
19. Rawls, *Political Liberalism*, p. 57 n. 10.
20. Rawls, *Political Liberalism*, pp. 38–40.
21. Rawls, *Political Liberalism*, pp. 151 n. 16, 156–7, 161.
22. I develop this criticism and those that follow more fully in R. Bellamy, 'Pluralism, Liberal Constitutionalism and Democracy: A Critique of John Rawls' (Meta)political liberalism', in J. Meadowcroft (ed.), *The Liberal Political Tradition: Contemporary Reappraisals*, Cheltenham: Edward Elgar, 1996, pp. 77–100 and my *Liberalism and Pluralism*, Ch. 2.
23. Rawls, *Political Liberalism*, p. 19.
24. Rawls, *Political Liberalism*, p. 8.
25. J. Elster, *Argomentare e negoziare*, Milan: Anabasi, 1993; J. Elster, 'The Market and the Forum: Three Varieties of Political Theory', in J. Elster and A. Hylland (eds), *Foundations of Social Choice Theory*, Cambridge: Cambridge University Press, 1986, p. 113.
26. A. O. Hirshman, 'Social Conflicts as Pillars of Democratic Market Society', *Political Theory*, 22 (1994): 203–18.
27. E.g. C. MacKinnon, *Feminism Unmodified: Discourses on Life and Law*, Cambridge, Mass.: Harvard University Press, 1989, p. 36.
28. B. Manin, 'On Legitimacy and Deliberation', *Political Theory*, 15 (1987): 338–68.
29. This is particularly true of those theorists influenced by the thought of J. Habermas. For the clearest account of his position, see 'Discourse Ethics: Note on a Programme of Philosophical Justification', in *Moral Consciousness and Communicative Action*, trans. C. Lenhardt and S. W. Nicholsen, Cambridge: Polity, 1990: 43–115.

30. Habermas does mention compromise very briefly in *Between Facts and Norms: Contributions to a Discourse Theory of Law and Democracy*, Cambridge: Polity, 1996, but restricts it to the 'balancing of interests' and bargaining rather than the negotiation of values, where consensus is the goal (pp. 140–1). Elster, 'The Market and the Forum, p. 112 also contrasts a politics of interest that strives for an 'optimal compromise' and a Habermasian politics of public and rational discussion which aims for 'unanimous agreement'.

31. See D. Miller, 'Citizenship and Pluralism', *Political Studies*, 43 (1995): 432–50.

32. The next few paragraphs draw on Richard Bellamy and Martin Hollis, 'Consensus, Neutrality and Compromise', in R. Bellamy and M. Hollis (eds), *Pluralism and Liberal Neutrality*, London: Frank Cass, 1999, pp. 54–78. I have subsequently developed the argument in *Liberalism and Pluralism*, Chs 4 and 5. Helpful discussions of compromise include: M. Benjamin, *Splitting the Difference: Compromise and Integrity in Ethics and Politics*, Kansas: University of Kansas Press, 1990; P. Dobel, *Compromise and Political Action: Political Morality in Liberal and Democratic Life*, Savage, MD: Rowman and Little, 1990; and J. H. Carens, 'Compromises in Politics', in J. R. Pennock and J. W. Chapman (eds), *Compromise in Ethics, Law and Politics*, NOMOS XXI, New York: New York University Press, 1979, pp. 123–39.

33. R. Goodin, 'Political Ideals and Political Practice', *British Journal of Political Science*, 25 (1995): 37–56.

34. Manin, 'Om Legitimacy and Deliberation', p. 353.

35. P. Singer, *Democracy and Disobedience*, Oxford: Oxford University Press, 1974, p. 32 sees it as 'a paradigm of a fair compromise'.

36. For the classic discussion of the need for a distinction between being 'in' and 'an' authority when people morally disagree, see T. Hobbes, *Leviathan*, Harmondsworth: Penguin, 1968, Ch. 18.

37. For a classic statement of these worries, see J. Morely, *On Compromise*, London: Macmillan, 1886.

38. E.g. Rawls, *Political Liberalism*, p. 161. The paragraphs that follow draw on arguments that I've developed more fully in 'The Constitution of Europe: Rights or Democracy?', in R. Bellamy *et al.* (eds), *Democracy and Constitutional Culture in the Union of Europe*, London: Lothian Foundation Press, 1995 and *Liberalism and Pluralism*, Ch. 7. See too J. Waldron, 'Rights and Majorities: Rousseau Revisited', in J. Chapman and A. Wertheimer (eds), *NOMOS XXXII: Majorities and Minorities*, New York: New York University Press, 1990 and J. Waldron, 'A Right-based Critique of Constitutional Rights', *Oxford Journal of Legal Studies*, 13 (1993): 18–51.

39. Waldron, 'Rights and Majorities'.

40. This point is forcefully made by Waldron, 'A Right-based Critique of Constitutional Rights', pp. 31–4.

41. Bellamy, 'Constitution of Europe' and R. Bellamy, 'Liberal Politics and the Judiciary: the Supreme Court and American Democracy', *Res Publica*, 3 (1997): 81–96.

42. B. Crick, *In Defence of Politics*, Harmondsworth: Penguin, 1962, p. 24.

43. S. Hampshire notes the centrality of this concept to most forms of public reasoning in 'Justice is Strife', *Proceedings and Addresses of the American Philosophical Association*, 65 (1991): 20–1.

44. R. Bellamy, 'The Political Form of the Constitution: the Separation of Powers, Rights and Representative Democracy', *Political Studies*, 44 (1996): 436–56 and Bellamy, *Liberalism and Modern Society*, Ch. 4.

PART III

Reinventing Liberal Politics

rational-voter model that informed the government's strategy, non-registration in order to avoid the Poll Tax was a thoroughly rational strategy. As McLean and Mortimore point out: 'The expected value of voting discounted by the probability that it is my vote which swings the election will almost always be lower than my Poll Tax bill discounted by the probability that keeping off the electoral register enables me to evade it.'[23] This incentive to forgo one's political rights was strongest amongst the poorest section of the community. Not only had they lost most via the introduction of the charge, but it was only the very bottom-most rung of society who were likely to opt to avoid appearing on any of the other local authority or social service records to which the Community Charge Registration Officer had access. In practice, this meant not having a council tenancy, claiming housing benefit, using council leisure services or going to a social worker – a possibility only likely to be available to the young, casually employed or unemployed without a place of their own. The net result of non-registration, therefore, was to withdraw almost totally from official society.[24] To find a reason why this group should feel obliged to obey the law is very difficult indeed.

The problem of consistent minorities has been an issue both of the very poor and of certain regions of Britain. One of the political innovations of the 1980s was the discovery that a government could allow high levels of unemployment without suffering unduly adverse electoral consequences. The first-past-the-post system combined with the regional concentration of the unemployed allowed 10 per cent of the population to be marginalized. The fact that this exclusion of a minority from national prosperity was as much territorial as class or sectorally based had the additional effect in Scotland of strengthening the sense of national distinctiveness, at least in political if not necessarily cultural terms. Thus, the Poll Tax came to be regarded as but the most signal instance of the manner in which policies without any electoral mandate from the Scottish electorate were imposed on Scotland.[25] This view of the unrepresentativeness of rule from Westminster did not automatically bring with it a call for independence, since the argument was widely used by Labour and the Liberal Democrats as well as the SNP. The former parties merely argued for greater representiveness within the British system through electoral reform or some devolution of power from the centre or both. The conclusion of all groups was the same, however: namely, that the sense of obligation deriving from democracy as a fair compromise did not exist in Scotland because, although the system itself might have been formally fair, it failed to operate in a fair manner, with the result that the Scottish people found themselves constantly outvoted and their views consistently ignored.

With regard to Singer's third condition of democratic fairness, the government claimed the Community Charge increased the power of citizens by enhancing the democratic accountability of local authorities to the wishes of the taxpayers. As Nicholas Ridley, then Secretary of State for the Environment, put it:

Everyone should have the right, through the ballot box, to influence the level of service that is provided and the price that they must pay through their taxes. That is the essence of democratic accountability and of responsible democratic control of the services provided by local authorities.[26]

However, this argument was doubled-edged. The individual exercised control through elections but also had to pay through taxation. The idea, in Selwyn Gummer's words, was not just 'that local authorities should be responsible to all of their electors', but also 'that every adult should pay his fair share and play a responsible part in the local democratic process'.[27] Their contention was that the rates system, in giving a large number of people a vote without their being personally liable for taxation, undermined this democratic responsibility. The flat rate was justified on the grounds that it was a charge for services rather than a tax, and so the level should reflect the demand and use made of facilities more than ability to pay (although some account was taken of the latter, albeit less than under the rating system). Thus, the accountability aimed at by the government was not so much that of local authorities to citizens, as that of citizens to the Treasury for the financial costs of the policies they enacted. The extent to which the change aimed at empowering citizens was distinctly limited, therefore. Rather than creating democratic structures that might have enabled citizens to have a greater control over the framing and implementation of local policies, for example, the guiding inspiration for the scheme seems to have been to impose financial discipline on voters by creating a more direct link between local spending on services and local taxation.[28]

This aim might nevertheless have been squared with Singer's view of democracy as a fair compromise had the charge been at least proportionate to income and if increases in the charge had been proportionate to increases in local expenditure. In practice, neither was the case. The government refused to band the charge according to income, merely providing a safety net in the form of rebates for the very poor – most of whom were net losers under the new system, the rich being the main gainers.[29] Moreover, the fact that some 75 per cent of local income came from a government assessment of the authority's needs, together with the capping powers used against overspenders and central control of business rates, all meant that national decisions about grants had a far more dramatic effect on Poll Tax levels than the decisions of local voters, and that additional spending at a local level produced a dispropor-tionate increase in domestic Poll Tax. These distortions of financial accountability weighed much more heavily on deprived individuals and areas than affluent ones, with the result that poorer groups had less than an equal share of influence. They were harder hit not just by any decision to increase local expenditure but also by any reduction in spending. In such circum-stances, the argument for obedience based on fair compromise once again plainly ceases to apply.

Singer, in fact, goes much further to argue that no existing democracy meets his conditions of fairness. A less severe judgement might accord existing Western democracies the Rawlsian status of 'nearly just societies'. In such imperfect democracies, however, the scope for disobedience is likely to be greater than Singer permits within a more perfect democracy. This observation will allow us to deal with two subsidiary arguments that are sometimes invoked to disallow even civil disobedience on issues such as the Poll Tax within liberal democracies.

The first argument seeks to distinguish between 'integrity-based', 'justice-based' and 'policy-based' issues.[30] An example of the first is conscientious objection; of the second a protest at a policy that abrogates basic rights, as in the civil rights campaigns in the American South in the 1960s; and of the third disobedience against a policy that is judged simply misguided. According to this line of thought, a particular form of behaviour is legitimate for each type of disobedience. In the first case, the disobedient acts to avoid doing something that goes against his or her deeply felt principles. She is not interested in persuading others, she merely seeks to avoid guilt by association. The consequences of her actions only constrain her to the extent that they might conflict with other of her deeply felt beliefs. In the second case, the disobedient may legitimately refuse to obey laws prohibiting him from doing what he believes he has a right to do. It is not legitimate, however, for a minority simply to seize what it thinks are its rights. Rather, it must seek to persuade the majority to its point of view. Coercion is only justified when fundamental democratic rights, basic to any persuasive strategy, are at issue. In the third case, civil disobedience is simply politics by other means. Anything other than persuasion, for example an attempt to frustrate a policy by making it unworkable or too costly to implement, becomes an illegitimate form of 'civil blackmail'.[31] For not to abide by a democratic decision in such cases deprives others of their say and constitutes a willingness to impose your views. Hence, such policy-based disobedience is wrong, because it opens up the way to a resort to force by all the parties concerned.

Let us accept for the moment the validity of these dubious distinctions and the even more debatable, if not uncommon, view that the anti-Poll Tax campaign belonged to the third category of disobedience.[32] Let us also assume that Britain is at any rate a nearly just democracy that reasonably approximates to a fair compromise. Does this mean that the non-payment and even the 'Stop It' campaign were illegitimate? The usual assumption is that they were, and that only purely persuasive disobedience designed to get a fair hearing or to promote a reconsideration would be justified, not disobedience that aimed to obstruct and thereby force a change by making the costs of implementation unnecessarily high or impossible. This argument, however, is contestable even in its own terms. First, the persuasion/costly and coercive distinction seems to be one of degree rather than kind. After all, peaceful demonstrations, letter-writing campaigns to MPs, and so on all place a strain on the state's resources. To be coherent, it would seem to rule out any protest at all. Second, it rests on an implausible conception of how liberal democracy works: namely, the view that only facts and reasoned argument guide the making of policy in the first place. As Robert Goodin has pointed out, this is a highly contentious assumption. Political scientists ranging from pluralists to Marxists, for example, argue that policy is made rather by the pushing and hauling of private interests. To the extent that this is the case, so that policies get made at least in part on the basis of some balancing of comparative costs, then 'any objection to forcing yet another cost-based recalculation of policy falls away'.[33] In the case of the Poll Tax, with its origins in the threatened rates strike in Scotland amongst predominantly Conservative voters, such an interpretation of the policy-making process is all too credible, and the argument that *qua* policy-issue civil disobedience over the Community Charge had to be either very limited or non-existent consequently crumbles.

The distinctions between the three kinds of disobedience are in any case highly questionable. Most protestors are likely to be motivated by all three types of objection, since a misguided policy tends to have morally bad effects as well as those of an indifferent nature. In addition, many people will feel obligated as citizens to withdraw support from and seek to change a wrong done to others in their name, as any action by the government tends to be. Possibly to get around some of these problems, Rawls has suggested that civil disobedience is only legitimate when it 'addresses the sense of justice of the majority of the community and declares that in one's considered opinion the principles of social cooperation among free and equal men are not being respected'.[34] However, this seems a highly stringent criterion that assumes that a consensus on political principles of justice exists, which is doubtful. In partial recognition of this fact, Rawls simply rules out civil disobedience over matters of social justice, such as disputes about tax policies, because 'the complexities of these questions' mean that 'the appeal to the public's conception of justice is not sufficiently clear'.[35] Yet, as the Poll Tax issue shows, notions of political citizenship and conceptions of social justice can often be intertwined and objects of political debate. Rawls's attempt to limit civil disobedience within a democracy to supposed infringements of a publically acknowledged political constitution rests on distinctions that neither apply to the anti-Poll Tax campaign nor are warranted in the first place.

Finally, the fairness argument is directly linked to the view that disobedience undermines democracy. This thesis hardly differs from the one considered in the last section. The argument claims that it is inconsistent for citizens to regard a majoritarian vote as valid when it goes their way and to reject it when they find themselves in a minority. If everyone acted like that, then democracy would soon collapse. Now, it is true that any group decision-making procedure would soon fail if none of the participants felt its decisions were in any way binding on them. But this is not what civil disobedients argue. They merely hold that to the extent majoritarian decision-making is a just and fair institution it ought to be supported. However, not all democratically arrived at laws are just and fair and hence it is justified for anyone to disobey majority decisions when the relevant moral considerations apply. In other words, they argue that democracy is to be valued because it has certain systemic features that make it more likely to produce good and just laws than any other available system. But this does not commit you to obeying all laws just because they are democratically made, unless one believes the plainly false view that the fact that a decision was democratically made somehow renders it morally just. At most we have a duty to support those laws guaranteeing the functioning of democracy but not all law, unless it can somehow be shown that this is indeed a necessary aspect of democracy. Our earlier discussion suggests that this latter assumption is unwarranted. As Singer notes, for example, since most democracies are at best imperfect, disobedience often serves the democratic cause by getting a particular point of view a fair hearing.

Withholding Payment is Unfair

The final argument to be considered is the view that disobedience is wrong because it leads to an unfair distribution of burdens and benefits amongst the citizenry. Non-payers were accused of free-riding on council services, making them more expensive for everyone else, and in the process hurting the very people they claimed to be helping since these groups were most dependent on local facilities. Labour tended to argue this point rather more than the government.[36] This is not surprising. Apart from the fact that Labour authorities were in the main harder hit than Conservative ones by the campaign, such arguments generally make greater sense when argued from the sort of communitarian perspective that socialists often find congenial than from the liberal individualist assumptions that informed the government's reform and which are examined in this section.

According to the fair-play argument as developed by Hart and Rawls,[37] individuals who have accepted the benefits of a just, mutually beneficial scheme of social co-operation, are bound by a duty of fair-play to do their part and not to take advantage of the free benefits by not co-operating. The assumption that societies can in some relevant sense be construed as collaborative ventures pursuing a mutually beneficial common good is problematic, however. Undoubtedly some social endeavours have this quality, such as playing in an orchestra. It is less clear that the state can be construed in this manner. Although governments generally say they are acting for the general welfare, a vast array of their policies are usually highly contested by significant sections of the population and many take part only because they feel compelled to do so. Such clashes occur because the diversity of interests and moral considerations means that the personal good of each individual does not necessarily always coincide with that of the community. Indeed, people themselves often feel pulled in more than one direction by conflicting economic and moral considerations. Thus, even in a democracy a price may be paid for universal obedience. Just because everyone benefits from a scheme does not mean one can only avoid injustice by reciprocal conduct. It may well be the case that in many instances discriminate disobedience will actually promote either greater benefits to the community or avoid greater injustices than total obedience would.

To raise these points is not to deny that mutually beneficial co-operative schemes can exist. Thus, certain public goods might appear to fit the criteria of a mutually beneficial scheme. A clean environment, for example, requires fairly widespread co-operation amongst citizens and because of its indivisibility necessarily benefits one and all. However, not everyone may desire it or find the terms on which it is offered as acceptable. After all, forced labour in a work-camp might be deemed more mutually beneficial than some hypothetical alternative such as starving in a desert, without legitimizing pressganging threatened nomadic tribes, say, into joining such a scheme. For these reasons, it is essential to the fair-play thesis that the scheme be fair and the benefits accepted.

Meeting either of these additional criteria is extremely troublesome. Whether agreement can be reached on what counts as fair is highly debatable. Rival accounts can be given, for example, from the perspectives of desert, need and entitlement, and each of these alternatives is open in its turn to differing interpretations – such as whether desert should derive from effort or contribution. Rawls's theory, like utilitarianism, attempts to circumvent these difficulties, but both accounts of justice are notoriously contested. Yet without a substantial account of justice to ground it, the fair-play argument will be unable to provide an adequate account of political obligation.

The difficulties posed by the requirement that we 'accept' benefits have been raised by Robert Nozick.[38] Public goods, as I noted above, are plausible examples of a mutually beneficial co-operative scheme. But they pose the difficulty that those who might prefer not to co-operate have no choice but to accept the proffered benefit. Even if I enjoy clean air, for example, I might find a number of the costs involved in providing it to the level demanded by others too great if it deprives me of certain things I value just as dearly, such as a coal fire, employment at the local factory, spectacular sunsets. The higher the costs of providing a particular benefit, the more likely certain individuals will want to opt out of the scheme, and the more implausible the argument that the beneficiary of this imposed scheme has 'accepted' the benefit will be.

This objection proves similarly debilitating to the more blanket claim that we should somehow be grateful to the state for the benefits we receive. In liberal accounts, this argument seems to rest on an implied analogy between the state and an individual who deliberately puts him- or herself out to help someone else. Obviously it remains important in this argument too that the beneficiary both desires the help proffered and wants it from the person who offers it. But it is also doubtful whether the analogy works, and that one can ascribe to an institution the intention and special effort that generates a sense of gratitude to an individual. Moreover, even with individuals it is hard to know quite what gratitude should consist in. In other words, the whole issue of fairness gets raised again and it is a moot point that gratitude to the state will always issue in an unfailing obligation to obey the law any more than that gratitude to an individual will result in life-long service and devotion to their every whim.

Some commentators believe the gratitude argument has greater plausibility with office holders of the state. This thesis was used to suggest that non-payment by councillors or local government employees was more reprehensible than by ordinary citizens. But the real argument here seems to be one of contractual obligation. Whether the resulting duty of office holders is to obey all the decrees of the government of the day or to uphold the public interest, however, is unclear. Clive Ponting's acquittal would suggest that, amongst the population if not the government and its legal officers, there is a belief that the two can sometimes clash and at times it would be just to disobey the law.

Superficially, taxation for public services appears to provide a good example for the fair-play and benefit arguments. Involvement by a significant number of the population is required, almost everyone benefits from some if not all the services provided and opting out does increase the burdens on law-abiding citizens. However, as we noted, general obedience to any mutually beneficial scheme is not costless either to individuals or even to the group as a whole – hence the need for the fairness and acceptance requirements. The government's reform was supposed to meet these criteria by creating a stronger link between the charge for services and use and by strengthening local accountability. However, even if we put to one side the issue of whether the government's views of what counts as fair and accountable were correct or not, the policy can be criticized for failing to meet even the government's own standards in these respects.

The Poll Tax was supposed to increase fairness and accountability because it represented a charge for a bundle of services that each individual receives. By removing the marginal subsidy from non-domestic rates and billing every one on the basis of the cost of services rather than taxing householders on the basis of the rateable value of their property, the charge was held to be related directly to the benefits obtained from the services consumed. This scheme can be criticized on at least two counts. First, leaving aside the (insuperable?) difficulties of devising any tax structure that accurately reflects the marginal benefit of a service to different voters, the government's flat-rate charge totally neglected the important fact that both patterns of use and benefit vary with income. Research in this area shows that the Poll Tax actually had the effect of substantially increasing the relative benefit shares of upper-income groups and lowering that of the poorer groups, thereby providing an incentive for the inefficient under-provision of local authority services.[39] Second, the reasoning behind the Poll Tax falsely conflated market and public provision of services.[40] Even if one accepts the economic rational voter model underlying the proposal, an important difference remains between the choices available to consumers and those open to voters. Whereas individuals in the market place can to a degree plausibly be said to weigh up the cost and use of particular products to them, individual voters are frequently compelled to buy into a package of benefits which fits far less closely to their set of preferences – even when it is their own party that wins the election. For well-known reasons,[41] in a society of any complexity it is impossible to design a model of party competition that is capable of translating the preferences of citizens into a coherent statement of social choice. As a result, local government will fail to be accountable in the manner desired by the government and Nozick's problem of 'imposed' benefits will almost certainly arise.

Civilly disobedient Poll Tax non-payers generally justified their actions on the grounds of the regressive and unfair nature of the Community Charge. By its own criteria of fairness, the government ought to have agreed with them. Furthermore, the individualist reasoning behind the government's proposals weakens the appeals to fair play and benefits that many directed at the non-payers, arguments which have seen to be deeply flawed in any case. Finally, most of the non-payers were presumably not disputing the validity of having some local taxation system to pay for particular public services. Indeed, they may have wanted to increase their own contributions to such a system. But they felt that the current set-up implicated them in an injustice against which they were obliged to protest in order to force a change of policy for a system that would yield a greater benefit to all in the long run. The rights and wrongs of such action will then turn on varying consequential judgements that even with hindsight are hard to make. Arguably this difficulty counts against adopting such a strategy. But if such discriminate disobedience succeeds, can it be regarded as unjustified?

Conclusion

The prime irony of this whole episode was that a Prime Minister who was notoriously committed to the view that 'there is no such thing as society' should have made a policy apparently appealing to our duty to the community the 'flagship' of her government's programme. The arguments underlying the reform were, however, of an impeccably liberal individualist nature and, as we have seen, frequently fail to generate any such obligation. Rather, these self-same arguments can be used to justify civil disobedience against paying the tax. It would seem, therefore, that by a sort of dialectical revenge the tax can be, and possibly was, hoist with its own petard.

If true, then this conclusion raises some doubts about the merits of current liberal theories of political obligation. Most contemporary political philosophers argue individualist liberalism can provide no convincing account of political obligation. In general, liberal theorists have not been unduly disturbed by this fact. They have contended that prudential self-interest and general moral considerations simply apply everywhere and provide good reasons for obeying most laws in most places. Philosophical anarchism simply removes the grounds for believing I have a special reason for obeying the laws of my country which is different to whatever reason I might have for obeying the laws of any foreign nation I might happen to visit.[42] It does not mean I have no good reason to obey any laws.

Communitarian critics of this form of liberalism have been less happy with this argument.[43] Following Hobbes, they have noted how, without a common power to keep them all in awe, the ties of prudence and reciprocal self-interest can prove worryingly unstable. Following Hegel, they contend that the appeal to neutral, impartial and impersonal rules of justice produces an abstract morality lacking in any determinate content specifying to whom, to what, how and why our duty is owed. They argue such specification can only be provided by the state. Even the most minimal of our moral obligations towards others tend to require political support in the form of police forces, courts of law and prisons. In fact, most modern states offer considerably more in the way of collective provision than mere physical security from internal or external attack, providing welfare and a considerable degree of social and economic regulation as well. In each of these instances, however, the most important service provided by the state is to act as a focus for the individual citizen's allegiance by offering an authoritative mechanism for deliberating upon matters of common concern through the establishment of a public sphere with a shared set of rules and language. In other words, it is only through participation in the state that we are able to determine who gets what, when, why and how. A special kind of political obligation that binds us to a particular political community remains indispensable, therefore. Such ties, however, stem from a sense of patriotism born out of a feeling of membership or identification with the state that grounds our wider notions of justice and which is to be explained sociologically rather than philosophically. Indeed, communitarian theorists fear that an insistence on universal, impersonal and individually justifiable principles of justice will fatally erode the particularist bonds and solidarities that give these rules their content and enable us to apply them.

My analysis of liberal arguments against the non-payment campaign suggests that such criticisms are not without foundation. A number of commentators noted an apparent contradiction in Thatcherism between Thatcher's economic liberalism and her political authoritarianism, her advocacy of the free market and her increasing reliance on a strong centralizing state.[44] By contrast, the above examination of the thinking behind the Poll Tax and the protest that it elicited indicates that the two are likely to go together. For as the liberal individualism of the first erodes the communal bonds on which a sense of political obligation depends, the authority of the second becomes both more necessary and increasingly reliant on the apparently arbitrary power of the Leviathan. How to re-create a sense of civic virtue in modern societies remains the great unanswered question. But the replacement of a form of plebiscitary tyranny with a political system where participation counts and the people frame the rules that have authority over them for themselves might be a start.

Notes

1. An earlier version of this chapter was given to a workshop on 'Legitimacy and the British State' held at Earlham Hall, University of East Anglia, 26 May 1993. I am grateful to the other participants, particularly Rodney Barker, Francis Coleman and Tim O'Hagan, for their comments on that occasion. I am also indebted to Dario Castiglione, Martin Hollis, John Horton and Jo Wolff for their useful written observations on that paper. The initial stimulus to write this piece came from numerous conversations on the topic with two former Edinburgh colleagues, Richard Gunn and Paul Smart, many of whose arguments I have found myself adopting.

2. W. Hamish Fraser commenting on the Scottish campaign in *Labour History Review*, 56 (1991): 87, as cited by R. Barker, 'Legitimacy in the United Kingdom: Scotland and the Poll Tax', *British Journal of Political Science*, 22 (1992): 531.

3. Approximate figures derived from local and metropolitan authority statistics cited in Barker, 'Legitimacy', pp. 522–3.

4. See R. P. Wolff, *In Defence of Anarchism*, 2nd edn, New York: Harper and Row, 1973 and A. J. Simmons, *Moral Principles and Political Obligations*, Princeton, NJ: Princeton University Press, 1979, for this argument.

5. I am not suggesting that many of the campaigners actually employed the arguments discussed here. Paradoxically, I suspect that most may well have appealed to principles of a far less individualist nature that, from a theoretical point of view, do not justify disobedience nearly so well. The irony I wish to point up is merely that those who supported the reasoning behind the tax arguably provided the best grounds for withholding payment for it, and that this reveals a weakness of liberal theory.

6. For an example of these arguments, see R. M. Hare, 'Political Obligation', in T. Honderich (ed.), *Social Ends and Political Means*, London: Routledge, 1976, p. 7.

7. See David Lyons, *Forms and Limits of Utilitarianism*, Oxford: Oxford University Press, 1965.

8. See Steven Lukes, 'Marxism and Dirty Hands', in *Moral Conflict and Politics*, Oxford: Clarendon Press, 1991, Ch. 10, for examples.

9. The statistic comes from a survey by the Convention of Scottish Local Authorities, *Summary Warrants Now Top 3 Million*, 16 December 1991 and the argument from Steve Briggs and Derek Bateman, 'Middle Class Rebel Over Poll Tax Rise', *Scotland on Sunday*, 3 February 1991, p. 5, both reported in Barker, 'Legitimacy', p. 532.

10. E.g. The case of *Randolph Murray v. Edinburgh District Council* brought before the Court of Session in Edinburgh in May 1990. See Barker, 'Legitimacy', p. 531 for details.

11. This was certainly a concern of the Scottish Labour Party, albeit motivated by the self-interested point of view that they would lose votes to the nationalists as a result, e.g. Ken Smith, 'Labour Troubled by Poll Tax Backlash', *Glasgow Herald*, 3 January 1990. For a more general expression of this concern, see Jean McFadden, President of the Convention of Scottish Local Authorities, 'Bringing the Law into Disrepute', *The Scotsman*, 20 November 1990.

12. Clearly there are some laws where secrecy may be a necessary part of successful civil disobedience. Thus, those who wished to protest the Fugitive Slave Act could not have openly helped slaves without giving them away.

13. The view of a Tory councillor, as reported in the *Glasgow Herald*, 12 February 1991.

14. 'Not solely' as opposed to 'not at all' concerned with personal or group gain, as is sometimes argued, because, as I shall argue below, damage to one's interests can be a reasonable ground for disobedience. Unlike the criminals, however, civil disobedients are willing that whatever advantages they gain from their actions should be enjoyed by others who are similarly placed.

15. J. Rawls, *A Theory of Justice*, Oxford: Clarendon Press, 1971, pp. 373–5.

16. Labour eventually abandoned even this measure as unjustified, for reasons explored in the next two sections.

17. David Scott, 'Councils Predict Poll Tax Crunch Only Months Away', *The Scotsman*, 2 July 1991.

18. These are the three points that get a highly qualified defence in P. Singer, *Democracy and Disobedience*, Oxford: Clarendon Press, 1973, for example.

19. Singer, *Democracy and Disobedience*, p. 52.

20. Singer, *Democracy and Disobedience*, pp. 30–42.

21. Singer, *Democracy and Disobedience*, p. 43.

22. Singer, *Democracy and Disobedience*, p. 134.

23. I. McLean and R. Mortimore, 'Apportionment and the Boundary Commission for England', *Electoral Studies*, 11 (1992): 308.

24. P. Esam and C. Oppenheim, *A Charge on the Community: The Poll Tax, Benefits and the Poor*, Child Poverty Action Group and Local Government Information Unit, 1989, pp. 114–15.

25. For details of this claim, see Barker, 'Legitimacy', pp. 525–6, 529–31.

26. Rt. Hon. Nicholas Ridley MP, *House of Commons Hansard*, 18 April 1988, col. 581, quoted in Esam and Oppenheim, *Charge on the Community*, p. 34.

27. Rt. Hon. John Selwyn Gummer, then Minister of State for Local Government, at Blakeney, Norfolk, 7 October 1988, quoted in Esam and Oppenheim, *A Charge on the Community*, p. 30.

28. Progressive taxation was said to allow the poorer to 'overload' both the state and the richer wealth-creating sections of the community with financial burdens for services those who paid for them did not necessarily use. A flat-rate charge was intended to get around this problem and was justified on the grounds that payment for facilities like car parks, swimming pools and the like had none of the redistributive implications involved with taxation for services such as welfare and education and should simply be related to use. The view that non-rate-payers were more likely to vote for extravagant

policies than ratepayers has been subjected to damaging critical scrutiny by Arthur Midwinter, 'Economic Theory, the Poll Tax, and Local Spending', *Politics*, 9 (1989): 9–15. In general, as W. L. Miller, *Irrelevant Elections*, Oxford: Clarendon Press, 1988, points out, 'it is rich taxpayers who turn out to vote more readily than poor non-taxpayers' (p. 232).

29. Households with an average weekly income of between £50 and £200 were on average net losers under the new system, the rest were net gainers. Whilst those with an average weekly income of under £50 gained on average by 0.01 per cent, those with an average weekly income of over £500 gained on average by over 6.73 per cent. (For detailed figures, see John Gibson, *The Politics and Economics of the Poll Tax: Mrs Thatcher's Downfall*, Warley: Emas, 1990, Ch. 5.)

30. These distinctions come from R. Dworkin, 'Civil Disobedience and Nuclear Protest', in his *A Matter of Principle*, Oxford: Clarendon Press, 1986 but are implicit in many other liberal accounts including Rawls, *Theory of Justice*, pp. 363–94.

31. Dworkin, 'Civil Disobedience', p. 112.

32. On the evidence of *Democracy and Disobedience*, pp. 92–104, it is doubtful that Singer would accept them, for example.

33. R. E. Goodin, 'Civil Disobedience and Nuclear Protest', *Political Studies*, XXXV (1987): 466.

34. Rawls, *A Theory of Justice*, p. 364.

35. Rawls, *A Theory of Justice*, p. 372. A similar view was expressed by the Scottish Court of Session Judges. See Bruce McKain, 'Belief in the Injustice of Poll Tax "No Excuse" for Disobeying the Act', *Glasgow Herald*, 25 July 1990.

36. E.g. David Scott, 'Top Labour Councillor Slams Poll Tax Dodgers', *The Scotsman*, 29 March 1990.

37. H. L. A. Hart, 'Are there any Natural Rights?', in A. Quinton (ed.), *Political Philosophy*, Oxford: Oxford University Press, 1967, pp. 61–2 and J. Rawls, 'Legal Obligation and the Duty of Fair Play', in S. Hook (ed.), *Law and Philosophy*, New York: New York University Press, 1964, pp. 9–10.

38. R. Nozick, *Anarchy, State and Utopia*, Oxford: Basil Blackwell, 1974, pp. 90–3.

39. For details see Gibson, *Poll Tax*, Chs 8 and 9, and G. Bramley, J. Le Grand and W. Low, 'How Far is the Poll Tax a "Community Charge"?: the Implications for Service Usage Evidence', *Policy and Politics*, 17 (1989): 187–205.

40. I owe this point to Esam and Oppenheim, *A Charge on the Community*, pp. 124–5.

41. For details, see S. Hargreaves Heap *et al.*, *The Theory of Choice: A Critical Guide*, Oxford: Blackwell, 1992, Chs 13 and 14.

42. Simmons, *Political Obligations*, pp. 192–4; Wolff, *In Defense of Anarchism*, pp. 18–19.

43. E.g. A. MacIntyre, *After Virtue: A Study in Moral Philosophy*, London: Duckworth, 1981, pp. 236–7; A. MacIntyre, *Is Patriotism a Virtue?*, The Lindley Lecture, University of Kansas, 26 March 1984; Charles Taylor, 'Atomism', in his *Philosophical Papers: Volume Two*, Cambridge: Cambridge University Press, 1982; and Charles Taylor, 'Cross-Purposes: the Liberal–Communitarian Debate', in N. Rosenblum (ed.), *Liberalism and the Moral Life*, Cambridge, Mass.: Harvard University Press, 1989.

44. E.g. A. Gamble, *The Free Economy and the Strong State*, Basingstoke: Macmillan, 1988.

CHAPTER 12

Building the Union: The Nature of Sovereignty in the Political Architecture of Europe

Is national sovereignty dead? Many writers on Europe appear to believe so. This thesis draws on a number of increasingly familiar arguments. The related processes of globalization and social differentiation have undermined the state's claims to sovereignty. It neither controls the most important decisions in the economy or defence, nor expresses a common identity capable of sustaining a shared sense of justice and a commitment to the collective good. The future lies with new forms of political and social order that take us below and beyond the sovereign nation-state, to regional and global blocs regulated by a cosmopolitan legal system based on individual human rights. So far as Europe is concerned, imperatives of both a functional and a normative nature impel the creation of an ever-closer Union.

This chapter takes a different tack. These reports of the nation-state's demise are exaggerated. The impact of global forces and the associated pressures towards greater social individuation have been far from uniform, and the normative claims of national cultures and group identities show few signs of diminishing. The capacity of the nation-state to act as the primary locus of administrative, legal and political power and authority may have been weakened but not in ways that necessarily point in a cosmopolitan direction. Rather, both the allegiances of citizens and their forms of economic, social and political interaction, co-operation and organization have become a complex mixture of the subnational, national and supranational. Instead of convergence on a common normative framework and a single set of institutions, such a highly differentiated social system is characterized by numerous subsystems, each governed by its own rules and practices.

Sovereignty does not lose its relevance in such a situation. If anything, the need for authoritative mechanisms capable of mediating between diverse values and interests increases rather than diminishes. However, sovereignty does need to be reconfigurated to reflect the competing attachments and norms emanating from the various spheres of people's lives, and the complexities of the relationships that exist between them. If politics is defined by the questions of who gets what, when, where and how, then the answers increasingly must be in the plural – different people, in different ways and employing different criteria according to the context and the good concerned. That suggests that sovereignty will also be plural, because more dispersed, with different persons or bodies having the power to decide in different circumstances, without there necessarily being any single, hierarchical system of decision-making.

What follows pursues this notion of a pluralist conception of sovereignty as a way of conceiving the interaction between the various actors within the European Union. On this understanding, the Member States, citizens, regions, the various EU institutions, and so on each represents a semi-autonomous component of a far from homogeneous political system. They interact in different ways, respond to different sorts of problem and represent different constituencies. Drawing on our earlier work in this field,[1] we shall characterize the resulting mixed polity in terms of a combination of the normative and empirical elements to be found in cosmopolitan and communitarian political moralities. Each of these broad schools of thought offers a particular model of the political architecture for Europe, involving different understandings of sovereignty and legitimacy. Whereas the first favours federal arrangements of various kinds, the second emphasizes the centrality of the component nation-states. Sections one and two examine each of these schools respectively, noting that both contain a range of positions, some of which are more compatible with those from the alternative camp than others. Section three presents a view of Europe as a mixed commonwealth which draws on those more complementary elements in a manner we dub cosmopolitan communitarianism. The resulting amalgam may be more bricolage than grand architectonic design, but none the worse for that.

Federal Architecture

Supporters of various federal arrangements share the fundamental intuition that material and ideal developments since the Second World War have severed the historical connection between political legitimacy and collective self-determination on the one hand, and identification with a unitary state, defined by its territorial borders and a high degree of cultural and linguistic homogeneity, on the other. To differing degrees, they accept that national and state units will, and should, retain some capacity for autonomous self-organization. But they believe that the political and legal structure of the new European polity must rest on a number of key centralized institutions and be based on principles of rights, justice and the rule of law of a fairly universalistic nature. It is this two-level structure of the polity that makes it a

semi-private associations that act in the public realm – where opinions are formed and debated.[19] In modern national democracies, representative institutions are meant to link the two spheres by rendering the executive power publicly accountable through the formal mechanisms of a parliamentary regime. This procedure has now become both technically difficult, due to the complexity of the issues and the number of decision-making levels involved, and politically problematic, because of the apparent inability of the political machinery to give expression to a common will in highly differentiated societies. Cosmopolitans maintain that this enervation of political representation can be offset by the diversification of the technical and the critical functions of the state. The latter is increasingly located in the informal institutions comprising the public sphere, such as the media, professional associations, charities and similar bodies. These are located in civil society and are said to exercise a constant control over the political and administrative process. Together with the judicial power, they assume the dual function of legitimating political and administrative decisions, by exposing them to the test of public reason more than that of popular consent, and of limiting the power of the political and technocratic apparatuses, by giving publicity to their actions. As a consequence, the main democratic deficit in the EU, as presently structured, does not lie in the limited powers vested in the institutions of direct representation, but in the lack of a fully developed and integrated European society and public sphere.

The other main cosmopolitan challenge to nation-state sovereignty concerns the idea of political identity. Its questioning follows directly from the deconstruction of the demos into a 'civil multitude', with important consequences for citizenship and territoriality. In modern societies, the law already recognizes that there are rights of the person, to which all are entitled irrespective of their affiliation to a particular political community. Citizenship rights, however, still have an exclusionary character. In increasingly globalized societies, so it is argued, such a distinction is not warranted.[20] Obligations towards others' negative and positive rights should not be restricted by community or national boundaries. The globalization of responsibility implies that state sovereignty be both broadened, by requiring the state to intervene beyond the confines of the immediate interests of its citizenry (as in, for example, the Bosnian crisis), and narrowed, by sanctioning a general and universal right to free movement and to take up residence. In a very limited sense, European citizenship, as imperfectly introduced by the Maastricht Treaty, goes some way towards bridging the gap between human and citizenship rights, which seem integral to the idea of communal identity, and which the emergence of nation-states widened further.

On the basis of this criticism of the privileged status normally associated with membership of a political community, the very idea of political unity and the right of self-determination that goes with it may only be justified on instrumental grounds,[21] and be strictly within the legal framework of a cosmopolitan federation. This makes an entitlement to political self-determination for both ascriptive and voluntary groups conditional on a number of factors concerning, on the one hand, their relevance and encompassing nature, and, on the other, the effects that self-determination may have on both groups' members and non-members. The territorial boundaries of these units cannot be assumed on simply historical or allegedly 'natural' grounds, they may need to be continuously negotiated and re-negotiated. Cosmopolitan federalism, therefore, has no privileged place for national sovereignty in the political architecture of the EU. Nor does it regard issues of national sovereignty as carrying special weight in the process of constitutionalization of the EU, thus denying that the nation-states are (or should be) the *Herren der Verträge*.

This radical criticism of national sovereignty does not exclude the possibility of a place for nation-states. According to at least one version of cosmopolitan federalism, a certain socio-political homogeneity between the political units comprising the federation is needed to prevent its transformation into a federal state.[22] In other words, states may remain relatively independent so long as they are sufficiently similar for centralized schemes of redistribution or mechanisms for mediating conflicts of legal norms to be unnecessary. In the EU, however, that requirement could be met by autonomous regions, which may be better equipped to address local needs and demands, as much as by existing national states.

Cosmopolitan federalism may also support more radical solutions to the political architecture of the EU by advocating either a vertical or a horizontal dispersion of sovereignty. The former solution[23] insists that what matters is the best level at which a decision-making unit can satisfy the conditions of maximum decentralization (units that are as small as possible) and optimal centralization (units that include as equals all persons significantly and legitimately affected by the relevant decisions). This vertical dispersion of sovereignty would have the added benefits of creating a multi-layered structure, strengthening the vertical system of checks and balances and of the division of powers, and encouraging a cosmopolitan culture that favours multiple identifications. The horizontal dispersion of sovereignty[24] addresses a different aspect of the crisis of the nation-state, by suggesting a model of social federalism that shifts the focus of decision-making processes from a territorially based to a socially based representation of interests. This is not as far-fetched a proposal as it may perhaps seem, for some features of European integration have *de facto* anticipated such a move. There is an obvious danger of corporatism, which could perhaps be offset by guaranteeing both a diffuse system of representation and a centralized dialogue based on strong normative criteria. This may have costs in terms of both political democracy and formal legitimacy, but would be aimed mainly at increasing social legitimacy in the EU. The proposals for either a vertical or a horizontal dispersion of sovereignty, however, seem to be particularly vulnerable to the kind of criticisms more generally directed against the cosmopolitan position. Namely, that they are too abstract and disregard the open-textured nature of discussions about the substantive legitimacy of decision-making units.[25] To imagine the political architecture of the EU without taking questions of political identity seriously may court serious danger. This, by contrast, is the starting point for models of political architecture based on a communitarian mode of argument.

Nation-based Architecture

Current defences of nation-states and of their sovereignty within the political architecture of the EU rest on a belief in the importance and justifiability of collective forms of self-determination that are not simply seen as instrumental to individualist values and interests. Defenders of these positions place great weight on the communitarian argument that there are no disembedded selfs. Individuals need communities with which to identify, in order both to make sense of their lives and to give substance to their autonomy of judgment and action. Communal self-determination is an important part of this autonomy; but the kind of community needed and the form that self-rule should take are still open questions to which many different answers can be given. National sovereignty in Europe requires some arguing, therefore, even from a communitarian perspective.

A first set of arguments contests the claim that national sovereignty has been eroded by globalization.[26] Three main ripostes are offered. The first suggests that globalists fail to recognize the important conceptual distinction between the limitation and the transferral of sovereignty. The nation-state's incapacity to control economic and environmental dynamics, for instance, results in a *de facto* limitation of the state's external sovereignty, without this having any major legal or political implications that signify the transferral of sovereignty to some other body. The second suggestion is that globalists overrate the impact that globalization has on the capacity of the nation-state to control socio-economic processes. The development of inter-national and inter-governmental – more than supranational – institutions should be seen as attempts by nation-states to keep their power, rather than as revealing a loss of sovereignty. Nation statists, for example, can defend monetary unification for much the same reasons that state federalists do, by suggesting that this is the only way in which political communities can keep financial markets under control. The all-important difference, which has significant implications for institutional design, is that while federalists consider a central European bank as part of a broadly federal structure, supporters of nation-state sovereignty look on it as an inter-state institution. The third criticism questions the globalists' view that the state has lost control over its territory. It suggests that, although this may be the case in a number of areas involving economic

231

regulation, capital circulation, information and technological developments, it is not so in the crucial area of human mobility. Indeed, if anything, states in the late twentieth century have a firmer grip over the great majority of their own population; while there are no longer opportunities for mass migrations on the scale of those that took place in the past up until the First World War.

The second set of arguments in support of the nation-state suggests that at present the nation-state is still the main collective entity capable of offering a stable, encompassing and relevant identity to its members, of guaranteeing recognition by other such collective bodies, and of providing the basic unity necessary for the exercise of political self-determination.[27] The privileging of the national dimension can be argued on strongly organic grounds, emphasizing ethnic and racial identity, a narrow conception of past history and a commonality of language and culture. This clearly can give rise to extremely unpleasant forms of nationalism. But some of the same elements can also be integrated into a civic understanding of national identity that constructs it in broadly voluntary terms and is respectful of the person as separate from the community.[28]

Civic communitarians, however, may find it difficult to demonstrate that nations should be privileged over other communities. In principle, there seems to be no particular reason why identity, recognition and self-determination should be better served by nations than by any other group or corporate body. This difficulty is not greatly different from that encountered by cosmopolitans in establishing the optimal level for the vertical distribution of sovereignty. Cosmopolitans argue for it in purely instrumental terms, so that there is always the possibility that a group within the political community may argue for sovereignty on certain matters to be moved either upwards or downwards. Similarly, civic communitarianism allows all kinds of groups to claim recognition, without there being any substantive principle on the basis of which to match processes of contextual identification with the allocation of sovereignty.[29] It would seem to follow that 'tribalism', as the universal attribute of human beings to join in groups, requires that self-determination be attached to any group claiming to have a common identity and demanding to be recognized by others. But the primacy of identity, though maintained in principle, is denied by civic communitarians in practice. Indeed most of them accept that political self-determination is an important precondition for sustaining identity itself and for guaranteeing its recognition. They conclude, therefore, that political personality should be granted only to those 'tribes' that are politically viable. In the modern world, this implies a number of conditions: territorial contiguity, to facilitate decision-making and its application; mutual trust, to guarantee social dealings with the minimum of force; the sense of being an active and lasting community, where everyone feels some direct or indirect involvement in its affairs; some shared belief and common identification, but neither too fixed nor based on ascriptive characteristics, so that they are congruent with social differentiation and do not undermine the territoriality condition; and a capacity to mix particular attachments with consideration for the community as a whole, both of which may be needed to sustain a sense of justice and solidarity. Of the many communities we inhabit, nations seem to approach such conditions best, and so are commonly regarded as the natural focus of political sovereignty.[30]

A number of other arguments are often given in support of maintaining national sovereignty as a central feature of the EU. First, it is suggested that political and administrative uniformity bring with them social and cultural homogenization. This would undermine the pluralism of traditions, institutional settings and styles of life for which Europe is often praised, and which is considered to be a vital ingredient in sustaining an autonomous civil society. Historically, this pluralism has been fostered by the multiplicity of nations that comprise Europe, and by a fundamental balance of power between them. This circumstance has prevented the establishment of a single empire on the European continent, maintaining instead a 'concert of nations'. Federal structures at the European level and a diminution of national self-rule would have a negative impact on social and cultural pluralism, posing a threat to individual and collective liberties.[31]

Secondly, communitarians insist that democracy – which everyone agrees is one of the fundamental values on which the EU ought to rest – needs to foster a sense of unity and a minimum of common identity in the people, so that everyone is prepared to accept the democratic game of majorities and minorities. Without this background assumption, there is no fundamental bond on which to rely, and no trust between the citizens that the rules of the game will be kept. Deep and irreconcilable divisions may set in, driving the democratic community apart and making democratic rules and institutions irrelevant.[32] As with arguments on nationality, so conceptions of the 'people' can be based on either organic (ethnic–historical–cultural) or artificial (civic–voluntary) constructions. However, the kinds of criticism of federal projects that these conceptions imply amount to the same thing. These projects are considered either unrealistic (state federalism), because there is no European demos, or anti-democratic (cosmopolitan federalism), because it would undermine democratic forms of legitimacy. It is also added that projects to construct a European demos contradict the original, and often repeated, aim of an 'ever closer Union of the *peoples* of Europe'.[33] Federalists seem to advocate a melting-pot strategy, something which was never intended, and which may turn out to be either impracticable or counterproductive for democracy both at a European and, indirectly, at the national level.

Thirdly, communitarians regard the idea of European citizenship with a certain suspicion. At one level, they consider the introduction of European citizenship alongside national citizenship as deeply problematic because of the conflict of allegiances that this may give rise to. In a fully integrated federal system, dual citizenship expresses the participation of the citizen in two different sets of institutions – one at the national and the other at the local level. Those conflicts that emerge from this vertical dispersion of sovereignty are conflicts between institutions. They do not concern the citizen directly, and do not test his or her allegiance to the political community, except in the extreme case of secession. But in a less-integrated system, a plurality of citizenships would seem unworkable.[34] This reason for the communitarians' rejection of multiple citizenship is compounded by a more fundamental objection they raise against cosmopolitanism. Communitarians emphasize that citizenship implies both rights and obligations and that the disjunction of the idea of citizenship from a community-based sense of solidarity and reciprocity would render citizenship highly problematic. A sense of commonalty and a minimum degree of homogeneity seem to be required for citizenship, therefore, as they were for the definition of the demos.

What all these arguments amount to is that political self-determination requires a community of fate. The EU in its present form is at most an individualist-based form of state. There do not seem to be the conditions for Europe itself to become a community of fate capable of sustaining democratic forms of government and principles of social citizenship. Such a development is both highly problematic and detrimental to social and cultural pluralism. Recent attempts at forging a European identity to sustain and justify greater integration have resulted in the shallow symbolism of self-celebration. The celebration of Europe *per se*, rather than its various national cultures and values, tends to be strikingly contentless.[35] The famous fantasy bridges of the ill-fated first examples of the new European banknotes are a good illustration of this phenomenon.

Communitarian models of the EU agree that nation-states are the *Herren der Verträge* and that the Union can at most be regarded as an 'association of states' (*Staatenverbund*), retaining full external sovereignty, but willing to pool it together in order either to co-ordinate their actions in matters of common interest or to increase their influence and bargaining power in international affairs. The transference of sovereignty from the states to the Union is limited and conditional and has no implications for internal sovereignty therefore; nor does it envisage a vertical dispersion of sovereignty. These sorts of considerations, for instance, motivated the German Constitutional Court's Maastricht judgement reaffirming its competence at the national level.[36]

But there are other aspects of the political architecture of the Union on which communitarians diverge. On the whole, three main positions can be identified, arising out of different conceptions of the nature of the national community and of politics. The first is based on strongly organic conceptions of the nation and the people harking back to nationalist values and aspirations and demanding the scaling down of all federal-like institutions of the Union. At the core of this position is a deep suspicion of external influence and the conviction that any form of organic co-operation risks jeopardizing the sovereignty of the nation. The second model, usually associated with British Eurosceptics and their 'hostility' to things European, mixes a traditional defence of national sovereignty on broadly nationalist grounds with the neo-liberal conviction that economic matters escape politics and so should not be subject to state intervention but left to market mechanisms. In this scheme, the EU is a form of technical–administrative association (*Zweckverband*),[37] whose power is narrowly limited to guaranteeing the existence and the functioning of a European-wide free market. There may be spillovers into other areas, but these should remain strictly subordinate to the primary technical and economic objective of the formation of a common market. The individualist 'universalism' of this position clashes with the rhetoric on the strengthening of the national economy, so that, echoing nineteenth-century traditions, economic individualism is harnessed to a would-be politics of national supremacy. In European terms, this means the acceptance of those supranational institutions and established co-operative procedures which ensure open and competitive markets, but the preservation of national sovereignty by limiting the functional expansion of supranational institutions and by keeping the veto power of the nation-states.

While the previous two models appeal to a more nationalistic-oriented communitarianism, the third is based on a civic–democratic (as opposed to a national) idea of sovereignty, which needs preserving both because it is crucial for self-determination and because of its formative and civilizing role. As was suggested earlier, from such a perspective post-national and supranational developments are seen as jeopardizing the way in which democracy itself works – either because the new polity would lack the social preconditions for democratic decision-making, or because it would not need democratic processes of will formation. Supporters of this position, however, accept that a 'natural' move towards a larger European polity is possible, and indeed to a certain degree desirable, in so far as this is functional to propping up the 'civic' aspects of the nations of Europe. Ideas of civicness and civility are bridges to more universalist considerations, suggesting an alternative model to the 'individualist' EU as it has so far been constructed. It substitutes 'voice' for 'exit' mechanisms, for example, and tries to preserve difference where homo-geneity seems to set in.[38] Civic nationalists are critical of those moves that expropriate nations of their external sovereignty, which in their view also undermine internal sovereignty and self-determination. But, in principle, it is not adverse to a pulling together of external sovereignty in forms that preserve the democratic configuration of internal sovereignty itself.[39] They also depart from the nationalist version of communitarianism by accepting that the construction of the EU is a two-way process of preserving national identities in Europe, but also of making the nations of Europe more European. In their view, both processes need to be seen as contributing to keeping alive civic and democratic values and practices.

A Mixed Commonwealth

Models of the EU inspired by a mixture of communitarian and cosmopolitan arguments give a more positive gloss to the two-way transformation of national politics acknowledged by civic communitarians. They tend to combine a communitarian appreciation of the importance of identity politics within a civic and democratic setting, with the recognition that globalization and supra- and post-national processes have already altered the structure of state sovereignty beyond what communitarians are prepared both to admit and to allow. In other words, communitarianism has to be modified to take into account cosmopolitan concerns arising out of the increasing interaction between states and peoples brought on by the processes of globalization. This cosmopolitan communitarianism, however, needs to be distinguished from a communitarian cosmopolitanism that seeks simply to flesh out cosmopolitan sentiments. It works out from existing identities and attachments and acknowledges that global forces have modified these to different degrees and in diverse ways.[40]

In many respects, the gradual constitutionalization of Europe that has so far occurred confirms the intuition at the root of this third group of models, that there is something fundamentally new, or, as is often said, *sui generis*, in the constitutional structure of the EU, and that such novelty is captured by neither federal nor nation-based forms of political architecture. What distinguishes this third position is a certain support both for the open, piecemeal nature of the constitutionalization process and for a constitutional structure that mixes national and federal elements. But, given the post-Maastricht crisis of confidence, supporters of this position have felt compelled to distance themselves from a purely functionalist justification of the piecemeal process and from the vacuity of the *sui generis* formula, both of which tend to ignore questions of legitimacy.[41] Thus, there have recently been a number of attempts to give theoretical and institutional substance to the re-configuration of sovereignty that comes with the construction of the EU as a new form of polity.

A first consideration, captured by Duverger's suggestion that a neo-federalist structure is in the making in Europe,[42] follows from the simple observation that the basic units of the new polity are fully formed nation-states, commanding strong allegiances from their citizenries and with long-established histories, well-developed identities and rooted institutional traditions. The development of a federation-like structure at the European level cannot avoid confronting and accommodating the demands that come from these national dimensions of politics. In recognition of all this, Joseph Weiler has proposed a dual form of citizenship, as in traditional federal structures, but based on different sources of allegiance and identification.[43] This, he believes, can be achieved by decoupling the idea of citizenship at the European level from its elements of nationhood. The European demos, formed on the basis of universalistic values and principles, as implicit, for instance, in Habermas's idea of constitutional patriotism, should not supplant the national demos, but only act as a civilizing force keeping under control the emotional drive and particularist focus of national citizenship. Such a dual form of citizenship and legitimacy would not simply require a vertical dispersion of sovereignty, but its more nuanced articulation, by giving to representation at national and European levels different functions, as perhaps suggested by a post-national vision of the European polity. It may also imply, as Neil MacCormick has argued, a vision of internal sovereignty in the EU as dependent on distinct legal and political systems, the validity of whose actions is a function of co-ordination and cross-referencing, both between centre and periphery and between individual states.[44] This takes us beyond the sovereign state, into a pluralist, and implicitly contested vision of sovereignty.

The polycentric polity that is therefore emerging is a definite departure from the nation-state, mainly because it implies a dissociation of the traditional elements that come with state sovereignty: a unified system of authority and representation controlling all functions of governance over a given territory. The personalized character of traditional sovereignty, associated with the idea of a *government*, is substituted by a more diffuse, and hence impersonal, idea of multi-layered *governance*.[45] The underlying logic of such a system of governance is nonetheless unclear. Majone has argued that while national institutions still maintain a semblance of unified control over the territory, they are complemented by European institutions, whose character is mainly regulatory, and which concern areas with increasing problems of externalities in decision-making (e.g. the economy and the environment).[46] Philippe Schmitter has noticed, however, that although the European level of governance is increasingly affecting all areas of policy-making, a multiplicity of institutional and semi-institutional arrangements between different partners are encouraged.[47] This institutional flexibility tends to blur the lines of identity and jurisdiction and, according to Schmitter, may develop either towards a form of *consortium*, with nation-states still in control of the areas and forms of co-operation, or towards a *condominium*, which implies a 'variation in both territorial and functional constituencies'.[48]

In spite of the many differences of analysis, we wish to suggest that all these attempts agree on the basic intuition that the polity that is gradually emerging is a 'mixed commonwealth':[49] that is, a polity where the subjects of the constitution are not homogeneous, but a mixture of political agents sharing in the sovereignty of the polity under different titles. In practical terms, this thesis implies that neither the nation-states nor the citizens of the EU are the sole, exclusive subjects of the constitution, but that they both, together with other new socio-political agents, may contribute to the democratic construction of a democratic Europe. It also requires that political practices of mediation and reconciliation have a primary role, to which legal means and institutions need to be subordinated. For democratic deliberation has a capacity that legal mechanisms lack to build new allegiances and identities, and to negotiate workable compromises when a consensus on new forms of common life cannot be achieved.[50]

Proponents of the 'mixed commonwealth' hypothesis also demonstrate a certain scepticism towards traditional views of political architecture. Both federal and nation-state versions presuppose a unified and systematic vision of the principles that should guide the construction of the European polity.[51] But the political architecture of a mixed commonwealth clearly implies a mixture of principles, which must in part reflect the willingness of the political agents to re-define their identities and practices. Such a mixture is more likely to emerge and be accepted as legitimate as the result of time and as part of a process of selection of procedures and institutions by trial and error. What distinguishes this position from traditional functionalist justifications is the appreciation of the element of design, which is central to constitution-making processes that take on board the need for both formal and social legitimacy. It is this conception of the open-ended nature of the constituent process, which may look more like bricolage than political architecture, that for the time being unifies those who favour the construction of a mixed common-wealth.[52]

The result may not have the symmetry and proportionality that come with the principles of classical architecture. It may perhaps lack the dynamism and sense of material, surfaces and space typical of modernism. But it is not necessarily going to be a hotchpotch of half-digested architectural idioms, like many post-modern buildings. Perhaps, more than structural architecture – whose image is conjured up by the 'pillars' of the Maastricht Treaty – urban development is a better metaphor for the construction of a 'mixed com-monwealth'. This may not involve as much careful planning, precise engineering and unity of conception than is thought necessary in creating a single building or a group of buildings. It may rather require that mixture of design and spontaneous development that is so much part of successful urban environments, where a plurality of groups and individuals dwell, and in which they pursue their different needs and aspirations.

Notes

This chapter was written with Dario Castiglione as part of an ESRC research project on 'Languages and Principles for the Constitution of Europe' (R000221170). We are grateful to Neil MacCormick and the participants in the ESRC-funded research seminar series on 'The Legal Theory of the European Union' for their comments on and discussion of earlier versions.

1. 'The Communitarian Ghost in the Cosmopolitan Machine: Constitutionalism, Democracy and the Reconfiguration of Politics in the New Europe', in R. Bellamy

(ed.), *Constitutionalism, Democracy and Sovereignty: American and European Perspectives*, Aldershot: Avebury, 1996, Ch. 8 and 'Between Cosmopolis and Community: Three Models of Rights and Democracy within the European Union', in D. Archibugi, D. Held and M. Koehler, *Re-Imagining Political Community: Studies in Cosmopolitan Democracy*, Cambridge: Polity, 1998, Ch. 8.

2. Herman Heller, *Die Souveränität. Ein Beitrag zur Theorie des Staats-und Völkerrecht*, Berlin and Leipzig: W. de Gruyter, 1927, Ch. 10.

3. On the role of ideals in the construction of the EU, cf. J. H. H. Weiler, 'Idéaux et construction européenne', in M. Telò (ed.), *Démocratie et Construction Européenne*, Brussels: University of Brussels, 1995.

4. P. C. Schmitter, 'If the Nation State were to Wither Away in Europe, what might Replace it?', in S. Gustavsson and L. Lewin (eds), *The Future of the Nation-State: Essays on Cultural Pluralism and Political Integration*, Stockholm: Nerenius & Santérus, 1996, pp. 228–9.

5. G. Folke Schuppert, 'The Evolution of a European State: Reflections on the Conditions of and the Prospects for a European Constitution', in J. J. Hesse and N. Johnson (eds), *Constitutional Policy and Change in Europe*, Oxford: Oxford University Press, 1995, p. 331.

6. W. Heun, 'The Evolution of Federalism', in C. Starck (ed.), *Studies in German Constitutionalism*, Baden-Baden: Nomos Verlagsgesellschaft, 1995, pp. 185–7.

7. On the anti-political conception of civil society, cf. C. Taylor, 'Invoking Civil Society', in *Philosophical Arguments*, Cambridge, MA and London: Harvard University Press, 1995, pp. 215–20.

8. On various understandings of cosmopolitanism, cf. T. W. Pogge, 'Cosmopolitanism and Sovereignty', in C. Brown (ed.), *Political Restructuring in Europe: Ethical Perspectives*, London and New York: Routledge, 1994, pp. 89–98.

9. Cf. Pogge, 'Cosmopolitanism and Sovereignty' and D. Archibugi, 'Immanuel Kant, Cosmopolitan Law and Peace', *European Journal of International Relations*, 1 (1995): 429–56.

10. T. Koopmans, 'Federalism: The Wrong Debate', *Common Market Law Review*, 29 (1992): 1047–52, at p. 1051.

11. Cf. C. H. MacIlwain, *Constitutionalism: Ancient and Modern*, Ithaca, NY: Cornell University Press, 1958, Ch. 4.

12. Cf. Hans Kelsen, *Das Problem der Souveränität und die Theorie des Völkerrechts. Beitrag zu einer reiner Rechtslehre*, Tübingen: Mohr, 1920, Ch. 9; and L. Ferrajoli, *La Sovranità nel Mondo Moderno. Nascita e Crisi dello Stato Nazionale*, Milan: Anabasi, 1995.

13. Cf. D. Held, *Democracy and the Global Order: From the Modern State to Cosmopolitan Governance*, Cambridge: Polity Press, 1995, Chs 5 and 6; and L. Ferrajoli, 'Beyond Sovereignty and Citizenship: A Global Constitutionalism', in Bellamy (ed.), *Constitutionalism, Democracy and Sovereignty*, Ch. 10.

14. I. Kant, 'On the Common Saying: "This may be True in Theory but not in Practice" ', in *Kant's Political Writings*, ed. by H. Reiss and trans. H. B. Nisbet, Cambridge: Cambridge University Press, 1991, p. 90.

15. A. Winckler, 'L'Empire revient', *Commentaire*, 15 (1992): 17–25, at p. 19.

16. Cf. J.-H. Ferry, 'Une "philosophie" de la communauté', in: J.-H. Ferry and P. Thibaud, *Discussion sur l'Europe*, Paris: Calmann-Lévy, 1992, pp. 169–89.

17. In Kantian terms, a 'civil multitude' is composed of cosmopolitan citizens – those, that is, that are bound by both the civil constitution and the idea of cosmopolitan

right: I. Kant, 'Perpetual Peace: A Philosophical Sketch', in *Kant's Political Writings*.

18. Cf. Pogge, 'Cosmopolitanism and Sovereignty'.
19. Cf. Ferry, 'Une "philosophie" de la communauté', pp. 148–66.
20. Cf. B. S. Turner, 'Citizenship Studies: A General Theory', *Citizenship Studies*, 1 (1997): 15–18, esp. pp. 15–17; and L. Ferrajoli, 'Dai diritti del cittadino ai diritti della persona', in D. Zolo, *La Cittadinanza. Appartenenza, Identità, Diritti*, Roma and Bari: Laterza, 1994.
21. Cf. A. Margalit and J. Raz, 'National Self-determination', *Journal of Philosophy*, 87 (1990): 439–61; and C. R. Beitz, 'Cosmopolitan Liberalism and the States System', in Brown (ed.), *Political Restructuring in Europe*, pp. 131–5.
22. On the condition of 'political homogeneity', cf. O. Beaud, 'La Fédération entre l'état et l'empire', in B. Théret (ed.), *L'État, la finance et le sociale*, Paris: La Decouverte, 1995, pp. 299–302.
23. Cf. Held, *Democracy and the Global Order* and Pogge, 'Cosmopolitanism and Sovereignty'.
24. On social federalism in Europe, cf. M. Telò, 'L'intégration sociale en tant que réponse du modèle européen à l'interdépendance globale? Les chances, les obstacles et les scénarios', in M. Telò (ed.), *Quelle Union Sociale Européenne?*, Brussels: University of Brussels, 1994.
25. On the relationship between substantive legitimacy and the boundedness of the democratic community, cf. A. Weale, 'Democratic Legitimacy and the Constitution of Europe', in R. Bellamy, V. Bufacchi and D. Castiglione (eds), *Democracy and Constitutional Culture in the Union of Europe*, London: Lothian Foundation Press, 1995, pp. 86–9.
26. This paragraph essentially summarizes arguments found in P. Hirst and G. Thompson, *Globalisation in Question: The International Economy and the Possibilities of Governance*, Cambridge: Polity Press, 1996.
27. A discussion of the distinction between identity, recognition and self-determination is found in C. Taylor, 'Why do Nations have to become States?', in G. Laforest (ed.), *Reconciling the Solitudes: Essays on Canadian Federalism and Nationalism*, Montreal and Kingston: McGill-Queen's University Press, 1994.
28. On a possible distinction between ethnic and liberal nationalism, cf. N. MacCormick, 'Liberalism, Nationalism and the Post-sovereign State', in R. Bellamy and D. Castiglione (eds), *Constitutionalism in Transformation: European and Theoretical Perspectives*, Oxford: Blackwell, 1996.
29. The indeterminacy of the communitarian argument on the natural unit for self-determination is evident in M. Walzer, 'Notes on the New Tribalism', in Brown (ed.), *Political Restructuring in Europe*.
30. The arguments suggested at the end of this paragraph are based on D. Miller, 'The Nation-state: A Modest Defence', in Brown (ed.), *Political Restructuring in Europe*; cf. also D. Miller, *On Nationality*, Oxford: Clarendon Press, 1995.
31. Cf. P. Thibaud, 'L'Europe par les nations (et réciproquement)', in Ferry and Thibaud, *Discussion sur l'Europe*, pp. 101–17.
32. On the relationship between democracy and Demos, cf. D. Grimm, *Braucht Europa eine Verfassung?*, Berlin: Carl Friedrich von Siemens Stiftung, 1995, pp. 36–47; and G. E. Rusconi, 'La cittadinanza europea non crea il "popolo europeo" ', *Il Mulino*, 45 (1996): 831–41.

33. On this contradiction, cf. J. H. H. Weiler, 'European Neo-constitutionalism: In Search of Foundations for the European Constitutional Order', in Bellamy and Castiglione (eds), *Constitutionalism in Transformation*, pp. 110–13.

34. Cf. R. Aron, 'Une citoyenneté multinationale est-elle possible?', *Commentaire*, 14 (1991–2): 695–704.

35. Cf. Thibaud, 'L'Europe par les nations', p. 50.

36. For discussions of the judgement of the Federal Constitutional Court of Germany on Maastricht, cf. N. MacCormick, 'The Maastricht-Urteil: Sovereignty Now', *European Law Journal*, 1 (1995): 255–62; and M. Herdegen, 'Maastricht and the German Constitutional Court: Constitutional Restraints for an "Ever Closer Union"', *Common Market Law Review*, 31 (1994): 235–49.

37. On this form of association in Europe, cf. G. Winter's 'Introduction' to *Reforming the Sources and Categories of EC Legal Acts*, Report for the General Secretariat of the European Consortium (March 1995), pp. 7–9.

38. Cf. Thibaud, 'L'Europe par les nations', p. 41.

39. In a state, or a political unit, *external* sovereignty is the power to act autonomously, while *internal* sovereignty means 'who' has the authority to make decisions. On this distinction, cf. N. MacCormick, 'Sovereignty, Democracy and Subsidiarity', in Bellamy, Bufacchi and Castiglione (eds), *Democracy and Constitutional Culture*, pp. 98–100; and Ferrajoli, *La sovranità nel mondo moderno*, Ch. 2.

40. See Bellamy and Castiglione, 'The Normative Challenge of the European Polity' and 'Between Cosmopolis and Community', for further elaboration of this distinction.

41. Cf. P. C. Schmitter, 'Is it Really Possible to Democratize the Euro-Polity?', University of Stanford, March 1996, mimeo, pp. 21–2.

42. M. Duverger, *L'Europe dans tous ses Etats*, Paris: Presses Universitaires de France, 1995.

43. Weiler, 'European Neo-constitutionalism', pp. 113–16.

44. Cf. N. MaCormick, 'Beyond the Sovereign State', *Modern Law Review*, 56 (1993): 1–23; and 'Liberalism, Nationalism and the Post-sovereign State', pp. 143–50.

45. On this, cf. Hirst and Thompson, *Globalisation in Question*.

46. For a discussion of the European polity as a 'regulatory state', cf. G. Majone, 'The Rise of the Regulatory State in Europe', *West European Politics*, 17 (1994): 77–101; and 'La communauté européenne come état régulateur', in Théret (ed.), *L'État, la finance et le sociale*. For a discussion of regulation and economic models in Europe, cf. S. Wilks, 'Regulatory Compliance and Capitalist Diversity in Europe', *Journal of European Public Policy*, 3 (1996): 536–59.

47. P. C. Schmitter, 'Imagining the Future of the Euro-Polity with the Help of New Concepts', in G. Marks *et al.*, *Governance in the European Union*, London: Sage, 1996.

48. Schmitter, 'Imagining the Future', p. 136.

49. We owe this concept to Neil MacCormick.

50. See R. Bellamy, 'The Constitution of Europe: Rights or Democracy', in Bellamy, Bufacchi and Castiglione (eds), *Democracy and Constitutional Culture*, pp. 153–75.

51. For a defence of a fully coherent and cohesive system, cf. D. Curtin, 'The Constitutional Structure of the Union: A Europe of Bits and Pieces', *Common Market Law Review*, 30 (1993): 17–69.

52. For further elaboration of this view, see R. Bellamy and A. Warleigh, 'From an Ethics of Integration to an Ethics of Participation – Citizenship and the Future of the European Union', *Millennium*, 27 (1998): 447–70.

Index